MANDARIN CHINESE

SECOND EDITION

THE EASY WAY

Philip F. Williams, Ph.D.
Professor and Head of School
  of Language Studies
Massey University
Palmerston North, New Zealand

Yenna Wu, Ph.D.
Distinguished Professor of Chinese
Director, Asian Languages and
  Civilizations Program
University of California
Riverside, California

BARRON'S

Acknowledgments

The authors gratefully acknowledge assistance from Dimitry
Popow, Max Reed, Denise Gilgannon, the outside referees,
Robert Shih, Dawn Sun, James Lin, Yen Paul Hsu, Ying Li,
Jie Chai, Jeff LaMarca, Kwing-wah, Grace, Eugene, and Nigel.

In memory of
Chi-liang and Yah-shun Wu,
and of Franklin and Elizabeth Williams.

CONTENTS

15   Wǒ yào zuò jǐlù chē? (What bus route number must I take?)   196

16   Qìshuǐ huòzhě píjiǔ dōu kěyǐ. (Either soda pop or beer is okay.)   212

17   Nǐ késòu ké le duōjiǔ le? (How long have you been coughing so far?)   225

INTRODUCTION

Mandarin Chinese the Easy Way emphasizes the development of skills in speaking and listening comprehension that are key to building a solid foundation in Mandarin Chinese (known in China as "pǔtōnghuà" or "Hànyǔ"). Lively colloquial dialogues present Chinese as it is actually spoken on the street and in such places as hotels, bookstores, private homes, and restaurants. These dialogues convey the spirit of good humor that so many Chinese people bring to their lives to soften everyday irritations, such as overcrowding.

Explanations of sentence structures and grammar aim at clarity and succinctness, and readers have an opportunity to immediately test themselves on what they have learned with exercises after each section in the 17 chapters with dialogues. Answers to these exercises are given at the back of the book. Appendices 1–3 provide handy indexed glossaries that encourage review of previously studied patterns and vocabulary. Appendix 4 contains a glossary of Chinese characters. Appendix 5 is the Chinese-character version of the 17 dialogues and accompanying vocabulary lists.

Each chapter begins with a list of the chapter's contents. Chapters 1 and 2 introduce pronunciation and the sound system of Chinese. Chapters 3–19 provide lesson dialogues in Chinese and in English translation, along with vocabulary lists, explanations of sentence structures and grammar, exercises on key patterns covered, notes on cultural patterns that language learners should know, and summaries of the chapter contents. Chapter 20 introduces the Chinese writing system, and offers numerous suggestions for self-study.

Various Chinese songs and rhymes are interspersed throughout the book to reinforce new sentence structures. Customized cartoons based on the dialogues, as well as photographs of Chinese festivals and landscapes, provide a broad visual context for learning the basics of the language.

ABBREVIATIONS OF GRAMMATICAL TERMS

ADJ	Adjective (can also function as sentence predicate)
ADV	Adverb (little flexibility in terms of word order)
AUXV	Auxiliary Verb (precedes the main verb)
BF	Bound Form (word that must be hooked onto another)
COMP	Complement (part of the verb unit just after the main verb)
CONJ	Conjunction (links words or larger units in the sentence)
COV	Coverb (functionally an adverbial preposition)
EXPL	Expletive (exclamatory utterance)
IDIO	Idiomatic Expression (better learned as a unit than analyzed)
INTJ	Interjection (inarticulate utterance that may interrupt)
LOC	Localizer (can convert a noun into a place word)
MADV	Moveable Adverb (may either precede or follow the subject)
MEAS	Measure (follows a number or specifier and precedes a noun)
NOUN	Noun (usually needs a measure if numbered or specified)
NUM	Number (usually needs a measure if modifying a noun)
OBJ	Object (sometimes has to be prestated before a verb)
PART	Particle (usually has an emotive or a grammatical function)
PRO	Pronoun (the only nominal often marked as plural)
PW	Place Word (has functions ordinary nouns lack)
QW	Question Word (makes a declarative sentence a question)
SUBJ	Subject (often omitted when clearly understood)
SPEC	Specifier (specifies a noun as "this" one, "that" one, and so on)
TW	Time Word (precedes action verbs when indicating a point of time instead of duration)
VERB	Verb (an even more central unit in Chinese than in English)
VERB-OBJ	Verb-Object Compound (explained in Section 11.1)

CHAPTER 1

PRONOUNCING SINGLE SYLLABLES

CHAPTER OVERVIEW
---

1. The Importance of Paying Attention to Pronunciation in Chinese

2. Tones of Single Syllables

3. The Initials

4. The Finals

1.1 The Importance of Paying Attention to Pronunciation in Chinese

Many a casual foreign observer on a first trip to China focuses upon the uniqueness of China's writing system if asked about the language. For practical and successful learners of Chinese, however, the singularity of the system of Mandarin Chinese pronunciation deserves and gets far more attention, particularly at the early stages of language study. ("Mandarin Chinese" will henceforth be shortened to "Chinese" unless otherwise noted.)

How, for instance, can a sound system with no final consonants other than -*n*, -*ng*, and -*r* produce a wide enough variety of syllables to avoid confusion of one syllable with another? And how can the learner ensure that when saying "Mom" (mā) in Chinese, the syllable doesn't accidentally come out as "mǎ" (horse) or "mà" (scold) instead?

Tones

The crucial role of four distinguishable pitches or tones at the level of individual syllables and words in Chinese helps explain why such a small number of basic syllables is adequate: there is a quadrupling in the number of possible syllables once the four tones are factored in. This should also alert the learner to the fact that the tone of a Chinese syllable is every bit as important as its beginning consonant(s), or *initial,* and vowel plus any ending consonant(s), or *final.*

To avoid the kind of laughable tone-related mistakes mentioned previously, learners of Chinese have to focus on pitch throughout the entire sentence, instead of mainly at the end or during rhetorical flourishes, as is the case in English. Moreover, there are many consonant sounds and some vowel sounds in Chinese that do not appear in English, so careful attention to the basic pronunciation system of Chinese is necessary to avoid confusing the listener and to pave the way for fluency farther down the road.

1.2 Tones of Single Syllables

Single Tones and Voice Range

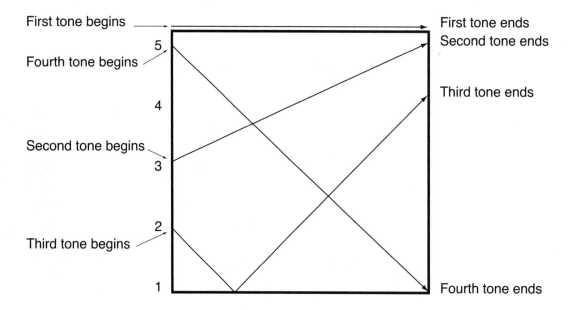

The single tones and voice range chart depicts the contours of the four tones in terms of the pitch of the human voice, with level 5 representing the top of your normal voice range, and level 1 representing the bottom of your comfortable voice range. Your voice range is bound to differ at least slightly from the voice ranges of most other people, but this is nothing to worry about; it is the relative pitch that really matters.

First Tone

The first tone, indicated by the horizontal line at the top of the chart, begins at the top of your comfortable voice range, or level 5, and stays at that level throughout the pronunciation of the entire syllable. Analogies include a singer who is holding a note of conversational volume near the upper end of her voice range, and a patient asked to say "ah" while the doctor looks inside his throat for signs of infection.

Try the following syllables in the first tone: *mā, fā, tā, fēi, lā.* It is a good idea to model your pronunciation of such syllables after the native speakers of Chinese in the CD accompanying this book. Much repeated practice is recommended.

Second Tone

The second tone begins at medium voice range, or level 3, and moves steadily upward to finish around the top of your voice range, at level 5. Try not to let your voice sag or arc on the way upward to level 5, but instead move your voice up in a lively manner. Do not begin at too low a level in your voice range, or else it could be confused with the third tone. The duration of the second tone tends to be slightly less than that of the first tone, and the pitch contour resembles that of a person who answers the phone and says "Yes?"

Try these syllables in the second tone: *má, méi, fá, féi, léi.* None of the syllables used in these pronunciation drills is a nonsense syllable; each has a specific real-world meaning, but this section ordinarily omits these meanings in order not to distract you from the primary task of learning pronunciation.

Third Tone

The third tone first dips before rising, making it the only bidirectional tone. Begin the third tone at level 2 just below the medium of your comfortable voice range, and rapidly push your voice down in pitch to level 1, the low end of your voice range. At that point, relax a bit and let the pitch of your voice bounce back up to level 4, slightly above your medium voice range.

It takes awhile to push your voice down to level 1 and then gradually let it bounce back up to level 4, so the third tone tends to be longer in duration than the other tones. The third tone is also the lowest in pitch, and it is hard to make it *too* low; many beginners err by not going low enough. The closest analogy to a third tone in English occurs when you grudgingly say "yes" to the persons with whom you are arguing when acknowledging their previous statements to be true, but not relevant to the issue at hand. Try the third tone in these syllables: *mǎ, fǎ, mǐ, lǐ, tǐ, bǎ.*

Fourth Tone

The fourth tone begins at level 5 near the top of your voice range, and descends rapidly to level 1 at the bottom, where it breaks off abruptly. Of all four tones, the fourth is usually the shortest in duration and is rivaled only by the second tone in this regard. The pitch contour of the fourth tone resembles that of a vehement "No!" used in response to an outrageous suggestion, such as dashing across a clogged mid-city freeway during rush hour. Try the fourth tone in these syllables: *mà, fà, fèi, là, tì, pà.*

Tone Marks

Note that each of the four tones has a distinctive mark above the vowel. The first tone mark is ‾, the second ´, the third ˇ, and the fourth `. The mark appears only above one of the vowels in a given syllable. For more details, see Section 2.4 in the following chapter. The only syllables without a tone mark are those in the neutral tone, which will be introduced in Section 2.2.

1.3 The Initials

TRACK
2

TABLE OF INITIALS

Columns	1	2	3	4	5
Rows					
1	bo	po	mo	fo	
2	de	te	ne		le
3	zi	ci		si	
4	zhi	chi		shi	ri
5	ji	qi		xi	
6	ge	ke		he	

The table of initials groups initial consonants or "initials" in six rows according to the various configurations of the mouth that generate a type of sound.

Row 1

Row 1 lists sounds articulated by the lips, and contains *bō, pō, mō,* and *fō*. These resemble their English counterparts, except for this row's initial in Column 1 *(bō)* and in Column 2 *(pō)*. All of the initials in Column 1 are unvoiced, meaning that the vocal chords are not vibrating when the initial consonant is pronounced, and start vibrating only after the vowel sound of the final kicks in. *Bō* thus sounds more like the unvoiced "p" in "sport" than like the voiced "b" of "buoyant."

Furthermore, all of the initials in Column 2 are plosives, and tend to cause a more explosive puff of air to rush out of the mouth than is the case with English; talking with your mouth full of food can be more reckless when saying *pō* than when uttering an English word such as "poor."

Row 2

Row 2 initials are articulated at the top front teeth, and include *dē, tē, nē,* and *lē*. As with the preceding row of initials, the Column 1 initial in this row *(dē)* is unvoiced, and thus sounds more like the "t" in "stump" than the "d" in "dud." This row's Column 2 initial *(tē)* expels a more explosive puff of air than is emitted with a word such as "ton."

Row 3

Row 3 initials are known as "dental sibilants" because of the hissing or buzzing sounds that result from exhaling through the mouth while the tip of the tongue is touching the top front teeth from behind. *Sī* is similar to an English "s," though the tongue is pressed further forward toward the top front teeth in the Chinese sound.

The other two sounds in this row do not occur at the beginning of a syllable in English words, but do appear at later junctures in the syllable. *Zī* is like the "ds" sound in "adds," and as a Column 1 sound is unvoiced. *Cī* is like the "ts" sound in "bits," though with a stronger puff of air, since it is a Column 2 plosive.

Row 4

The initials in Rows 4 and 5 are the most different from English initial consonants, and need special attention. Row 4 initials—*zhī, chī, shī,* and *rī*—are called "retroflexes," because the tongue is flexed or curled backward until its tip barely touches the front portion of the roof of the mouth. Speakers using a strong retroflex may almost seem to be holding something in their mouths, rather like a baseball player talking with a wad of chewing tobacco in his mouth. The tip of the tongue makes contact with the roof of the mouth in both *zhī* and *chī*.

Zhī somewhat resembles the "j" in "adjure," except that the tongue is curled much further back and the sound is unvoiced, as with all Column 1 initials. *Chī* bears a similarity to the "ch" of "chirp," but the tongue must again be curled much further back, and a stronger puff of air must come out, as with other Column 2 plosives.

Shī is not too far from the "sh" sound in "shirt." Again, the tongue must be flexed back much further, but it should stop just short of actually making contact with the roof of the mouth, unlike the case with *zhī* and *chī*.

Rī is like *shī* in that, while the tongue is curled back toward the roof of the mouth, its tip stops just short of making contact.

Row 5

Row 5 contains the "palatals" *jī*, *qī*, and *xī*, so named because of the way the back of the tongue arches upward toward the palate while its tip nestles behind the front bottom teeth. If you compare *jī* with the "j" of "jeep," *qī* with the "ch" of "cheap," and *xī* with the "sh" of "sheep," you will note that the flaring outward of the lips that occurs in the English consonants does not occur with the Chinese initials, which have more of a hissing sound because of the narrowed airway between the arched back of the tongue and the palate.

Row 6

Row 6 initials are articulated far back in the mouth toward the throat, and are related to the sounds that result from clearing one's throat. As an unvoiced Column 1 initial, *gē* is less like the "g" in "gun" than like the first "k" in "skunk." *Kē* requires a stronger puff of air than the initial consonant in "cut." *Hē* has a harsher sound than the English "h" in "hunt," and has something of the throaty contours of the German "ch" in "Johann Bach" when a syllable beginning with "h" receives emphasis.

Three Initials to Watch

The three initials whose spellings tend to be the most confusing in the standard pīnyīn system of romanization are *c*, *q*, and *x*. These three initials can be remembered as a breathy "ts," a palatal "ch," and a palatal "sh," respectively.

This Buddhist pagoda in southern Ānhuī province reputedly received a visit from the great eighth-century Táng poet, Lǐ Bái (a.k.a. Lǐ Bó).

Most educated Chinese people have encountered the table of initials at an early point in their schooling. If you lack access to a web site, a friend or relative with this educational background could thus serve as a sounding board and help you fine-tune your pronunciation of these consonants.

1.4 The Finals

TRACK
3

TABLE OF FINALS

Row-a:	-i	a	e	ai	ei	ao	ou	an	en	ang	eng	ong	er
Row-i:	i	ia	ie			iao	iu	ian	in	iang	ing	iong
Row-u:	u	ua	uo	uai	ui			uan	un	uang	ueng
Row-ü:	ü		üe					üan	ün

The table of finals reveals that fewer than half of them have any final consonants. Therefore, it is particularly important to distinguish clearly between the various vowel sounds. Please note that the spelling of the finals is not equivalent to free-standing syllables in pīnyīn romanization, which will be covered in Chapter Two.

Row-a

Row-a finals begin with *-i*, which is the only final that cannot occur alone and must follow an initial that is either a dental sibilant *(z, c, or s)* or a retroflex *(zh, ch, sh, or r)*. This unique final functions merely as a prolongation of the initial, resulting in a "schwa"-like buzzing after a sibilant and a sound such as "earn" without the "n" after a retroflex. The *a* final resembles "p*a*pa," and *e* sounds more like a U.S. southerner's "u" in "show 'nuff" than the standard "u" in "uh-oh." *Ai* is equivalent to "aye-aye," while *ei* is the same as the vowel in "weight." *Ao* is roughly halfway between "awe" and "ow!" (short for "ouch"), while *ou* is like the first vowel in "okay."

Each of the other finals in Row-a ends with a consonant. *An* is about two-thirds of the way between "an" and "on," and *en* resembles the second syllable of "women," but should not be pronounced like "men."

Ang has the vowel quality of "wok," but ends with the "ng" sound of "song." *Eng* resembles the "ung" sound of "rung." *Ong* has the vowel quality of "ohm," but must end with a nasal sound like "rung."

Er usually sounds like the first part of "earn." However, in fourth tone its vowel quality sounds more like "are."

Row-i

Row-i finals all begin with the *i* of "machine." *Ia* is like German "ja" or the Southern U.S. "y'all," and *ie* resembles the first two letters in "yet." *Iao* resembles "yowl" without the "l," while the somewhat tricky *iu* is equivalent to the first syllable of "yeoman." *Ian* sounds much like "yen," while *in* is about halfway between "in" and "sheen."

Iang begins like "young," but the vowel quality is like that of "wok" and it ends like "song." The vowel quality of *ing* resembles "singing," while *iong* sounds like a combination of the first syllable of "yeoman" and the consonantal ending of "rung."

Row-u

The *u* that begins the Row-u finals is quite different from the "u" sound in an English word such as "chew," in which the lips flare out. The Chinese *u* requires that the lips be rounded into a small, tight opening, while the tongue is retracted toward the back of the mouth. A good way to make a Chinese *u* is to get ready to whistle as low a note as you can, but instead of whistling, just vocalize.

Ua is like "wash" without the "sh," while *uo* sounds like the vowel component of "store" or "door" in a heavy New York City accent. *Uai* resembles the first part of "wine," and the rather tricky *ui* sounds like "weigh."

Uan is like the vowel and final consonant of Spanish "Juan," while *un* is closer to "won" than to "when." *Uang* begins like "wall" without the final consonant and ends like "wrong." *Ueng* begins like "won" and ends like "rung."

Row-ü

The Row-ü finals all begin with the *ü* found in German. To generate this sound, get your tongue in position to say the Chinese *i* as in "machine," but instead of saying that, tense your lips into a small round opening and try to say the Chinese *u* instead. The *üe* final begins differently from *ie,* but the two finals rhyme. Similarly, *üan* rhymes with *ian,* while *ün* simply adds the -n ending to the *ü* sound.

A Chinese Song

Many Chinese recall the song they used to sing in public school when learning the standard pronunciation of the initials and the finals. One version goes as follows:

The Chinese Syllabary Song
Sung to the tune of "The Alphabet Song" (A,B,C,D,E,F,G...)
or "Twinkle, Twinkle, Little Star"

Bō, pō, mō, fō,
dē, tē, nē, lē,
gē, kē, hē,
jī, qī, xī,
zhī, chī, shī, rī,
zī, cī, sī,
ā, ō, ē, yē,
āi, ēi, āo, ōu,
ān, ēn, āng, ēng, ōng,
yī, wū, yū,
hái yǒu yíge yīnfú "ēr."

(There's also the syllable "*ēr.*")

Celebrants dance in elaborate dragon costumes during Lunar New Year festivities.

SUMMARY

The first step in learning Chinese is to get acquainted with its sound system and to practice the often unfamiliar sounds out loud. The pitch or tone is a basic and integral component of the Chinese syllable, and is similar in importance to any consonant or vowel in a given syllable. As a beginner, you need to study Section 1.2's chart, *Single Tones and Voice Range,* then read aloud a set of basic individual syllables in the first tone, and finally move on to practice the second tone, the third tone, and the fourth tone in turn.

After you can generate each of the four tones and distinguish one from another by ear, it is time to move on to the initials, which are the consonants at the beginning of most Chinese syllables. Each of the six rows in Section 1.3's *Table of Initials* includes a group of initials that are articulated at a certain place in the mouth or throat, ranging from the lips in Row 1 to the throat in Row 6. As a beginner, you need to practice the initials out loud, row-by-row, giving special attention to Row 4's retroflexes and Row 5's palatals.

The third and last part of the Chinese syllable to learn is the final, which consists of the vowel and any consonants at the end of the syllable. Just as it is best to begin learning the initials by patiently working your way rightward across the *Table of Initials* row by row, you should start practicing the finals out loud by going carefully through Section 1.4's *Table of Finals* in a similar manner. The Row-ü finals require extra practice, particularly for learners who have not studied German or French. Listening to the native speakers on the CD and actively imitating them out loud is strongly recommended.

This concludes the introduction to pronouncing the individual Chinese syllable, which consists of a final, a tone, and usually an initial as well. The next chapter focuses on pronouncing combinations of syllables.

CHAPTER 2

PRONOUNCING SYLLABLES IN COMBINATION

CHAPTER OVERVIEW

1. Tonal Changes for Third-tone Syllables in Combination

2. Neutral Tones

3. Tonal Changes in "Yī" and "Bù"

4. Some Rules of Thumb for Pīnyīn Romanization

2.1 Tonal Changes for Third-tone Syllables in Combination

TRACK
4

Syllables in Combination Other than Third-tone

When a syllable in the first tone, second tone, or fourth tone is followed by another syllable of any tone, the first syllable almost always retains its original tonal configuration. Some examples are "Tā shuō" (She's saying it), "Tā ná" (She's holding it), "Tā mǎi" (She's buying it), "Tā qù" (She's going), "Bié shuō" (Don't say it), "Bié ná" (Don't hold it), "Bié mǎi" (Don't buy it), "Bié qù" (Don't go), "Yào shuō" (Want to say it), "Yào ná" (Want to hold it), and "Yào mǎi" (Want to buy it).

The only minor exception to this rule occurs when two fourth-tone syllables such as "Yào qù" (Want to go) appear in a row. In this case, the first fourth-tone syllable receives less stress and dips only as far as mid-range or level 3 in the voice range, while the fully stressed second fourth-tone syllable dips all the way to the low end at level 1.

Third-tone Syllables in Combination

The third-tone syllable is another matter altogether; it retains its full original tonal configuration only when it is the last syllable in a sentence or comes before some other prominent pause, as in "Tā mǎi," "Bié mǎi," and "Zǎo!" (Good morning!). When two or more third-tone syllables appear in a row, the first syllable(s) must change to second tone, leaving only the final third-tone syllable unchanged.

For example, the "nǐ" in the common greeting "Nǐ hǎo" (Hello) must be read as second tone, even though we do not change the tone mark when writing "nǐ" in romanization. In a sentence like "Nǐ mǎi yǐzi" (You're buying chairs), both "nǐ" and "mǎi" should be pronounced in the second tone.

The Half-third Tone

When a third-tone syllable is followed by a syllable in any tone other than third tone, that third-tone syllable must be read in what is called the "half-third tone." A half-third-tone syllable does not bounce back up to level 4 in one's voice range the way a full third tone does, but merely drops from level 2 to level 1, where it stays for a brief moment before the next syllable is spoken. Half-third-tone syllables appear at the outset in these brief sentences: "Nǐ shuō" (Say it), "Nǐ ná" (Take it), and "Nǐ mài" (Sell it).

2.2 Neutral Tones

TRACK
5

Pronouncing Neutral-tone Syllables

Two types of words tend to be read in the neutral tone: first, grammatical particles and other bound forms that must be attached to more substantial words before they can even appear in a sentence; second, a wide variety of words that occasionally lose their tonal configurations in the heat of rapid speech. A neutral-tone syllable is relatively short in duration and light in stress, does not change in pitch, and nearly always has its pronunciation determined by the tone of the preceding syllable.

After a first-tone syllable, a neutral-tone syllable falls slightly below mid-range to level 2, as in "tāde" (hers). Following a second-tone syllable, a neutral-tone syllable lands at mid-range at level 3, as in "shíge" (ten of them). After a half-third-tone syllable, a neutral-tone syllable falls above mid-range at level 4, as in "wǒde" (mine).

Following a fourth-tone syllable, a neutral-tone syllable just remains at the bottom of one's voice range at level 1, as in "liùge" (six of them).

Romanization for Neutral-tone Syllables

Generally, you can assume that any syllable in the pīnyīn romanization that has no tone mark above it is probably a neutral-tone syllable, such as the "you" of "péngyou" (friend). An alternative way of indicating a neutral-tone syllable on paper is to retain any tone mark above the neutral-tone syllable and to precede the syllable with a raised tone-mark dot, as in "péng·yǒu." Southern Chinese tend to use the neutral tone for the second syllable of compounds such as "péng·yǒu" considerably less frequently than northern Chinese, and may thus give "yǒu" its full stress by pronouncing the term "péngyǒu."

2.3 Tonal Changes in "Yī" and "Bù"

TRACK
6

Tonal Changes in "Yī"

Special rules apply for the tonal configurations of "yī" (one) and "bù" (not, no), two of the highest frequency words. When "yī" occurs by itself, as part of a larger number such as "shíyī" (11), or as part of a series of digits such as a phone number or house number, it is pronounced in the first tone. On the other hand, when you want to express the idea of one something or other, "yī" switches from first tone to either fourth tone or second tone. Before a syllable in the first, second, or third tone, it should be read in the fourth tone as "yì," as in "yìzhāng zhuōzi" (one table), "yìnián" (one year), and "yìbǎ yǔsǎn" (one umbrella). Before a fourth-tone syllable, it must be read in the second tone as "yí," as in "yíjiàn yīfu" (one piece of clothing) and "yíyàng" (the same).

Tonal Changes in "Bù"

The type of tonal change that "bù" undergoes resembles that of "yī," though it is simpler. By itself, or in front of any syllable in the first, second, or third tone, "bù" is pronounced in the fourth tone, as in "bù gāo" (isn't tall), "Bùxíng!" (That won't do!), and "bù zǎo" (isn't early). If "bù" precedes a fourth-tone syllable, however, it must change to the second tone as "bú," as with "bú qù" (not going) and "bú dà" (isn't big).

2.4 Some Rules of Thumb for Pīnyīn Romanization

Readers who are already familiar with the pīnyīn romanization system, which became the People's Republic of China's (PRC) official romanization system in 1958, may wish to skim over or even skip this section and plunge quickly into this book's first dialogue in Chapter 3. However, for those who are new to pīnyīn or romanization schemes in general, a few general remarks may prove helpful.

Placement of Tone Marks

Unless a syllable is in the neutral tone, a tone mark should appear above one of the vowels in the syllable, as in the combinations "qiūtiān" (first tone, autumn), "méi lái" (second tone, didn't come), "xiǎo gǒu" (third tone, little dog), and "mài bào" (fourth tone, sell newspapers). If there are two or three vowels to choose from in a given syllable, write the tone mark above the *a* or the *e*, either of which always takes preference over any other vowel; there is no syllable in pīnyīn that contains both an *a* and an *e*. Furthermore, in the *ou* final, place the tone mark over the *o*. In all other cases, the tone mark goes over the final vowel. By observing these three easy guidelines, you can place the tone mark over the correct vowel within any pīnyīn syllable.

Writing Romanization Longhand

It is best to print the romanized letters longhand and add tone marks as you go; by all means refrain from writing cursive letters and adding tone marks only at the end of each word as a sort of afterthought. Tone marks are every bit as important as correct pronunciation and spelling of the initials and finals, and it is best to print the tone marks as you go to avoid slipping into the fatal mistake of misperceiving tones as an afterthought or an optional decoration.

Rules for Forming Syllables and Words in Pīnyīn

Most of the time, you can form acceptable syllables in pīnyīn simply by combining a final from the table of finals with a tone mark and the consonant portion of an appropriate initial from the table of initials: for example, *-ian* + ` + *j* = jiàn (see). However, there are several exceptions that are worth noting for future reference. The only two instances in which the two dots or "umlaut" in ü are actually needed are after the initials *l* and *n*, as in "lǜ" (green) and "nǚrén" (woman). When Row-ü finals have no initial, the umlaut drops out and a *y* is added, as with "yú" (fish) and "yuǎn" (far). Moreover, the umlaut drops out after the palatal initials *j, q,* and *x,* as in "jùzi" (sentence), "qù" (go), and "yěxǔ" (perhaps).

Occasional Apostrophe Use to Demarcate Syllables Within a Compound

In the vast majority of cases, a word of two or more syllables, or "compound," is written as one unit, because it is clear where one syllable ends and the next syllable begins. For example, it is entirely clear where the demarcation lies between the two syllables in the compound *nǚrén* (woman)—between *nǚ* and *rén*—because while *en* exists as a pīnyīn syllable, *nǚr* does not. However, the line of division between one syllable and another in a compound sometimes can become ambiguous in cases such as the northwestern city of *Xī'ān* and Běijīng's famous east-west boulevard *Cháng'ānjiē*. We use an apostrophe to mark divisions between syllables that would otherwise be ambiguous, since the four-letter compound *Xian* could be mistakenly read as a monosyllabic word if the apostrophe were omitted, and the latter place-name could be erroneously read as a combination of the syllables *chan* and *gan* instead of the correct *chang* and *an*.

Rules for Spelling Row-u Finals

There are a few changes connected with the Row-u finals. First, the *u* of the *-uo* final drops out only when following the Row 1 initials *b, p, m,* and *f,* as in "guǎngbō" (broadcasting), "dǎpò" (to break), "mó" (to grind), and "fó" (Buddha). Second, when Row-u finals stand alone instead of combining with an initial, the *u* changes to *w,* as in the cases of "-uǒ" changing to "wǒ" (me), and "-uáng" changing to "wáng" (king). The only three variations on this pattern involve the finals *-ui* and *-un,* which need to have an *e* added also, as when "-ùi" changes to "wèi" (honorific measure) and "-ún" changes to "wén" (language), and the final *-u,* which requires that a *w* be added to the *u* rather than substituted for it, as when "-ǔ" changes to "wǔ" (five).

Rules for Spelling Row-i Finals

Row-i finals that occur without initials change in ways similar to the Row-u finals: instead of the *u* changing to a *w,* the *i* changes to a *y,* as when "-iǎo" changes to "yǎo" (bite), and "-iě" changes to "yě" (also). Variations on this pattern include the three finals *-i, -in,* and

-ing, which require that a *y* be added to the *i* instead of substituted for it, as can be seen in "yī" (one), "yīnwèi" (because), and "yīnggāi" (should), and the *-iu* final, to which an *o* must be added along with a *y*, as when "-iǔ" changes to "yǒu" (have).

Pīnyīn Tables

Tables illustrating all the possible initial-and-final combinations of a syllable within the pīnyīn system of romanization may be consulted below.

TABLE 1
CHINESE INITIALS (left column) AND FINALS *a* THROUGH *ong* (top)

	a	o	e	-i*	er	ai	ei	ao	ou	an	en	ang	eng	ong
b	ba	bo				bai	bei	bao		ban	ben	bang	beng	
p	pa	po				pai	pei	pao	pou	pan	pen	pang	peng	
m	ma	mo	me			mai	mei	mao	mou	man	men	mang	meng	
f	fa	fo					fei		fou	fan	fen	fang	feng	
d	da		de			dai	dei	dao	dou	dan	den	dang	deng	dong
t	ta		te			tai		tao	tou	tan		tang	teng	tong
n	na		ne			nai	nei		nou	nan	nen	nang	neng	nong
l	la		le			lai	lei	nao	lou	lan		lang	leng	long
z	za		ze	zi		zai	zei	zao	zou	zan	zen	zang	zeng	zong
c	ca		ce	ci		cai		cao	cou	can	cen	cang	ceng	cong
s	sa		se	si		sai		sao	sou	san	sen	sang	seng	song
zh	zha		zhe	zhi		zhai	zhei	zhao	zou	zan	zen	zhang	zheng	zhong
ch	cha		che	chi		chai		chao	chou	chan	chen	chang	cheng	chong
sh	sha		she	shi		shai	shei	shao	shou	shan	shen	shang	sheng	
r			re	ri				rao	rou	ran	ren	rang	reng	rong
j														
q														
x														
g	ga		ge			gai	gei	gao	gou	gan	gen	gang	geng	gong
k	ka		ke			kai	kei	kao	kou	kan	ken	kang	keng	kong
h	ha		he			hai	hei	hao	hou	han	hen	hang	heng	hong
	a	o	e		er	ai	ei	ao	ou	an	en	ang	eng	

TABLE 2
CHINESE INITIALS (left column) AND FINALS *i* THROUGH *iong* (top)

	i	ia	iao	ie	iou	ian	in	Iang	Ing	iong
b	bi		biao	bie		bian	bin		bing	
p	pi		piao	pie		pian	pin		ping	
m	mi		miao	mie	miu	mian	min		ming	
f			.							
d	di		daio	die	diu	dian			ding	
t	ti		tiao	tie		tian			ting	
n	ni		niao	nie	niu	nian	nin	niang	ning	
l	li	lia	liao	lie	liu	lian	lin	liang	ling	
z										
c										
s										
zh										
sh										
ch										
r										
j	ji	jia	jiao	jie	jiu	jian	jin	jiang	jing	jiong
q	qi	qia	qiao	qie	qiu	qian	qin	qiang	qing	qiong
x	xi	xia	xiao	xie	xiu	xian	xin	xiang	xing	xiong
g										
k										
h										
	yi	ya	yao	ye	you	yan	yin	yang	ying	yong

TABLE 3
CHINESE INITIALS (left column) AND FINALS *u* THROUGH *ueng* (top)

	u	ua	uo	uai	uei	uan	uen	uang	ueng
b	bu								
p	pu								
m	mu								
f	fu								
d	du		duo		dui	duan	dun		
t	tu		tuo		tui	tuan	tun		
n	nu		nuo			nuan			.
l	li		luo			luan	lun		
z	zu		zuo		zui	zuan	zun		
c	cu		cuo		cui	cuan	cun		
s	su		suo		sui	suan	sun		
zh	zhu	zhua	zhuo	zhuai	zhui	zhuan	zhun	zhuang	

TABLE 3 (continued)
CHINESE INITIALS (left column) AND FINALS *u* THROUGH *ueng* (top)

	u	ua	uo	uai	uei	uan	uen	uang	ueng
ch	chu	chua	chuo	chuai	chui	chuan	chun	chuang	
sh	shu	shua	shuo	shuai	shui	shuan	shun	shuang	
r	ru	rua	ruo		rui	ruan	run		
j									
q									
x									
g	gu	gua	guo	guai	gui	guan	gun	guang	
k	ku	kua	kuo	kuai	kui	kuan	kun	kuang	
h	hu	hua	huo	huai	hui	huan	hun	huang	
	wu	wa	wo	wai	wai	wan	wen	wang	weng

TABLE 4
CHINESE INITIALS (left column) AND FINALS *ü* THROUGH *ün* (top)

	ü	üe	üan	ün
b				
p				
m				
f				
d				
t				
n	nü	nüe		
l	lü	lüe		
z				
c				
s				
zh				
ch				
sh				
r				
j	ju	jue	juan	jun
q	qu	que	quan	qun
x	xu	zue	xuan	xun
g				
k				
h				
	yu	yue	yuan	yun

The view into a family courtyard from outside the boundary wall in an upland southern Ānhuī village.

SUMMARY

A combination of Chinese syllables often amounts simply to the sum of its parts, especially when the syllables involved are in the first, second, or fourth tones. However, the tone of a syllable may change, depending on what sort of syllable precedes it. This is especially true of syllables in the third tone and the neutral tone. When two third-tone syllables occur together, as in "Nǐ hǎo" (Hello), the first syllable ("nǐ") is pronounced in the second tone, while the second syllable ("hǎo") retains its third-tone configuration. If a third-tone syllable precedes a syllable in any other tone than third, it loses its final rise in pitch and is pronounced in the low-pitched half-third tone.

Short in duration and lightly stressed, a neutral-tone syllable also changes its pitch in accordance with the tone of the syllable that precedes it. A neutral tone is high-pitched after a half-third tone ("wǒde"), medium-pitched after a second tone ("shíge"), and low in pitch after a first or fourth tone ("tāde," "liùge").

Special rules govern tonal change for the common words "yī" (one) and "bù" (not). While there are some important differences in tonal changes between these two words, each of them usually switches to second tone when preceding a fourth-tone syllable, as in "yíyàng" (the same) and "búyào" (don't want).

Chapter 2 concludes with some rules of thumb for navigating the pīnyīn romanization system, which this book uses. Pīnyīn romanization has been the PRC's standard system since 1958, and has solidly established itself as the dominant method of Chinese romanization, especially for Chinese dictionaries, textbooks, and popular media.

CHAPTER 3

LĂOSHŬ HĂO!
(Hello, Mouse!)

CHAPTER OVERVIEW

1. Greetings, Farewells, and Asking After a Third Party

2. Negating Ordinary and Adjectival Verbs with the Adverb "Bù"

3. Chinese Word Order and Adverbs Such As "Bù" and "Hěn"

4. The Question Particle "Ma" and Simple Possessives

NEW VOCABULARY

1. lǎoshǔ	mouse (easily confused with "lǎoshī," #6)	NOUN
2. hǎo	be good, be well (in the sense of doing well, things going fine)	ADJ
3. wǒ	I, me	PRO
4. bù	no, not ("bù" becomes "bú" before a fourth-tone syllable such as "shì")	ADV
5. shì	to be, is, am, are	VERB
6. lǎoshī	teacher (also used as a title, as in Lǐ Lǎoshī, "Teacher Lǐ")	NOUN
7. duìbùqǐ	sorry, excuse me	IDIO
8. nǐ hǎo	hi, hello (idiomatic greeting to one person)	IDIO
9. nǐ	you	PRO
10. nǐ māma	your mom	NOUN
11. māma	mom, mama (informal)	NOUN
12. tā	he, she, him, her (gender can be inferred from the context), it	PRO
13. hěn+ ADJ	very (+ adjective; an unstressed "hěn" often precedes an adj.)	ADV
14. bàba	dad, papa (informal)	NOUN
15. phrase + ne	and how about (phrase)?	PART
16. yě	also, too	ADV
17. máng	be busy	ADJ
18. ma	(particle that transforms a sentence into a question)	PART
19. nín	you (polite or honorific counterpart of "nǐ")	PRO
20. zàijiàn	see you later, good-bye	IDIO

DIALOGUE

Mínglěi: Lǎoshǔ hǎo!
Lǐ Lǎoshī: Wǒ búshì lǎoshǔ. Wǒ shì lǎoshī.
Mínglěi: Duìbùqǐ. Lǎoshī hǎo!
Lǐ Lǎoshī: Nǐ hǎo! Nǐ māma hǎo ma?
Mínglěi: Tā hěn hǎo.
Lǐ Lǎoshī: Nǐ bàba ne?
Mínglěi: Tā yě hěn hǎo.

Lǐ Lǎoshī: Nǐ máng ma?
Mínglěi: Wǒ bù máng. Nín ne?
Lǐ Lǎoshī: Wǒ hěn máng. Zàijiàn!
Mínglěi: Lǎoshī zàijiàn!

DIALOGUE TRANSLATION

Mínglěi (confusing "lǎoshǔ" with "lǎoshī"): Hello, Mouse!
Teacher Lǐ: I'm not a mouse. I'm a teacher.
Mínglěi: Sorry. Hi, Teacher!
Teacher Lǐ: Hi! Is your mom doing well?
Mínglěi: She's doing fine.
Teacher Lǐ: How about your dad?
Mínglěi: He's also doing well.
Teacher Lǐ: Are you busy?
Mínglěi: I'm not busy. How about you?
Teacher Lǐ: I'm very busy. See you later!
Mínglěi: Good-bye, Teacher!

3.1 Greetings, Farewells, and Asking After a Third Party

Greetings

Nǐ hǎo!	Hello!
Lǐ Lǎoshī hǎo!	Hi, Teacher Lǐ.
Nǐ hǎo ma?	How are you?
Wǒ hěn hǎo.	I'm fine.
Nǐ māma ne?	And how about your mom?
Zàijiàn!	Good-bye!
Lǐ Lǎoshī, zàijiàn!	Good-bye, Teacher Lǐ.

The simplest way to greet somebody with whom you are already acquainted is to say "nǐ hǎo," keeping in mind that when two third-tone syllables appear together the first syllable automatically changes to second tone; only the latter syllable retains its third-tone configuration. If the person you are greeting is older or is of higher social status, you may either substitute the honorific second-person pronoun "nín," as in "nín hǎo," or address the person with an appropriate title such as "lǎoshī" (teacher), as in "lǎoshī hǎo." A title following the surname is also common in such cases: "Lǐ Lǎoshī hǎo" (Hi, Teacher Lǐ).

Farewells

When bidding someone farewell, "zàijiàn" or "see you later" is fine for both formal and informal occasions. To non-Chinese ears, the two falling fourth tones of "zàijiàn" may at first sound abrupt for a farewell, but this is not the case for Chinese speakers. Remember that Chinese tone or pitch is chiefly associated with the syllable instead of the entire sentence, and thus carries less emotional expression than do rises and falls in pitch in a language such as English.

Asking After a Third Party

In between the greeting and the farewell, it is common to ask after one or more of the listener's relatives. In sentences where the context has been clearly set out already, the particle "ne" can be used after the noun or phrase to mean, "And how about (phrase)?" In this dialogue, the discussion has touched on how Mínglěi and his mother are doing in general, so when Teacher Lǐ then asks after Mínglěi's father, she simply appends the particle "ne" to the phrase "nǐ bàba" (your dad), to result in "Nǐ bàba ne?" (And how about your dad?).

Exercises for 3.1

1. Say hello to Mínglěi.

_____

2. Ask whether Mínglěi's dad is doing well.

_____

3. Mínglěi says, "He is doing well."

_____

4. Use a tag question to ask about Mínglěi's mom.

_____

5. Say hello to an older person. [Use the honorific second-person pronoun.]

_____

6. Say hello to Teacher Wáng.

_____

7. Say good-bye to Mínglěi.

_____

3.2 Negating Ordinary and Adjectival Verbs with the Adverb "Bù"

Subject	Adverb/"bù"	Ordinary Verb	(Object)	
Nǐ		shì	lǎoshī.	(You are a teacher.)
Wǒ	bú	shì	lǎoshǔ.	(I am not a mouse.)

Subject	Adverb/"bù"	Adjectival Verb	
Nǐ	hěn	máng.	(You are [very] busy.)
Wǒ	bù	máng.	(I am not busy.)

Noun-modifying Adjective	Noun	
hǎo	māma	(good moms)
máng	bàba	(busy dads)

Either an ordinary verb such as "shì" (to be) or an adjectival verb such as "máng" (be busy) can be negated by placing the adverb "bù" (not) before it. "Bù" is unique in being pronounced as fourth-tone by itself or before any syllable that is not fourth-tone, but as second-tone when coming before a fourth-tone syllable.

Mínglěi thus uses the standard fourth-tone pronunciation in "Wǒ bù máng" (I'm not busy), while his teacher must use the second-tone pronunciation in "Wǒ búshì lǎoshǔ" (I'm not a mouse). Note that it is wrong and redundant to say "Wǒ búshì máng," because the verbal quality of "to be" is already included in the adjectival verb "máng." Chinese adjectives can function either as adjectival verbs or as noun-modifying adjectives, as in "máng lǎoshī" (busy teachers). The equational verb "shì" may take an object, such as "lǎoshǔ"; Chinese has no need for the term "predicate nominative," which is used with English "to be" constructions.

Exercises for 3.2

1. Tell Mínglěi that you are not his mom.

   _____

2. Tell Mínglěi that he is not a teacher.

   _____

3. Tell Teacher Lǐ that she isn't busy.

   _____

4. Tell your daughter that you are a mommy ("māmī"), not a kitty cat ("māomī")

   _____

5. Tell your students that you are Teacher Mǐ (Mǐ Lǎoshī), not Mickey Mouse (Mǐ Lǎoshǔ).

   _____

Some varieties of festive dragon dances require a small army of performers.

3.3 Chinese Word Order and Adverbs Such As "Bù" and "Hěn"

Chinese Word Order

Subject	Adverb(s)	Ordinary Verb	Object	
Tā	yě	shì	lǎoshī.	(She is also a teacher.)
Nǐ	yě bú	shì	lǎoshī.	(You are not a teacher, either.)

Subject	Adverb(s)	Adjectival Verb	
Tā	yě hěn	hǎo.	(She is also fine.)
Tā	yě bù	máng.	(She is not busy, either.)

In languages such as Latin, word order in a given sentence is often quite flexible, because the various suffixes or endings commonly appended to words typically provide an indication of the grammatical function of words, such as subject, object, past-tense verb, and so on. However, the Chinese language does without these grammatical suffixes or inflections, and thus must depend heavily on word order as an indicator of grammatical function.

Adverbs Such As "Bù" and "Hěn"

In the common Chinese sentence pattern of subject-adverb-verb (object), the subject must go before the adverb, and the adverb must precede the verb. There is some flexibility in the placement of the object, but not with the other three elements.

English grammar permits us to say either "I'm not kidding you" (SUBJ-ADV-VERB-OBJ) or "I kid you not" (SUBJ-VERB-OBJ-ADV), but Chinese requires us to say "Wǒ bú piàn nǐ"; no other word order besides SUBJ-ADV-VERB is possible for the first three words of this Chinese sentence.

Because word order is often inflexible, such adverbs as "yě," "bù," and "hěn" must go somewhere after the subject and before the verb. If combined together in a sentence, "yě" needs to come before either "bù" or "hěn." Both the English sentences "She's very busy, too" and "She's also very busy" are fine, but the only correct Chinese equivalent is "Tā yě hěn máng" (SUBJ-ADV1-ADV2-VERB).

Exercises for 3.3

1. Ask whether the teacher is busy.

    _____

2. The teacher answers that she is busy.

    _____

3. The teacher asks, "How about you?"

    _____

4. Tell her that you're also very busy.

    _____

5. Tell a friend that you're not a teacher.

    _____

6. Tell him that your dad isn't a teacher, either.

    _____

2. The teacher answers that she is busy.

_____

Subject	Adverb	Ordinary Verb	Object	Question Particle "ma"	
Tā		shì	lǎoshī	ma?	(Is she a teacher?)
Nǐ	yě	shì	lǎoshī	ma?	(Are you also a teacher?)

Affirmation, (Shì or Duì)	Subject	Adverb	Verb	Object	
Shì,	tā		shì	lǎoshī.	(Yes, she's a teacher.)
Duì (correct),	tā	yě	shì	lǎoshī.	(Yes, she's also a teacher.)

Negation, (Búshì or Búduì)	Subject	Adverb(s)	Verb	Object	
Búshì,	tā	bú	shì	lǎoshī.	(No, she's not a teacher.)
Bù (or, Búduì),	tā	yě bú	shì	lǎoshī.	(No, she's not a teacher, either.)

Subject	Adverb(s)	Adjectival Verb	Question Particle "ma"	
Nǐ	yě hěn	máng	ma?	(Are you also busy?)
Tā	yě bù	máng.		(She isn't busy, either.)
Wǒ	yě bù hěn	máng.		(I'm not very busy, either.)

3. The teacher asks, "How about you?"

_____

4. Tell her that you're also very busy.

_____

"ma"; "ma" does well at transforming a declarative sentence into a question, but it cannot make a good question into a better one.

Simple Possessives

Pronoun as Possessive	Noun	
wǒ	māma	(my mom)
nǐ	bàba	(your dad)

For nouns having a close connection with the speaker, especially two-syllable words for body parts and relatives, simple possessive expressions like "my NOUN" and "your NOUN" can be generated through the structure PRO + NOUN. Thus we have "nǐ bàba" (your dad) and "wǒ māma" (my mom), and "wǒ dùzi" (my stomach).

Exercises for 3.4: Translate into Chinese, then transform into an affirmative question with "ma."

1. You are her mom.

_____

_____

2. He isn't your dad.

_____

_____

3. Teacher Lǐ isn't a mouse.

_____

_____

4. My mom isn't busy.

_____

_____

5. His dad isn't a teacher.

_____

_____

Raised pathways border seasonally flooded rice paddies throughout much of rural China, especially in warmer and more humid climes.

SUMMARY

Greetings and other social lubricants introduced in this chapter include "nǐ hǎo!" (hello!), "zàijiàn" (good-bye), and "duìbùqǐ" (sorry). The basic word order in Chinese sentences, SUBJ-VERB-OBJ, matches mainstream English word order, as can be seen in such a sentence as "Wǒ shì lǎoshī" (I am a teacher).

On the other hand, Chinese sentence structure differs from English in many ways. For example, the appending of sentence-end question particles such as "ma" and "ne" can transform a declarative sentence or phrase into a question: "Nǐ shì lǎoshǔ ma?" (Are you a mouse?) and "Bàba ne?" (And how about Dad?). Moreover, ordinary adverbs such as "bù" (not) and "yě" (also) must be sandwiched between the subject and the verb, unlike their English counterparts, as in "Wǒ búshì lǎoshǔ" (I am not a mouse) and "Māma yě shì lǎoshī" (Mom is a teacher, also). Furthermore, pronouns may sometimes function as possessives: "Nǐ māma ne?" (And how about your mom?).

Differences between the two languages loom especially large with respect to the adjective. Although a Chinese adjective functions much like its English counterpart when modifying a noun, as in "máng lǎoshī" (a busy teacher), it is verbal in nature, and should *not* be preceded by the Chinese "to be" verb (shì) when used as the predicate of a sentence: "Wǒ bù máng; lǎoshī hěn máng" (I am not busy; the teacher is very busy). The basic grammatical structure of such sentences is SUBJ + ADV + ADJ; an *unstressed* "hěn" (sometimes written as "·hěn") should ordinarily fill the adverbial slot as a "dummy" term when the speaker does not wish to specify the adverb, as in "Tā hěn hǎo" (She is fine).

CHAPTER 4

HĚN GĀOXÌNG RÈNSHÌ NÍN.
(Glad to meet you.)

CHAPTER OVERVIEW

1. Introducing Oneself and Asking About a New Acquaintance's Name

2. The Apostrophe-"s"-like Modification Particle "de"

3. The Alternate-choice VERB-bù-VERB Question Pattern, as in "Shì búshì"

4. Keeping the Same Word Order in Questions as in Declarative Sentences

5. Words Such as "Nǚ" That Must Be Bound to Another Word, and Cannot Stand Alone

---

NEW VOCABULARY

TRACK ○ 9

1. jīnglǐ	manager (can also be a title such as "lǎoshī")	NOUN
2. shéi	who? (question word)	QW
3. de	(apostrophe-like modification particle)	PART
4. nǐde	your	PRO + PART
5. nǚpéngyou	girlfriend	NOUN
6. nǚ	female (must be attached to another word such as "péngyou")	NOUN/BF
7. péngyou	friend	NOUN
8. jiějie	elder sister	NOUN
9. Sānjiě	Third Elder Sister (address used by younger sibling)	NOUN
10. gōngsī	company	NOUN
11. qǐngwèn	May I ask . . . ? (to show politeness before an inquiry)	IDIO
12. wèn	to ask	VERB
13. (nín) guìxìng?	What is your family name? (polite idiomatic question)	IDIO
14. guì	be honorable (as in #13), be expensive	ADJ
15. xìng	to be surnamed, to have the family name of	VERB
16. gāoxìng	be happy, be glad	ADJ
17. rènshì	to be acquainted with, to recognize	VERB
18. xiǎojiě	Miss, young woman (term of address for an unmarried woman)	NOUN
19. jiào	to call, to be called, to shout	VERB
20. shénme	what? (question word)	QW
21. míngzi	name (either given name or given name and surname)	NOUN
22. xuéshēng	student	NOUN
23. xué	to learn, to study	VERB
24. yóuyǒng jiàoliàn	swimming coach	NOUN
25. yóuyǒng	to swim	VERB
26. jiàoliàn	coach	NOUN
27. nán	male (must be attached to another word)	NOUN/BF

DIALOGUE

Wáng Jīnglǐ (pointing to a girl approaching them): Tā shì shéi? Tā shì búshì nǐde nǚpéngyou?

Mínglěi: Búshì. Tā shì wǒ jiějie. (Turning to address his elder sister Lìlián) Sānjiě, tā shì wǒ gōngsī de jīnglǐ.

Lìlián: Nín hǎo! Qǐngwèn, nín guìxìng?

Wáng Jīnglǐ: Wǒ xìng Wáng.

Lìlián: Wáng Jīnglǐ, hěn gāoxìng rènshì nín.

Wáng Jīnglǐ: Xiǎojiě, nǐ jiào shénme míngzi?

Lìlián: Wǒ jiào Hán Lìlián.

Wáng Jīnglǐ: Nǐ shì búshì xuéshēng?

Lìlián: Bù, wǒ shì yóuyǒng jiàoliàn.

DIALOGUE TRANSLATION

Manager Wáng (pointing to a girl approaching them): Who is she? Is she your girlfriend?

Mínglěi: No. She's my elder sister. (Turning to address his elder sister Lìlián) Third Elder Sister, he's the manager of my company.

Lìlián: Hello! May I ask what your name is?

Manager Wáng: My name's Wáng.

Lìlián: Glad to meet you, Manager Wáng.

Manager Wáng: What's your name, young lady?

Lìlián: My name is Hán Lìlián.

Manager Wáng: Are you a student?

Lìlián: No, I'm a swimming coach.

4.1 Introducing Oneself and Asking About a New Acquaintance's Name

Subject	shì	Noun of Relationship	
Tā	shì	wǒ māma.	(She is my mom.)
Tā	shì	wǒ(de) jīnglǐ.	(He is my manager.)
Wǒ	shì	nǐ(de) lǎoshī.	(I'm your teacher.)

When introducing someone to a third party, it is common to use the pattern "subject + shì + noun of relationship," as in "Tā shì gōngsī de jīnglǐ" (He is the company's manager), or "Tā shì wǒde nǚpéngyou" (She is my girlfriend). If you wish to be more specific, you may plug in a proper name for the subject, as in "Lìlián shì wǒde nǚpéngyou"

(Lìlián is my girlfriend), or address the listener directly, as in "Lìlián, Wáng Jīnglǐ shì wǒ gōngsī de jīnglǐ" (Lìlián, Manager Wáng is the manager of my company).

Qǐngwèn, nín guìxìng?	(May I ask what your name is?/ May I ask what you are honorably surnamed?)
Wǒ xìng Hán.	(I am surnamed Hán./ My name is Hán.)
Nǐ jiào shénme míngzi?	(What's your name?/ What are you called?)
Wǒ jiào Lǐ Míng.	(My name is Lǐ Míng./ I'm called Lǐ Míng.)
Hěn gāoxìng rènshì nǐ.	(Glad to meet you.)

If you are asking the name of someone older than you or higher in social status, or even of a person who seems to be about the same age or social status as you, it is best to use the idiomatic question phrase "Nín guìxìng?" This literally means, "You are honorably surnamed . . . ?" The "what" is implied but not stated after the verb "xìng" (to be surnamed). As an honorific idiomatic phrase, "Nín guìxìng?" honors the listener both through the polite second-person pronoun "nín" and via the adjective "guì," here used in the adverbial position before the verb to mean "honorably."

To show extra respect for Manager Wáng, Lìlián prefaces the idiom "nín guìxing" with the common phrase, "Qǐngwèn" (May I ask . . .). This phrase indicates that you respect a stranger or new acquaintance, and appreciate the trouble that person will be taking to answer your question.

You will notice in the dialogue that Manager Wáng does not use the honorific "guì" when he refers to himself, but simply says, "Wǒ xìng Wáng," literally, "I am surnamed Wáng" (My name is Wáng). Except for a person of highest rank, such as an emperor in old China, a speaker should never use an honorific term in reference to himself, but rather to other people, especially the listener. Notice, too, that "xìng" takes only a surname as its object. If Manager Wáng wanted to tell Lìlián his given name along with his surname, he would need to replace the verb "xìng" with the verb "jiào," which will be discussed below. Yet since the Chinese tend to be quite status-conscious, addressing one another with titles such as "Manager" and "Teacher" comes more naturally than with speakers of English, who would find "Manager Smith" a stiffly formal term of address.

After you find out the name of someone you have just met for the first time, the next step is to say how glad you are to have met her. The full version of the standard phrase is "Wǒ hěn gāoxìng rènshì nín"; but since the identity of the subject is obvious in such a conventional phrase, it is usually omitted, just as English speakers will say "Happy to meet you" and the French will say "Enchanté." In general, Chinese speakers omit the understood first-person subject of a sentence more often than Westerners.

It is wrong, however, to omit the adverb "hěn," which typically precedes an adjectival verb not marked by some other adverb, as in "zhēn gāoxìng" (truly happy) or "fēicháng gāoxìng" (extremely happy). The "hěn" in this model sentence usually receives an unstressed vocalization of low volume and short duration; only when "hěn" is fully stressed does it carry its literal meaning of "very." Lìlián's direct address of Mínglěi's boss as "Wáng Jīnglǐ" here makes her statement more respectful, but is not mandatory.

If you are asking the name of someone younger or lower in status than you, it is standard to say, "Nǐ jiào shénme míngzi?" (literally, "What name are you called by?"). Depending on the context, "míngzi" refers either to the full name (surname or family name plus given name), as in Hán Lìlián, or to just the given name, as in Lìlián. As an option, you can make this standard question form more courteous if you preface it with a fairly polite form of address, such as "xiǎojiě" for a young lady or other unmarried woman.

The proper way to reply to such a question is to say "I am called such-and-such" (Wǒ jiào X); that is, you supply your full name (such as Hán Lìlián) in place of the questioner's "shénme míngzi" (what name?), maintaining the same word order throughout. Though many ethnic Chinese living in the West follow the Western practice of placing the given name first and the family name last, practically all Chinese in China adhere to the traditional practice of putting the family name first and the given name second. If and when you have a Chinese-style name, you should also adopt the traditional Chinese practice when in China.

Exercises for 4.1: Fill in the blanks to complete the sentences according to the English meanings given.

1. You try to get acquainted with someone older than you.
   You say: _____, nín _____?
   (May I ask what your surname is?)

   She answers: Wǒ xìng Wáng. Nǐ jiào _____
   míngzi? (My surname is Wáng. What's your name?)

2. Mínglěi introduces himself and inquires about the name
   of a young man. Mínglěi: _____ Hán Mínglěi.
   Qǐngwèn, _____?
   (I am called Hán Mínglěi. May I ask what your name is?)

3. Your elder sister introduces you to her friend.
   Jiějie: Tā shì wǒ péngyou. Tā _____ Lǐ.
   (Her surname is Lǐ.)

   You say: Lǐ _____, hěn _____.
   (Miss Lǐ, I'm glad to meet you.)

   Lǐ: Wǒ yě hěn gāoxìng rènshì nǐ.

4. Lǐ Jīnglǐ (to a young lady): Qǐngwèn, _____?
   (May I ask what your name is?)

   Hán Lìlián: _____. (My name is Hán Lìlián
   [Lillian Han].)

5. Lǐ Jīnglǐ (pointing to a young man): _____? (What
   is his name?)

   Hán Lìlián: _____. (His name is Chén Dàwèi
   [David Chen].)

4.2 The Apostrophe-"s"-like Modification Particle "de"

Modifier		Modified Word	
Noun	de	Noun	
nǐ	de	péngyou	(your friend)
tā	de	xuéshēng	(her student)
wǒ	de	gōngsī	(my company)
wǒ gōngsī	de	jīnglǐ	(my company's manager)
nǐ bàba	de	jiàoliàn	(your dad's coach)
tā lǎoshī	de	māma	(his teacher's mom)

The important and ubiquitous particle "de" directly follows a modifier and precedes the word being modified. In other words, "de" indicates that the word preceding "de" tells you something specific about the word coming after "de." Manager Wáng is not just any

Dragon-boat racing is a popular annual pastime during the late spring Duānwǔ Festival, which commemorates the ancient southern poet and courtier Qū Yuán.

old manager, but the manager of a company or a company's manager, "gōngsī de jīnglǐ."

Notice that the Chinese "de" makes the process of modification proceed in the opposite direction from the French "de," which like the English "of" serves to place the modifier at the end of the phrase instead of at the beginning. The Chinese "de" functions rather like an apostrophe "s" ('s), which also indicates that the preceding word modifies the following word. Thus we have "Mínglěi de nǚpéngyou" (Mínglěi's girlfriend), or "tāde nǚpéngyou" (his girlfriend). Instead of having a separate group of possessive pronouns such as "her," "your," and "my," Chinese simply affixes "de" to pronouns like "tā," "nǐ," and "wǒ" to result in "tāde," "nǐde," and "wǒde," as in "wǒde jiàoliàn" (my coach), "nǐde míngzi" (your name), and "tāde gōngsī" (his company).

Longer and more complex modifiers will be examined in later chapters. For the time being it is worth noting that if there are two or more modifiers such as "wǒ" and "gōngsī" both modifying the word "jīnglǐ," the "de" after the first modifier ("wǒ") usually drops out to result in "wǒ gōngsī de jīnglǐ" (my company's manager). It is possible but uncommon to say "wǒde gōngsī de jīnglǐ" instead.

Exercises for 4.2: Translate the following sentences into Chinese.

1. He is my student.

   _____

2. Is she your elder sister? (Use the question particle "ma.")

   _____

3. Her name is not Hán Lìlián.

   _____

4. I am the manager of his company.

   _____

5. Teacher Hán is my friend's mother.

   _____

6. Isn't he your friend's swimming coach? (Use the question particle "ma.")

   _____

4.3 The Alternate-choice VERB-bù-VERB Question Pattern, as in "Shì búshì"

Subject	Verb-bù-Verb	Object?	
Nǐ	shì búshì	lǎoshī?	(Are you a teacher?)
Tā	shì búshì	jīnglǐ?	(Is she a manager?)
Tā	shì búshì	xuéshēng?	(Is he a student?)

Instead of affixing a "ma" particle to the end of a sentence, you can transform a declarative sentence into a question by repeating the main verb with "bù" sandwiched in between; that is, instead of SUBJ-VERB-OBJ ma, you would have SUBJ-VERB-bù-VERB-OBJ. Rather than "Nǐ shì xuéshēng ma?" you would say "Nǐ shì búshì xuéshēng?" Though the latter sentence may at first glance seem to be saying, "Are you or are you not a student?" the challenging and severe tone of that English utterance does not exist in the Chinese VERB-bù-VERB pattern. "Tā shì búshì nǐde péngyou?" thus translates as "Is she your friend?" not "Is she your friend or not?"

Exercises for 4.3: Translate into Chinese, then transform into the alternate-choice VERB-bù-VERB question pattern.

1. She is your girlfriend.

_____

_____

2. I am Teacher Wáng's student.

_____

_____

3. He is Coach Lǐ's friend.

_____

_____

4. You are Mínglěi's father.

_____

_____

5. She is Manager Hán's third elder sister.

_____

_____

4.4 Keeping the Same Word Order in Questions as in Declarative Sentences

Subject	Verb	Object	
Nǐ	shì	shéi?	(Who are you?)
Wǒ	shì	Lǐ Lǎoshī.	(I'm Teacher Lǐ.)
Nǐ	jiào	shénme (míngzi)?	(What's your name?)
Wǒ	jiào	Hán Mínglěi.	(My name is Hán Mínglěi.)

In European languages such as English, the standard SUBJ-VERB-OBJ word order in declarative sentences is almost always inverted in "who?" or "what?" questions, with the subject and object positions reversing. To make the declarative sentence "She is my coach" into an English "who?" question, you have to move the subject "she" to the end of the sentence where the object normally is.

You must also move the question word that substitutes for "my coach" (who) to the beginning of the sentence where the subject normally is, resulting in the question "Who is she?"

In contrast, Chinese word order does not change when you transform a declarative sentence into a question asking "who?" or "what?" To make "Tā shì wǒde jiàoliàn" into a question, you simply plug in the question word "shéi" (who?) for the object in its normal position after the verb, resulting in "Tā shì shéi?" If the object of a sentence is a thing rather than a person, you use "shénme" (what?) instead of "shéi" in the same way. The statement "Tā jiào Hán Lìlián" (She's called Hán Lìlián) thus becomes "Tā jiào shénme?" (What's she called?), with an optional "míngzi" at the end in this particular case.

Exercises for 4.4: Translate the following dialogue into Chinese.

1. A: Who is he?

    _____

2. B: He is the manager of my company.

    _____

3. A: What is his name?

    _____

4. B: His name is Lǐ Míng.

    _____

5. A: Who is she?

    _____

6. B: She is my eldest sister.

    _____

7. A: Is she a student?

    _____

8. B: No, she's not a student.

    _____

9.   A: Is she a teacher?

_____

10.   B: Yes, she is a teacher.

_____

4.5 Words Such As "Nǚ" That Must Be Bound to Another Word, and Cannot Stand Alone

An important distinction is made in spoken Chinese between "free" words that can stand alone and independent, versus "bound" words that lack this independent quality and must be attached to another word to be pronounced. Nearly all particles such as "ma," "ne," and "de" are bound words.

Moreover, while "female" and "male" are independent words in English, "nǚ" and "nán" (male) must be bound or attached to another word such as "xuéshēng" or "péngyou" to make "nǚxuéshēng" (female student) or "nánpéngyou" (boyfriend). To speak of women in general, we can use a term such as "nǚde," "nǚrén," or "fùnǚ," but not "nǚ" alone. The designation BF, or "bound form," is used in the vocabulary lists to indicate when a word that is independent in English actually requires attachment to another word in Chinese. All particles such as "ma," "ne," and "de" can be assumed to be bound forms unless noted otherwise.

Finally, "nǚ" and "nán" also differ from their English counterparts in referring only to human females and males; their most common counterparts in the animal world are "mǔ" and "gōng," as in "mǔjī" (hen) and "gōngjī" (rooster).

Exercises for 4.5: Use "nán," "nǚ," "nánlǎoshī," "nǚlǎoshī," "nǚpéngyou," and "nǚxuéshēng" to fill in the blanks.

1. Lìlián shì _____ de, búshì _____ de. (Lìlián is a female, not a male.)

2. Tā shì _____, búshì _____. (He is a male teacher, not a female teacher.)

3. Tā shì _____, yě shì wǒde _____. (She is a girl student, and is also my girlfriend.)

4. Lǐ Dàwèi shì _____ jiàoliàn ma? (Is Lǐ Dàwèi a male coach?)

5. Wáng Míng shì búshì _____ jīnglǐ? (Is Wáng Míng a female manager?)

CULTURE NOTES

The Chinese language manages very well without verb conjugations, verb tenses, and other such taxes on the memory; however, Chinese word order is extremely important, and often leaves little room for variation. We can often understand these patterns in word order grammatically; an example is the consistency in word order between statements and questions.

On the other hand, cultural factors sometimes play a significant role in word order. Hailing or directly addressing someone has a special kind of cultural importance, and demands priority placement within the Chinese sentence. When directly addressing somebody, you should begin the sentence with the direct address, as can be seen in Lìlián's address of Wáng Jīnglǐ and his address of her as "xiǎojiě" in this chapter's dialogue. Although English allows the speaker to place the direct address either at the beginning or at the end of the sentence, Chinese requires placement at the beginning.

SUMMARY

When inquiring about the name of a new acquaintance who is your age or older and is of similar or higher social rank, it is best to use the polite or honorific formula "Nín guìxìng?" Only in very informal situations or when questioning someone who is younger or is of lower social status should you use "Nǐ jiào shénme míngzi?" to ask "What is your name?"

The common particle "de" denotes a modification process proceeding in the same direction as an " 's"; "de" follows the modifying word(s) and precedes the word being modified. Some examples are "wǒde jiàoliàn" (my coach), "nǐde nǚpéngyou" (your girlfriend), and "tā gōngsī de jīnglǐ" (her company's manager/the manager of her company).

Instead of using a sentence-end question particle such as "ma," you can formulate an affirmative question with the VERB-bù-VERB pattern. For instance, each of the following two questions asks, "Is Third Elder Sister a student?": "Sānjiě shì xuéshēng ma?" and "Sānjiě shì búshì xuéshēng?"

In "what?" questions using "shénme," the word order remains the same as in the declarative-statement reply, as contrasted with the flip-flopping of subject and object characteristic of English "what" questions: "Tā jiào shénme?" (What is she named?); "Tā jiào Lìlián" (She is named Lìlián). The same pattern holds for other question words such as "shéi" (who?): "Tā shì shéi?" (Who is he?); "Tā shì wǒ gōngsī de jīnglǐ" (He is my company's manager). An alternative pronunciation of "shéi" is "shuí."

CHAPTER 5

NǏ YǑU MÉIYǑU XIŌNGDÌ JIĔMÈI?

(Do you have brothers or sisters?)

CHAPTER OVERVIEW

1. The Special Verb "Yǒu" (to Have) and Some Key Adverbs Commonly Used with It

2. Small Numbers, and Using Measure Words with Numbered Nouns

3. The Specifier—Either Part of a Phrase with a Measure or Alone as a Noun

4. Asking How to Say Something in Chinese and How Many Things There Are

5. Showing a Photograph and Asking or Telling Someone About Relatives

---

NEW VOCABULARY

TRACK 11

1. yǒu	to have, there is, there are	VERB
2. méi	not (used instead of "bù" to negate "yǒu")	ADV
3. xiōngdì jiěmèi	brothers and sisters	NOUN
4. xiōngdì	elder and younger brother(s); brothers	NOUN
5. jiěmèi	elder and younger sister(s); sisters	NOUN
6. sān	three	NUM
7. ge	(generic measure word—goes between NUM and NOUN)	MEAS
8. gēge	elder brother	NOUN
9. dìdi	younger brother	NOUN
10. mèimei	younger sister	NOUN
11. jiā	family, home	NOUN
12. yígòng	altogether, in toto	ADV
13. jǐ	how many? (used with measure word and noun)	QW
14. rén	person(s)	NOUN
15. jiǔ	nine	NUM
16. hái	still, in addition	ADV
17. bàba	dad, papa	NOUN
18. māma	mom, mama	NOUN
19. zǔfù	grandfather (usually paternal side)	NOUN
20. zǔmǔ	grandmother (usually paternal side)	NOUN
21. hé	and, with (links nouns; pronounced "hàn" in Taiwan)	CONJ
22. shúshu	paternal uncle (younger than the father)	NOUN
23. kàn	to look at, to read	VERB
24. zhèi	this (requires a measure word between it and noun; orig. contraction of "zhè" [this] and "yī" [one]); pronounced "zhè" in Taiwan	SPEC
25. zhāng	(measure; word for flat things such as photos and paper)	MEAS
26. zhàopiàn	photograph	NOUN
27. nà	that	SPEC

28. yì	one, a (tone varies according to rules discussed below)	NUM
29. tiáo	(measure word for long things such as roads, rivers, and slacks)	MEAS
30. lù	deer (pronounced exactly the same as "road" in Chinese)	NOUN
31. zhī	(measure word for animals, boats, some body parts)	MEAS
32. Zhōngwén	Chinese (language, not just anything Chinese)	NOUN
33. zěnme	how? (mostly); how come? (sometimes)	QW
34. shuō	to say, to speak	VERB
35. chǒngwù	pet	NOUN
36. nèi	that (must have a measure word between it and noun; orig. contraction of "nà" [that] and "yī" [one]; pronounced "nà" in Taiwan)	SPEC
37. zhēn	truly, really	ADV
38. kě'ài	be cute, be lovable	ADJ
39. ài	to love; love, affection	VERB/ NOUN

DIALOGUE

Lǐ Lǎoshī: Nǐ yǒu méiyǒu xiōngdì jiěmèi?

Mínglěi: Wǒ yǒu sānge jiějie. Wǒ méiyǒu gēge, yě méiyǒu dìdi, mèimei.

Lǐ Lǎoshī: Nǐ jiā yígòng yǒu jǐge rén?

Mínglěi: Wǒ jiā yǒu jiǔge rén. Wǒ hái yǒu bàba, māma, zǔfù, zǔmǔ, hé yíge shūshu. (Taking a picture out of his pocket) Lǎoshī, nín kàn zhèizhāng zhàopiàn.

Lǐ Lǎoshī (pointing to an animal in the picture): Nà shì shénme?

Mínglěi: Nà shì yìtiáo lù.

Lǐ Lǎoshī: Búshì yìtiáo lù, shì yìzhī lù.

Mínglěi: Lǎoshī, "pet," Zhōngwén zěnme shuō?

Lǐ Lǎoshī: Chǒngwù.

Mínglěi: Nèizhī lù shì wǒde chǒngwù. Tā zhēn kě'ài.

DIALOGUE TRANSLATION

Teacher Lǐ: Do you have any brothers and sisters?

Mínglěi: I have three elder sisters. I don't have an elder brother, or a little brother or younger sister, either.

Teacher Lǐ: How many people are there altogether in your family?

Mínglěi: There are nine people in my family. I have, in addition, a dad, a mom, a grandfather, a grandmother, and one uncle. (Taking a picture out of his pocket) Take a look at this photo, Teacher.

Teacher Lǐ (pointing to an animal in the picture): What's that?

Mínglěi: That's a road (using the wrong measure word for "lù," deer).

Teacher Lǐ: It's not a road; it's a deer.

Mínglěi: How do you say "pet" in Chinese, Teacher?

Teacher Lǐ: Pet (lit., "chǒngwù").

Mínglěi: That deer is my pet. It's really cute.

5.1 The Special Verb "Yǒu" (to Have) and Some Key Adverbs Commonly Used with It

Subject/ Place Word	Adverb(s)	yǒu	Object/ Noun	
Wǒ		yǒu	māma.	(I have a mom.)
Tā	méi	yǒu	māma.	(He doesn't have a mom.)
Wǒ	hái	yǒu	bàba.	(I have, in addition, a dad.)
Nǐ	yě	yǒu	māma.	(You, too, have a mom.)
Wǒ jiā	yígòng	yǒu	sānge rén.	(Altogether, there are three people in my family.)

Unlike other verbs, which are negated by "bù," "yǒu" is unique in being negated by "méi" in standard form, as in "Māma méiyǒu wǒde zhàopiàn" (Mom doesn't have my photograph). It would be just as wrong to substitute "bù" for "méi" in the preceding sentence as it would be to blurt "Wǒ méi shì xuéshēng" (I'm not a student) instead of saying "Wǒ bú shì xuéshēng."

Although "yǒu" means "have" or "has" in the common SUBJ-VERB-OBJ sentence pattern, its meaning changes to "there is/are" in the pattern PW (place word) + yǒu + NOUN, "There is/are noun(s) at/in/on the place word." "Wǒ jiā yǒu jiǔge rén" could be awkwardly translated as "My family has nine people," but "wǒ jiā" is actually conceptualized here as a kind of place, a social unit that contains individual family members. If there are nine managers in your company, you would say, "Wǒ gōngsī yǒu jiǔge jīnglǐ."

Some Key Adverbs Commonly Used with "Yǒu"

The common adverb "hái" usually means "still" in affirmative sentences, as in "Tāde zǔfù hái hǎo" (Her grandfather is still okay). Before a few special verbs, however, chiefly "yǒu" and "yào" (to want), "hái" means "in addition." This use of "hái" is sometimes translated as "also," and might seem to overlap with the adverb "yě." In fact, the two usages are quite distinct, with "yě yǒu" typically emphasizing the subject while "hái yǒu" stresses the object. In the dialogue, Mínglěi has already established the context of family members by mentioning his three elder sisters, and he then goes on to specify the other five family members, who are the objects of the sentence: "Wǒ hái yǒu bàba, māma, zǔfù, zǔmù, hé yíge shúshu." In this context, substituting "yě" for "hái" would not make sense.

On the other hand, if Teacher Lǐ had instead told Mínglěi that she has a dad, a mom, a grandfather, a grandmother, and an uncle in her family, then it would make sense for Mínglěi to place the emphasis on himself (the subject) and respond, "Wǒ yě yǒu bàba, māma, zǔfù, zǔmù, hé yíge shúshu" (I, too, have a dad, a mom, a grandfather, a grandmother, and an uncle). Note that the meaning and emphasis of this sentence differ from its counterpart in the dialogue.

When referring to the sum total of something, use the adverb "yígòng" (altogether, in all). For example, "Jiàoliàn yígòng yǒu jiǔge péngyou" (The coach has nine friends in all).

Exercises for 5.1: Fill in the blanks with the following words: "yǒu méiyǒu," "yǒu" "méiyǒu," "hái yǒu," "yě yǒu," "yígòng yǒu."

1. A: Nǐ _____ gēge, jiějie ma?
   B: Duì ("Correct"). Wǒ yǒu sānge gēge, yíge jiějie.

2. Tā yǒu bàba, māma, _____ (have . . . in addition) zǔfù, zǔmù.

3. Nǐ shúshu _____ Zhōngwén lǎoshī?

4. Nǐ lǎoshī jiā _____ (there are altogether) jǐge rén?

5. A: Nǐ jīnglǐ yǒu méiyǒu xiōngdì jiěmèi?
   B: Tā _____ (does not have) xiōngdì jiěmèi.

6. A: Wǒ yǒu yíge dìdi, yíge mèimei.
   B: Wǒ _____ (also have) yíge dìdi, yíge mèimei.

5.2 Small Numbers, and Using Measure Words with Numbered Nouns

Small Numbers

0	1	2	3	4	5	6	7	8	9	10
líng	yī	èr	sān	sì	wǔ	liù	qī	bā	jiǔ	shí

As the chart shows, the Chinese numbers from zero to ten are "líng," "yī," "èr," "sān," "sì," "wǔ," "liù," "qī," "bā," "jiǔ," "shí." When numbers are used in isolation from words, as in postal zip codes and telephone numbers, Chinese works just like English: 765-4321 is "Qī liù wǔ, sì sān èr yī."

Using Measure Words

Number	Measure	Noun	
yí	ge	rén	(one person)
yì	zhī	lù	(one deer)
sān	tiáo	lù	(three roads)
sì	zhāng	zhàopiàn	(four photographs)

If, however, a number modifies a noun, as in "three friends" or "eight people," you cannot simply place the number in front of the noun, but must additionally sandwich an appropriate measure word between the number and the noun: NUM + MEAS + NOUN. English actually does this on occasion for nouns that aren't countable unless measured out in some sort of unit, such as "three head of cattle," "two teaspoonfuls of sugar," and "four acres of farmland." There is no Chinese equivalent for the English "of" in these expressions, just the three units NUM + MEAS + NOUN.

By far the most common measure word is "ge," the neutral-tone generic measure that is not restricted to a certain type of objects, as in "sānge míngzi" (three names) and "wǔge jiějie" (five elder sisters). The measure "zhāng" is used for flat objects, as in "yìzhāng zhàopiàn" (one photograph) and "bāzhāng zhuōzi" (eight tables). "Tiáo" is a measure for long and relatively slender things, such as in "liùtiáo lù" (six roads) and "qī tiáo yú" (seven fish); it is also used for "kùzi" (pants) and "qúnzi" (skirts). Though "tiáo" is sometimes used for particularly long animals such as some snakes and fish, by far the most common measure for animals is "zhī," as in "sānzhī lǎoshǔ" (three mice), "sìzhī lù" (four deer), "wǔzhī gǒu" (five dogs), and "liùzhī māo" (six cats).

Some other frequently used measure words are as follows:

- "jiàn" (piece), as in "wǔjiàn chènshān" (five shirts) and "yíjiàn dàyī" (one overcoat)
- "zhī" (lit. "branch"), as in "sānzhī bǐ" (three pens) and "yìzhī kuàizi" (one chopstick)
- "piàn" (thin slice), as in "sìpiàn miànbāo" (four slices of bread) and "liǎngpiàn ròu" (two slices of meat)
- "kuài" (lump), as in "bākuài táng" (eight lumps of sugar), "liùkuài ròu" (six chunks of meat), and "jiǔkuài (qián)" (nine dollars; see further explanation in Chapter 7)
- "bēi" (cup), as in "yìbēi kāfēi" (one cup of coffee) and "wǔbēi shuǐ" (five glasses of water)
- "píng" (bottle), as in "liǎngpíng qìshuǐ" (two bottles of soda pop)
- "shuāng" (pair), as in "sānshuāng xié" (three pairs of shoes) and "qīshuāng kuàizi" (seven pairs of chopsticks)
- "jià" (lit. "frame"), as in "liùjià fēijī" (six airplanes) and "sìjià diànshìjī" (four television sets)

Exercises for 5.2: Fill in the correct numbers and measure words.

1. _____ péngyou (seven friends)

2. _____ lù (one road)

3. _____ lǎoshī (four teachers)

4. _____ gǒu (six dogs)

5. _____ zhàopiàn (nine photographs)

6. _____ yú (eight fish)

7. _____ xiōngdì jiěmèi (five siblings)

Many contemporary choreographers have incorporated traditional operatic stage movements into their new dance routines.

8. _____ chǒngwù (three pets)

9. _____ zhǐ (ten sheets of paper)

10. _____ lù (two deer) [Use "liǎng" instead of "èr" for "two" nouns]

5.3 The Specifier—Either Part of a Phrase with a Measure or Alone as a Noun

The Specifier as Part of a Phrase with a Measure

Specifier	Measure	Noun	
zhèi	zhī	chǒngwù	(this pet)
nèi	ge	lǎoshī	(that teacher)
zhèi	tiáo	lù	(this road)
nèi	zhāng	zhàopiàn	(that photograph)

Generally, you need to use a measure in only two types of situations:

- You are indicating a specific number of things—the noun in question may either be stated outright ("sānge jiějie," three elder sisters) or implied through the context ("sānge," three of them).
- You are specifying a person or object by using a specifier such as "zhèi" (this) or "nèi" (that), as in "nèizhāng zhàopiàn" (that photograph) and "zhèige rén" (this person).

The NUM + MEAS + NOUN pattern is explained in Section 5.2, and the second pattern is SPEC + MEAS + NOUN. Note that neither of these patterns amounts to a complete sentence; each is only a noun phrase, in which the noun is being modified by a measure and either a number or a specifier.

The Specifier Alone as a Noun

Specifier/ Subject	Verb	Object	
Zhè	shì	shénme?	(What is this?)
Nà	shì	shénme?	(What is that?)
Zhè	shì	wǒde zhàopiàn.	(This is my photograph.)
Nà	shì	tā(de) jiā.	(That's his home.)
Zhè	shì	shéi?	(Who is this?)
Nà	shì	wǒ dìdi.	(That's my younger brother.)

The other type of specifier is a noun that is not modified by a measure or anything else, and it nearly always appears in the subject position of a sentence that states "This is X" or "That is Y." The pronunciation of these stand-alone noun specifiers contrasts significantly with that of their measure-hooked modifying specifiers: "Zhè shì wǒde chǒngwù" (This is my pet) versus "Zhèizhī chǒngwù bù kě'ài" (This pet isn't cute), and "Nà shì yìzhāng zhàopiàn" (That is a photograph) versus "Nèizhāng zhàopiàn shì tāde" (That photograph is his).

The subject-position noun specifier does not get inverted to the object position in an interrogative sentence, unlike the case with English and most other Western languages. Therefore, the question that would probably have elicited the answer "Zhè shì wǒde chǒngwù" is "Nà shì shénme?" (What is that?). Similarly, the question that would have incurred the response "Nà shì yìzhāng zhàopiàn" is "Zhè shì shénme?" (What is this?).

Exercises for 5.3: Rearrange the words in each entry to make a correct sentence according to the meanings given.

1. bàba   zhè   wǒ   shì   (This is my father.)

   _____

2. shéi   rén   shì   nèige   (Who is that person?)

   _____

3. lǎoshī   tā   rén   shì   de   nèige   Zhōngwén
   (That person is her Chinese teacher.)

   _____

4. shì   zhè   shénme   (What is this?)

   _____

5. dìdi   shì   wǒ   zhè   gǒu   de
   (This is my younger brother's dog.)

   _____

6. jīnglǐ   máng   nèige   de   gōngsī   hěn
   (The managers of that company are very busy.)

   _____

7. búshì   zhāng   mèimei   zhàopiàn   zhèi   de   wǒ
   (This photograph is not my younger sister's.)

   _____

5.4 Asking How to Say Something in Chinese and How Many Things There Are

Asking How to Say Something in Chinese

Topic	Comment	
"Pet,"	Zhōngwén zěnme shuō?	(How do you say "pet" in Chinese?)
"Pet,"	Zhōngwén shì chǒngwù.	("Pet" is "chǒngwù" in Chinese.)

When trying to discover the Chinese equivalent of a given English word or phrase, you can use this pattern: English word (pause) "Zhōngwén zěnme shuō?" (How do you say [English word] in Chinese?). Note that there is actually no "nǐ" (you) or any other subject in this sentence.

Like many other subjectless sentences in Chinese, this sentence adopts the common topic-comment structure, for which the nearest equivalent in English is "As for [topic], [comment]." In this sentence, the topic is the English word, and the comment, if literally and ungracefully rendered, is "In Chinese, how to say it?" The question word that makes this sentence interrogative is "zěnme," which fits in the adverbial position before the verb and usually means "how?" and less commonly "how come?"

Asking How Many Things There Are

Subject	Adverb	yǒu	Question Word "jǐ"/Number	Measure	Noun
Nǐ (How many pets do you have?)		yǒu	jǐ	zhī	chǒngwù?
Wǒ (I have six pets.)		yǒu	liù	zhī	chǒngwù?
Nǐ jiā (How many people are there altogether in your family?)	yígòng	yǒu	jǐ	ge	rén?
Wǒ jiā (There are five people altogether in my family.)	yígòng	yǒu	wǔ	ge	rén.

Questions about how many things there are follow the same pattern as most other transformations of declarative sentences into interrogatives. There is no change in sentence word order; instead, a question word is substituted for the item at issue, in this case the number of nouns. Starting with the pattern NUM + MEAS + NOUN, we plug in the question word "jǐ" (how many?) for the number, resulting in jǐ + MEAS + NOUN. For example, "yìzhāng zhàopiàn" (one photograph) becomes "jǐzhāng zhàopiàn?" (how many photographs?).

"Jǐ" is generally used when the questioner expects the answer to be a fairly small number—no more than 100, and often no more than 20 or so. Larger numbers and the question words for them are discussed in Chapters 6 and 7.

Rainwater continually replenishes this clan ancestral temple's courtyard pool, symbolizing the individual's cradle-to-grave integration with the clan.

Exercises for 5.4: Complete the following sentences.

1. A: "Cat," Zhōngwén _____? (How do you say "cat" in Chinese?)
   B: "Cat," Zhōngwén shì "māo." ("Cat" is "māo" in Chinese.)

2. A: Nǐ _____ nǚpéngyou? (How many girlfriends do you have?)
   B: Wǒ yǒu yíge.

3. A: Nǐ jiā yígòng _____ gǒu? (How many dogs are there altogether in your family?)
   B: Wǒ jiā yígòng yǒu wǔzhī gǒu.

4. A: "Sleep," _____? (How do you say "sleep" in Chinese?)
   B: Zhōngwén shì "shuìjiào." ("Sleep" is "shuìjiào" in Chinese.)

5. A: _____? (How many siblings do you have?)
   B: Wǒ yǒu yíge dìdi, yíge mèimei.
   (I have a younger brother and a younger sister.)
   Wǒmen _____. (There are, altogether, three of us.)

5.5 Showing a Photograph and Asking or Telling Someone About Relatives

Showing a Photograph

Since the family plays an especially important social role in Chinese culture, it is a good idea to take a family photo along on visits. You should be prepared to discuss the photograph and to explain the relationships of the persons pictured.

Asking or Telling Someone About Relatives

When asking about somebody's brothers and sisters, it is best to use the four-syllable classical phrase, "xiōngdì jiěmèi," which literally means "elder brothers, younger brothers, elder sisters, and younger sisters." No matter how complicated sibling relations may be in actual life, when it comes to the Chinese language there is a standard order for expressing hierarchical distinctions of gender and age: male before female, and elder before younger—except for parents, who are generally mentioned before the grandparents. When you are explaining who your brothers and sisters are, though, you will want to avoid that classical phrase and use plain terms such as "gēge," "jiějie," "dìdi," and "mèimèi."

Just as we customarily put an "and" before the last noun in a list in English, we may handle a similar situation in Chinese with a conjunction, "hé," that can serve to link nouns, but not verbs or verb clauses. It is often not necessary to use a "hé" where we would need an English "and," though; Chinese is more sparing than English in the use of conjunctions.

Chinese imperatives in which the speaker is commanding or requesting something of the listener use second-person pronouns such as "nǐ" and "nín" far more frequently than is the case in English. If Mínglěi were showing his family photograph to an ordinary friend instead of a teacher high in status, he would simply have said, "Nǐ kàn zhèizhāng zhàopiàn" (Look at this photograph). Mínglěi's request is more courteous because of both the polite "nín" (you) and the use of a title in addressing the teacher, "Lǎoshī, . . ."

A Chinese Song

Two Tigers
Sung to the tune of "Frère Jacques"

Liǎngzhī lǎohǔ, liǎngzhī lǎohǔ,
pǎo de kuài, pǎo de kuài,
yìzhī méiyǒu ěrduo,
yìzhī méiyou wěiba,
zhēn qíguài, zhēn qíguài.

(Two tigers, two tigers,
Run very fast, run very fast.
One has no ears,
One has no tail,
Truly strange, truly strange.)

SUMMARY

When modifying a noun with a number or a specifier such as "this" or "that," you must ordinarily sandwich a measure word between the number or specifier and the noun, as in "zhèitiáo lù" (this road), "yìzhī lù" (one deer), and "nèizhāng zhàopiàn" (that photo). To ask how many things there are, substitute the question word "jǐ" for the number in the above pattern (jǐ + MEAS + NOUN), as in "Nǐ yǒu jǐzhī lù?" (How many deer do you have?). The adverb "yígòng" (altogether) is often used when the speaker is totaling up objects or persons: "Wǒ jiā yígòng yǒu jiǔge rén" (There are nine people altogether in my family).

"Yǒu" is the only verb in standard form that is negated by "méi" instead of "bù," as in "Wǒ méiyǒu nǐde zhàopiàn" (I don't have your photo). The phrase "yǒu méiyǒu" generates affirmative questions in the same manner as the VERB-bù-VERB construction: "Nǐ yǒu méiyǒu wǒde zhàopiàn?" (Do you have my photo?). Although the adverb "hái" means "still" when appearing before most verbs, it conveys the sense of "also" or "in addition" when used before "yǒu": "Mínglěi hái yǒu yíge shúshu" (Mínglěi also has an uncle).

To ask about the Chinese equivalent of an English word such as "grandmother," say "Grandmother, Zhōngwén zěnme shuō?" (How do you say "Grandmother" in Chinese?). This useful question formula also exemplifies the topic-comment construction and the subjectless sentence, both of which occur often in Chinese. The most appropriate answer to this particular question is " 'Grandmother,' Zhōngwén shì 'zǔmǔ' " ("Grandmother" is "zǔmǔ" in Chinese).

CHAPTER 6

NǏ XIÀNZÀI YǑU MÉIYǑU SHÌ?
(Is there anything you have to do now?)

CHAPTER OVERVIEW

1. Counting to 100 and Beyond, Telling Clock Time, and Word Order for Time Words

2. Using "Men" for Plural Pronouns and "Liǎng" for Two + MEAS + NOUN

3. Suggestive Imperatives ("ba") and Negative Imperatives ("Bié")

4. "Yào" and "Qù" as Auxiliary Verbs and as Ordinary Verbs

5. Reduplicated Verbs Such As "Kànkan" for Imminent, Informal Action

6. The Sentence-end "le" for Expressing a Change in Situation

---

NEW VOCABULARY

1. Lín Xiānsheng	Mr. Lín	NOUN
2. xiānsheng	Mr. (after a surname), teacher, husband	NOUN
3. Xiǎo Hán	Young Hán (familiar address)	NOUN
4. xiǎo	be young (esp. before a surname), be little	ADJ
5. xiànzài	now	TW
6. shì	things that need doing, tasks, troubles	NOUN
7. yào + VERB	be going to VERB, must VERB, want to VERB	AUXV
8. yào (as VERB)	to want	VERB
9. qù	to go, to go to	VERB
10. qù + VERB	go VERB	AUXV
11. fēijīchǎng	airport	PW
12. fēijī	airplane	NOUN
13. jǐdiǎn	what time? / What time is it? (short form of #18)	QW
14. qǐfēi	to take off (usually from an airport runway)	VERB
15. hǎoxiàng	seems as though. . . , seemingly	ADV
16. sāndiǎn bàn	half-past three	TW
17. sāndiǎn	three o'clock	TW
18. jǐdiǎn zhōng	What time is it? / what time? (full form of #13)	QW
19. zhōng	clock (#18 is literally "how many points on the clock?")	NOUN
20. yìdiǎn wǔshíwǔfēn	1:55	TW
21. yìdiǎn	one o'clock	TW
22. wǔshíwǔfēn	55 minutes	TW
23. zāogāo!	darn!	EXPL
24. yǐjīng	already	ADV
25. liǎngdiǎn	two o'clock	TW
26. liǎng + MEAS + NOUN	two nouns	NUM
27. le	(sentence-end particle indicating change in situation)	PART
28. gǎnkuài + VERB	hurriedly VERB, VERB at once	ADV

TRACK 13

29. jiào	to call, to order	VERB
30. chūzū qìchē	taxicab (lit., "for-hire automobile"; "jìchéng chē" in Taiwan)	NOUN
31. qìchē	automobile	NOUN
32. kànkan	to take a look	VERB
33. fēijī piào	airplane ticket	NOUN
34. piào	ticket	NOUN
35. xiàwǔ	afternoon, P.M.	TW
36. wǎnshàng	evening, night	TW
37. bādiǎn èrshífēn	8:20	TW
38. bié + VERB	don't VERB	ADV
39. jí	be anxious	ADJ
40. wǒmen . . . ba.	Let's	
41. wǒmen	we, us	PRO
42. xiān + VERB	first VERB	ADV
43. hē	to drink	VERB
44. bēi	cup	MEAS
45. bēizi	cup	NOUN
46. chá	tea	NOUN
47. liáoliáo tiān	to have a chat	VERB
48. liáo tiān	to chat	VERB

DIALOGUE

TRACK
14

Lín Xiānsheng:	Xiǎo Hán, nǐ xiànzài yǒu méiyǒu shì?
Mínglěi:	Wǒ yào qù fēijīchǎng.
Lín Xiānsheng:	Nǐde fēijī jǐdiǎn qǐfēi?
Mínglěi:	Hǎoxiàng shì sāndiǎn bàn. Xiànzài jǐdiǎn zhōng?
Lín Xiānsheng	(looking down at his watch): Yìdiǎn wǔshíwǔfēn.
Mínglěi:	Zāogāo! Yǐjīng liǎngdiǎn le. Wǒ yào gǎnkuài jiào chūzū qìchē.
Lín Xiānsheng:	Wǒ kànkan nǐde fēijī piào. (Looks down at Mínglěi's ticket) Búshì xiàwǔ sāndiǎn bàn, shì wǎnshàng bādiǎn èrshífēn. Nǐ bié jí, wǒmen xiān qù hē yìbēi chá, liáoliáo tiān ba!

DIALOGUE TRANSLATION

Mr. Lín:	Young Hán, is there anything you have to do now?
Mínglěi:	I'm going to go to the airport.
Mr. Lín:	What time does your plane take off?

Mínglěi:	It seems as though it's half-past three. What time is it now?
Mr. Lín	(looking down at his watch): 1:55.
Mínglěi:	Darn! It's 2:00 already. I've got to call a taxicab right away.
Mr. Lín:	I'll take a look at your plane ticket. (Looks down at Mínglěi's ticket) It's not for half-past three in the afternoon, it's for 8:20 in the evening. Don't be anxious; let's first go drink a cup of tea and have a chat!

6.1 Counting to 100 and Beyond, Telling Clock Time, and Word Order for Time Words

Counting to 100 and Beyond

11	12	13	14	20	21	90	99	100
shíyī	shíèr	shísān	shísì	èrshí	èrshíyī	jiǔshí	jiǔshíjiǔ	yìbǎi

Additional Figures:

1,000	yìqiān	one thousand
10,000	yíwàn	ten thousand ("one wàn")
100,000	shíwàn	one hundred thousand ("ten wàn")
1,000,000	bǎiwàn	one million ("one hundred wàn")
10,000,000	qiānwàn	ten million ("one thousand wàn")
100,000,000	yíyì	one hundred million ("one yì")
1,000,000,000	shíyì	one billion ("ten yì")
3,247,958,601	sānshíèryì, sìqiānqībǎijiǔshíwǔwàn, bāqiānliùbǎilíngyī	three billion, two hundred and forty-seven million, nine hundred and fifty-eight thousand, six hundred and one

To count from 11 to 19, simply start with the number for 10, "shí," and follow that with the relevant integer from one to nine: "shíyī," "shíèr," "shísān," "shísì," "shíwǔ," "shíliù," "shíqī," "shíbā," "shíjiǔ." To count by tens from 20 to 90, reverse that order, placing "shí" after the relevant integer, as if saying "2 tens, 3 tens, 4 tens . . .": "èrshí," "sānshí," "sìshí," "wǔshí," "liùshí," "qīshí," "bāshí," "jiǔshí." For a number between 21 and 99 that does not end in zero, the number in the tens place precedes "shí," while the number in the units place follows "shí," as in "èrshíyī" (21), "sìshísān" (43), and "wǔshíqī" (57).

Telling Clock Time

Time Word	Question Word "jǐ"/Number	diǎn (zhōng)
Xiànzài (What time is it now?)	jǐ	diǎn (zhōng)?
Xiànzài (It's seven o'clock now.)	qī	diǎn (zhōng).

Larger Units	Smaller Units in Telling Time				
	Number 1	diǎn	Number 2	fēn	
zǎoshàng	liù	diǎn	shí	fēn	(6:10 in the morning)
xiàwǔ	sān	diǎn	èrshísì	fēn	(3:24 in the afternoon)
	Number	diǎn	bàn		
wǎnshàng	jiǔ	diǎn	bàn		(9:30 in the evening)

To indicate the hour of the day, use the pattern NUM + diǎn (+ zhōng), as in "qīdiǎn" (7:00), "shídiǎn zhōng" (10:00), "shíyīdiǎn" (11:00), and "shíèrdiǎn zhōng" (12:00). The "zhōng" is optional in this pattern and is usually omitted, especially in rapid speech. To ask what time it is now, simply plug in the question word "jǐ" (how many?) for NUM: jǐ + diǎn (+ zhōng). To stress the sense of "now," you can use the time word "xiànzài" and an optional "shì," resulting in "Xiànzài (shì) jǐdiǎn zhōng?" (What time is it now?).

The answer to a query about the time usually includes information about the number of minutes after the hour. If it is half past a certain hour of the day, you simply add "bàn" (half) right after the "diǎn," to make NUM + diǎn + bàn, as in "liùdiǎn bàn" (half-past six) and "shíyīdiǎn bàn" (half-past eleven). To indicate a certain number of minutes after the hour, use the measure "fēn" after the number of minutes in the same way that "diǎn" is used after the hour: NUM1 + diǎn + NUM2 + fēn. For example, 7:12 is "qīdiǎn shí'èrfēn," 12:19 is "shí'èrdiǎn shíjiǔfēn, 9:45 is "jiǔdiǎn sìshíwǔfēn," and 1:24 is "yìdiǎn èrshísìfēn."

English A.M. and P.M. designations follow the clock-time reading, but their Chinese counterparts precede it. We thus have "zǎoshàng qīdiǎn èrshísānfēn" (7:23 in the morning), "xiàwǔ sāndiǎn bàn" (half-past three in the afternoon), and "wǎnshàng jiǔdiǎn shíbāfēn" (9:18 in the evening). The Chinese language is admirably consistent in the way it orders units of time and space, starting with the largest unit and moving to progressively smaller units until the smallest is finally reached. For instance, the full address of a residence begins with the country it is in, then moves on to the province or state, the city or town, the name of the street, and finally the number of the house on that street. For time, Chinese begins with the year, then moves to the month, the day in the month, the part of the day such as morning or afternoon, and finally the hour and minute.

Word Order for Time Words

Subject	Time Word	Verb	
Fēijī	jǐdiǎn	qǐfēi?	(When does the plane take off?)
Fēijī	sìdiǎn	qǐfēi.	(The plane takes off at four o'clock.)

Consistency in word order also exists in the placement of time words in a sentence. Time words indicating when an action is happening or has happened need to go somewhere before the verb, and are usually sandwiched between the subject and verb, SUBJ + TW + VERB, as in "Nǐde fēijī jǐdiǎn qǐfēi?" (What time does your plane take off?).

Mínglěi and Mr. Lín know that the take-off time is the subject of their conversation, so there is no need to keep repeating the verb "qǐfēi." However, if somebody not yet in the know, such as Lìlián, were to walk up to the two men right at that point, Mínglěi would very likely tell her, "Wǒde fēijī sāndiǎn bàn qǐfēi" (My plane is taking off at half-past three). Moreover, there is an understood "qǐfēi" just before the comma and period in Mr. Lín's later statement, "Búshì xiàwǔ sāndiǎn bàn, shì wǎnshàng bādiǎn èrshífēn."

Exercises for 6.1

I. Say the following numbers in Chinese.

19, 24, 35, 47, 56, 63, 71, 82, 99

II. Complete the following sentences and phrases according to the meanings given.

1. A: Xiànzài _____ zhōng? (What time is it now?)
   B: Xiànzài _____ diǎn _____ fēn.
   (It's 12:48.)

2. _____ diǎn _____. (9:30 in the
   morning)

3. _____ diǎn _____ (fēn). (8:27 in
   the evening)

4. _____ diǎn _____ (fēn) (3:36 in
   the afternoon)

5. A: Nǐde fēijī _____ qǐfēi? (What time does your
   plane take off?)
   B: _____ qǐfēi. ([It] takes off at 10:55.)

6. A: Nǐ jǐdiǎn yào jiào chūzū qìchē? (When are you going to call a
   taxicab?)
   B: Wǒ _____ (11:25) yào jiào.

6.2 Using "Men" for Plural Pronouns and "Liǎng" for Two + MEAS + NOUN

Using "Men" for Plural Pronouns

Plural Pronouns		
wǒmen (we)	nǐmen (you)	tāmen (they)

Although the vast majority of English nouns can be designated as plural by adding an "s" or "es" to the singular form of the noun, Chinese nouns are not marked for singular or plural. A noun such as "fēijī" can mean either "airplane" or "airplanes"—you have to look at the context in which "fēijī" appears before you can figure out whether the speaker is referring to one airplane or to two or more airplanes. Instead of specifying whether a noun is singular or plural, the Chinese language often uses measures to classify nouns as naming flat objects, elongated objects, animals, and so on.

The major exception to the relative absence of plural markers in Chinese is the pluralizing suffix for pronouns, "men." On rare occasion, "men" can follow a noun that refers to human beings, such as "háizimen" (children), but it is almost always used after pronouns ("háizi" is by far the most common equivalent of both "child" and "children"). We thus have "wǒmen" for "we" or "us," "tāmen" for "they" or "them," and "nǐmen" for the plural "you," the Bronx dialect's "youse," or the American southerner's "y'all."

Using "Liǎng" for Two + MEAS + NOUN

Two	Measure	Noun	
liǎng	ge	rén	(two persons)
liǎng	zhī	chǒngwù	(two pets)

When talking about two particular things, as opposed to the number 2 in a purely numeric chain such as a phone number or a postal code, we have to substitute "liǎng" for "èr." In other words, liǎng + MEAS + NOUN leads us to say things like "liǎngdiǎn bàn" (half-past two), "liǎngzhī lǎoshǔ" (two mice), and "liǎngge péngyou" (two friends). Keep in mind that "liǎng" is used only when there are two things in question, not for any other number that might include the numeral 2, such as 12 or 22. We would thus say "shíèrdiǎn bàn" (half-past 12), "èrshíèrge péngyou" (22 friends), and "sānshíèrzhī lǎoshǔ" (32 mice).

Exercises for 6.2: Answer the following questions using the cues given.

1. A: Nǐmen yào qù nǎr? (Where are you going?)
   B: _____. (We're going to the airport.)

2. A: Tāmen jǐdiǎn yǒu shì? (When will they have things to do?)
   B: _____. (They'll have things to do at 2:12.)

3. A: Nǐmen gōngsī yǒu jǐge jīnglǐ? (How many managers are there in your company?)
   B: _____. (There are two managers in our company.)

4. A: Tāmen jǐdiǎn yào hē chá? (When are they going to drink tea?)

   B: _____. (They're going to drink tea at 2:20.)

5. A: Nǐmen lǎoshī jiā yǒu jǐzhī māo? (How many cats are there in your teacher's home?)

   B: _____. (There are two cats in our teacher's home.)

6.3 Suggestive Imperatives ("ba") and Negative Imperatives ("Bié")

Suggestive Imperatives ("ba")

Subject	Adverb	Verb	Object	ba	
Wǒmen		hē	chá	ba.	(Let's drink tea.)
Wǒmen	xiān	qù	nǐ jiā	ba.	(Let's first go to your home.)

To soften a command or request in the imperative mode, you can add the particle "ba" to the very end of the sentence. This kind of suggestive imperative sentence is very similar to English imperatives beginning with the word "better" in the second-person mode (with "you" as the understood subject) and the word "let's" in the first-person plural mode.

Compare a sentence in the standard imperative, "Nǐ xiān hē chá" (Drink tea first), with the suggestive imperative version, "Nǐ xiān hē chá ba" (Better drink tea first). More common still is the first-person plural "let's VERB" sentence, such as "Wǒmen jiào chūzū qìchē ba" (Let's call a taxicab). In sentences such as this, northern Chinese speakers sometimes use "zámen," a special form of "we" that includes the speaker in the "we" group. A northerner thus might say, "Zámen jiào chūzū qìchē ba."

Negative Imperatives ("Bié")

(Subject)	bié	Verb	Object	
(Nǐ)	bié	jiào	wǒ.	(Don't call me.)
(Nǐmen)	bié	hē	chá.	(Don't drink tea.)

For negative imperatives of the "Don't VERB" variety, the adverbial "bié" fits in the slot we would expect: between the subject ("nǐ" or "nǐmen") and the verb: "Nǐ bié jiào wǒ lǎoshǔ" (Don't call me a mouse). Note that Chinese usually includes the second-person pronoun subject in the negative imperative, while English includes this subject only in rare cases of vehemence and implied threat, as in "Don't you (dare) call me a mouse!"

Exercises for 6.3: Translate the following.

1. Let's drink tea. (Use "ba.")

_____

2. Don't call a taxicab. (Use "bié.")

_____

3. You (plural) better go to the airport. (Use "ba.")

_____

4. Please don't call me "Teacher." (Use "bié.")

_____

5. Please don't look at my photo.

_____

6.4 "Yào" and "Qù" as Auxiliary Verbs and as Ordinary Verbs

Using "Yào"

Subject	yào (Verb)	Object	
Wǒ	yào	péngyou.	(I want friends.)
Tā	yào	māma.	(He wants Mom.)

Subject	yào (Auxiliary Verb)	Verb	Object	
Wǒ	yào	kàn	péngyou.	(I want to see a friend.)
Nǐ	yào	hē	chá.	(You want to drink tea.)

"Yào" often means "want," either as an ordinary verb, as in "Wǒ yào chá" (I want tea), or as an auxiliary verb: "Wǒ yào hē chá" (I want to drink tea). Yet "yào" has two other very common functions that beginning textbooks often ignore or introduce too late.

1. Chinese verbs have no tenses, but it is possible to introduce a future aspect to a verb by using "yào" as an auxiliary verb, as in "Wǒ yào qù fēijīchǎng" (I'm going to go to the airport). In this pattern SUBJ + yào + VERB, the subject will verb or is going to verb in the near future.
2. "Yào VERB" quite often means "must verb" or "have got to verb," as in "Wǒ yào gǎnkuài jiào Lìlián" (I must call Lìlián at once).

In general, you must look at the context in which "yào" occurs as an auxiliary verb to decide whether the speaker wants to verb, is going to verb in the near future, or has got to verb.

Using "Qù"

Subject	qù (Verb)	Place Word	
Wǒ	qù	nǐ jiā.	(I go to your home.)

Subject	qù (Auxiliary Verb)	Verb	(Object)
Tā (She goes swimming.)	qù	yóuyǒng.	
Wǒ (I go to see/visit a friend.)	qù	kàn	péngyou.

To express movement away from the speaker toward a destination, the simplest pattern is SUBJ + qù + PW, as in "Tāmen qù yíge péngyou de jiā" (They're going to a friend's home), and "Wǒmen qù Shànghǎi" (We're going to Shànghǎi). Another important pattern for coming and going will be introduced in Chapter 10.

When "qù" is used as an auxiliary verb, it often implies a sense of purpose, "go (in order to) VERB": SUBJ + qù + VERB. For example, in "Wǒmen qù liáoliáo tiān ba" (Let's go have a chat), the speaker's focus is not on the actual going, but on his purpose: to have a chat with the listener.

Exercises for 6.4: Use the cues given to answer the following.

1. A: Nǐ gēge yào shénme?
   B: Tā _____. (He wants a photograph.)

2. A: Nǐmen yào hē shénme?
   B: Wǒmen _____. (We want to drink tea.)

3. A: Nǐde jīnglǐ jǐdiǎn yào jiào chūzū qìchē? (When is your manager going to call a taxicab?)
   B: _____. (He is going to call a taxicab at 4:35.)

4. A: Nǐmen (yào) qù nǎr? (Where are you going?)
   B: _____. (We are going to his company.)

5. A: Tāmen qù Hán Jiàoliàn jiā liáotiān ma?
   B: Bù, tāmen _____. (No, they go to Coach Hán's home to swim.)

6.5 Reduplicated Verbs Such As "Kànkan" for Imminent, Informal Action

To underline the fact that an informal action has not yet begun but will soon take place, Chinese speakers often repeat or "reduplicate" the verb, as in "Nǐ kànkan wǒde fēijī piào" (Take a look at my airplane ticket). Reduplication is used only for action verbs, and the reduplicated or repeated verb is often in the neutral tone.

However, reduplication is never used for action that is completed or past. For beginning students of Chinese, it is far more important to be able to understand sentences with reduplicated verbs than to be able to generate such sentences in their own conversations.

6.6 The Sentence-end "le" for Expressing a Change in Situation

Adverb	Time Word	le (Change-of-Situation Particle)	
	Sìdiǎn bàn	le.	(It's four thirty.)
Yǐjīng	liùdiǎn	le.	(It's six o'clock already.)

The particle "le" has various important functions. This section introduces one of its most common uses when appearing at the end of a sentence, that of indicating a change in situation. In the dialogue, Mínglěi was originally relaxed about his impending trip to the airport, and assumed he still had plenty of time. When Mr. Lín told him that it was almost 2:00, however, Mínglěi experienced a new or changed perception of urgency: "Zāogāo! Yǐjīng liǎngdiǎn le" (Darn! It's 2:00 already). In this sentence, "yǐjīng" (already) helps to convey the sense of a change in situation; if that word were left out, we could add an adverb such as "now" in the translation to indicate a change: "Liǎngdiǎn le!" (It's 2:00 now).

Subject	bù	Verb	Object	le (Change-of-Situation Particle)	
Tā	bù	hē	chá	le.	(He doesn't drink tea any more.)
Nǐ	bú	shì	jiàoliàn	le.	(You aren't a coach any more.)

The change-of-situation "le" in negative sentences expresses the equivalent of "not verbing any more." Examples include "Tāmen bújiào chūzū qìchē le" (They don't call taxicabs any more), and "Lìlián búshì xuéshēng le" (Lìlián isn't a student any more).

Exercises for 6.6: Translate the following sentences using the sentence-end "le" to indicate a change in situation.

1. It's 3:00 already.

_____

2. Mr. Lǐ is not the manager any more.

_____

3. We are not going to the airport.

_____

4. Her teacher is not going to call a taxicab (now).

_____

5. My younger brother is not going to look at your pet any more.

_____

"Flying eaves" may be found on many local temples, such as this one in honor of Lord Guān, the God of War, in southern Ānhuī.

CULTURE NOTES

In spite of the availability of an ever-widening variety of things to drink, China's beverage of choice is still chá (tea). Teabags are not as rare as they once were, but many Chinese simply drop a pinch or two of loose tea leaves into a cup (bēizi) and brew tea by pouring boiling water (kāishuǐ) from a thermos (rèshuǐpíng) over the tea leaves. At restaurants and in more formal settings, the tea steeps in a teapot before being poured into small individual cups. Whether you're playing the role of host or guest in China, you will want to be ready to enjoy tea together with your friends and new acquaintances, as Mr. Lín invites Mínglěi to do.

SUMMARY

To refer to just two nouns, not to 12 or 20, use "liǎng" instead of "èr," as in "liǎngbēi chá" (two cups of tea) and "liǎngdiǎn zhōng" (two o'clock). Indicating the hour of the day involves the pattern NUM + diǎn (+ zhōng), and in queries about the hour the question word "jǐ" is substituted for the number representing the hour: "Jǐdiǎn zhōng?" (What time is it?). Adding "bàn" after "diǎn" makes it "half-past" the hour, as in "shíèrdiǎn bàn" (half-past twelve). To indicate a certain number of minutes after the hour, substitute NUM + fēn for "bàn": "xiàwǔ sìdiǎn èrshíqī fēn" (4:27 in the afternoon). Note that all of the above time words must go somewhere before the verb, and that larger units precede smaller units in Chinese, regardless of whether the issue is time or space.

The suffix "men" transforms a singular pronoun into its plural form, as in "wǒmen" (we/us) and "tāmen" (they/them). The sentence-end particle "le" indicates a change in situation: "Tā búshì jiàoliàn le" (She isn't a coach any more). On the other hand, the sentence-end particle "ba" softens imperatives, as in "Nǐ qù fēi-jīchǎng ba" (Better go to the airport) and "Wǒmen xiān liáoliáo tiān ba" (Let's first have a chat). In contrast, the adverb "bié" makes imperatives negative, as in "Nǐmen bié jí" (Don't be anxious) and "Bié hē chá" (Don't drink tea).

Though "yào" and "qù" can function as ordinary verbs, they are often used as auxiliary verbs instead. Some examples are "Wǒ yào jiào chūzū qìchē" (I've got to call a taxicab), "Nǐ qù kànkan tāde fēijī piào ba" (Better go take a look at her airplane ticket), and "Mínglěi yào qù fēijīchǎng" (Mínglěi is going to go to the airport).

CHAPTER 7

NÀME, NĬMEN MÀI SHÉNME?

(Well, then what *do* you sell?)

CHAPTER OVERVIEW

1. Inquiries About Products for Sale and Their Prices

2. Countries and National Languages as Noun Modifiers

3. Paying for a Purchase and Getting Change Back

4. The Conjunction "Nàme" and Measures for Books and Newspapers

5. The New Adverbs "Zhĭ" and "Zài," and Another Use of "yĕ"

6. The Rhetorical Question Pattern, "Búshì . . . ma?"

NEW VOCABULARY

TRACK
15

1.	nǐmen	you (plural), youse, y'all	PRO
2.	Měiguó	America, the United States	NOUN
3.	bàozhǐ	newspaper	NOUN
4.	fúwùyuán	shop clerk, waiter (PRC usage), also "diànyuán"	NOUN
5.	Zhōngguó	China (as a modifier, "Chinese")	NOUN
6.	dìtú	map	NOUN
7.	nàme	well, then; in that case . . .	CONJ
8.	mài	to sell	VERB
9.	zhǐ	only	ADV
10.	Zhōngwén	Chinese language	NOUN
11.	shū	book	NOUN
12.	Yīngwén de	English-language ones, ones in English	NOUN
13.	Yīngwén	English language	NOUN
14.	zhè	this	SPEC
15.	Hànyǔ	Chinese language (lit., "Hàn Chinese language")	NOUN
16.	cídiǎn	dictionary	NOUN
17.	běn	(measure for books, dictionaries, journals, and so on)	MEAS
18.	duōshǎo qián	How much money is it?/How much does it cost?	QW
19.	duōshǎo	how much? / how many?	QW
20.	qián	money	NOUN
21.	shíèr kuài wǔ máo	12 yuán 50, 12 and ½ yuán (PRC currency)	NUM
22.	kuài	(measure for dollars, yuán, and pieces of things like cake)	MEAS
23.	máo	(measure for dimes; commonly used after "kuài" + NUM)	MEAS
24.	guì	be expensive	ADJ
25.	mǎi	to buy	VERB
26.	gěi	to give	VERB
27.	kěshì	but, yet	CONJ
28.	búshì . . . ma?	Is it not . . . ?	

29. cuò	be wrong; to get something wrong	ADJ/ VERB
30. zài	another, again (for action that's not yet completed)	ADV
31. zhǎo	to return in change, to look for	VERB

DIALOGUE

TRACK
16

Mínglěi: Nǐmen yǒu méiyǒu Měiguó bàozhǐ?

Fúwùyuán: Duìbùqǐ, wǒmen méiyǒu!

Mínglěi: Yǒu méiyǒu Zhōngguó dìtú?

Fúwùyuán: Duìbùqǐ, wǒmen yě méiyǒu!

Mínglěi: Nàme, nǐmen mài shénme?

Fúwùyuán: Wǒmen zhǐ mài Zhōngwén shū, bú mài Yīngwén de, yě
bú mài dìtú.

Mínglěi (pointing at a dictionary on the shelf): Nà shì shénme?

Fúwùyuán: Zhè shì Hànyǔ cídiǎn.

Mínglěi: Yìběn duōshǎo qián?

Fúwùyuán: Yìběn shí'èrkuài wǔmáo. Bú guì.

Mínglěi: Wǒ mǎi liǎngběn, gěi nǐ wǔshíkuài.

Fúwùyuán: Kěshì, zhè búduì. Zhè shì èrshíkuài, búshì wǔshíkuài.

Mínglěi: O, nà búshì wǔshíkuài ma? Duìbùqǐ, wǒ cuòle. Zài gěi
nǐ shíkuài.

Fúwùyuán: Hǎo, zhǎo nǐ wǔkuài.

DIALOGUE TRANSLATION

Mínglěi: Do you have American newspapers?

Shop clerk: Sorry, we don't have them.

Mínglěi: Have you got Chinese maps?

Shop clerk: Sorry, we don't have those, either.

Mínglěi: Well, then what *do* you sell?

Shop clerk: We sell only Chinese-language books, and don't sell
English-language ones; we don't sell maps, either.

Mínglěi (pointing at a dictionary on the shelf): What's that?

Shop clerk: This is a Hàn Chinese dictionary.

Mínglěi: How much money for one of them?

Shop clerk: They're 12 yuán 50 each. They're not expensive.

Mínglěi (handing the clerk a bill): I'll buy two of them. Here's
50 yuán.

Shop clerk: But this isn't right. This is 20 yuán, not 50 yuán.

Mínglěi: Oh, that isn't 50 yuán? Sorry, I got it wrong. I'll give you
another 10 yuán.

Shop clerk: Okay, I'm returning you five yuán in change.

7.1 Inquiries About Products for Sale and Their Prices

Inquiries About Products for Sale

Subject	yǒu méiyǒu	Object?	
Nǐmen	yǒu méiyǒu	dìtú?	(Do you have maps?)

Subject	yǒu	Object	ma?	
Nǐmen	yǒu	dìtú	ma?	(Do you have maps?)

You may notice that the shop clerk's negative replies to Mínglěi's "yǒu-méiyǒu" questions dispense with both the subject "wǒmen" and the objects "bàozhǐ" and "dìtú," which are understood from the context and need not be repeated. In other words, the question (Nǐmen) + yǒu méiyǒu + OBJ (Do you [plural] have OBJ?) typically receives the simple affirmative answer "yǒu" or the brief negative answer "méiyǒu"; the respondent is of course free to expand her answer to the questioner, though she need not do so. She could have responded to Mínglěi's first question by saying, "Méiyǒu, wǒmen zhǐ yǒu Zhōngguó bàozhǐ" (No, we have only Chinese newspapers).

Inquiries About Prices

Yì	Measure	Noun	duōshǎo qián?/ jǐkuài qián?	
Yì	běn	shū	duōshǎo qián?	(How much for one book?)
Yì	zhāng	dìtú	jǐkuài qián?	(How many yuán for one map?)

Yì	Measure	(Noun)	Number 1	kuài	Number 2	máo	Number 3	fēn
Yì	běn	(shū)	shíèr	kuài	jiǔ	máo	wǔ	(fēn).
(One book is 12 yuán 95.)								
Yì	zhāng	(dìtú)	liǎng	kuài	sān	máo	èr	(fēn).
(One map is 2 yuán 32.)								

When asking how much an item costs, Chinese speakers seldom use a complete sentence with a verb, but instead adopt the topic-comment structure "Yì + MEAS (+ NOUN) duōshǎo qián?" (One X, how much money?). The measure for the basic monetary unit, either the Chinese yuán or the American dollar ("Měiyuán"), "kuài," is not used after the question word "duōshǎo." If, however, you are limiting your purchase to a small amount in the neighborhood of one to 20 yuán and would like to use the question word "jǐ" instead of "duōshǎo," you must include the measure "kuài": "Yìzhāng dìtú jǐkuài qián?" (How many yuán for one map?). If in doubt, use the phrase "duōshǎo qián" rather than the far less common "jǐkuài qián."

The answer to a question about an item's price follows the same topic-comment construction Yì + MEAS (+ NOUN) + NUM1 + kuài + NUM2 + máo: "Yìzhāng qīkuài bāmáo" (They're seven yuán 80 each). Note that the most important monetary unit smaller than the yuán (also termed rénmínbì, "people's currency") is the dime or jiǎo, which is spoken of as "máo."

Since the 1990s, the Chinese yuán has amounted to somewhat more than an American dime, and one máo to just over one U.S. penny, so it hardly made sense for many Chinese vendors to bother with the Chinese penny (fēn), which was worth only about one-tenth of an American penny. If Chinese fēn do appear in a price, as the smallest unit they appear exactly where you would expect them, at the very end: Yì + MEAS (+ NOUN) + NUM1 + kuài + NUM2 + máo + NUM3 + fēn, as in "Yìzhāng liùkuài sìmáo jiǔfēn" (They're six yuán 49 each).

In rapid speech, the last and smallest measure in a price expression is often omitted, as in "qīkuài bā" for seven yuán 80 and "liùkuài sìmáo jiǔ" for six yuán 49. Another unusual thing about prices is that, while "liǎngkuài" is the standard form for "two yuán," either "liǎng" or "èr" is okay before the smaller measures "máo" and "fēn." For the sake of consistency, you may wish to use "liǎng" with all three price measures, kuài, máo, and fēn, but be ready for others to call out prices such as "èrmáo" or "sìmáo èr."

Exercises for 7.1: Complete the following dialogues according to the cues given.

1. A: Nǐmen yǒu méiyǒu dìtú? (Do you have maps?)
   B: Yǒu, _____. (Yes, we have maps.)

2. A: _____? (Do you have English dictionaries?)
   B: Méiyǒu, wǒmen méiyǒu Yīngwén cídiǎn, wǒmen zhǐ yǒu Hànyǔ cídiǎn. (No, we don't have English-language dictionaries. We have only Chinese-language dictionaries.)

3. A: Zhōngguó dìtú yì zhāng duōshǎo qián? (How much for one of the Chinese maps?)
   B: _____. (The maps are 13 yuán 50 each)

4. A: _____? (How much for one dictionary?)
   B: Cídiǎn yìběn shíliùkuài sìmáoèr. (One dictionary is 16 yuán 42.)

5. A: _____? (How many yuán for one book?)
   B: Yìběn liǎngkuài jiǔmáowǔ. (One [book] is two yuán 95.)

7.2 Countries and National Languages as Noun Modifiers

The names of countries and national languages often function as nouns, as in "Zhōngguó yǒu xióngmāo" (There are pandas in China) and "Wǒ yào shuō Zhōngwén" (I want to speak Chinese). When such a name is used to modify another noun, it usually goes right before the modified noun, and without the modification particle "de" sandwiched between: "Zhōngguórén mǎi Zhōngwén bàozhǐ, Měiguórén mǎi Yīngwén bàozhǐ" (Chinese people buy Chinese-language newspapers, and Americans buy English-language newspapers).

Note that if we translated the first part of the above sentence as "Chinese buy Chinese newspapers," the ambiguity of the English word "Chinese" would obscure the important distinction between the two modifiers "Zhōngguó" (Chinese nationality) and "Zhōngwén" (Chinese language). "Zhōngguó bàozhǐ" refers to a newspaper in any language that is published in China, while "Zhōngwén bàozhǐ" refers to a newspaper in Chinese that could be published anywhere in the world where there are readers of Chinese.

To refer specifically to the spoken language of a country or territory, append "huà" to the name of that country or territory. Some examples are "Zhōngguóhuà" (spoken Chinese), "Rìběnhuà" (spoken Japanese), "Táiwānhuà" (Taiwanese), and "Guǎngdōnghuà" (Cantonese).

Countries and Territories	Languages
Měiguó	Yīngwén
Zhōngguó	Zhōngwén (OR Hànyǔ)
Yīngguó	Yīngwén
Fǎguó (OR Fàguó, France)	Fǎwén (OR Fàwén)
Déguó (Germany)	Déwén
Jiānádà (Canada)	Yīngwén, Fǎwén (OR Fàwén)
Rìběn (Japan)	Rìwén
Mòxīgē (Mexico)	Xībānyáwén (Spanish)
Éguó (OR Èguó, Russia)	Éwén (OR Èwén)
Táiwān (Taiwan)	Zhōngwén
Xīnjiāpō (Singapore)	Zhōngwén
Xiānggǎng (Hong Kong)	Zhōngwén

1. _____ bào (English-language newspapers)

2. _____ rén (Chinese people)

3. _____ dìtú (a map of the United States)

4. _____ shū (Chinese-language books)

5. _____ rén (British people)

6. _____ cídiǎn (French dictionary)

7.3 Paying for a Purchase and Getting Change Back

Paying for a Purchase

Wǒ	mǎi	Number 1	Measure	Word (Noun),	gěi nǐ	Number 2	kuài
Wǒ	mǎi	yì	běn	(shū),	gěi nǐ	shíwǔ	kuài.
(I'll buy one [book]. Here's 15 yuán.)							

When purchasing something, you typically tell the shop clerk how many items you are buying and how much money you are handing over—often a round sum that is more than the items are worth: Wǒ mǎi + NUM1 + MEAS (+ NOUN), gěi nǐ + NUM2 + kuài. If you are buying three newspapers for three yuán each, you would likely say, "Wǒ mǎi sānfēn, gěi nǐ shíkuài" (I'll buy three of them. Here's 10 yuán). Since "gěi" literally means "give," the literal meaning for the expression is "I'm giving you X amount," but the closest natural-sounding English equivalent for the act of handing over money to a clerk is "Here's X amount."

Getting Change Back from a Purchase

Zhǎo	nǐ	Amount	
Zhǎo	nǐ	liǎngkuài wǔmáo èr.	(I'm returning you two yuán 52 in change.)

A clerk giving change to a customer typically uses the pattern, Zhǎo nǐ + amount, as in "Zhǎo nǐ yíkuài" (I'm returning you one yuán in change). Many Chinese sentences omit the subject (here, "wǒ") if it is obvious from the context. The basic meaning of the verb "zhǎo" is "to look for," though during such purchases "zhǎo" refers to not only the clerk's search for the correct change, but also the act of handing the change to the customer.

Exercises for 7.3: Translate the following dialogue.

1. Do you sell Chinese-language books? (Use "ma" question.)

_____

2. Yes, we do.

_____

3. How much money per book?

_____

4. Nine yuán 20 each.

_____

5. I'll buy four books. Here's 50 yuán.

_____

6. I'm returning you 13 yuán 20 in change.

7.4 The Conjunction "Nàme" and Measures for Books and Newspapers

The Conjunction "Nàme"

Later chapters will introduce an adverbial function of "nàme," but this section describes its common use as a conjunction at the very beginning of a sentence that provides a retort or otherwise builds upon what someone else has just said. In the dialogue, Mínglěi's use of "nàme" to mean "Well, then . . ." or "In that case . . ." makes his question a bit emphatic, thereby better expressing his disappointment with the limited range of the bookshop's wares.

Measures for Books and Newspapers

Books (shū) and magazines (zázhì) both take "běn" (volume) as their measure. Newspapers (bào or bàozhǐ) are different, and for measures take "fèn" in multipage format and "zhāng" in single-sheet format.

Exercises for 7.4: Ask questions using the cues given.

1. A: _____? (Do you want to buy newspapers?)
   B: Duì, wǒ yào mǎi Měiguó bàozhǐ.

2. B: _____? (Do you sell English-language newspapers?)
   A: Wǒmen bú mài Yīngwén bào.

3. B: _____? (Well, then do you sell Chinese-language newspapers?) [Use the alternative-choice Verb-bù-Verb question pattern.]
   A: Wǒmen mài. Nǐ yào jǐ fèn?

4. B: _____? (How much for one newspaper?)
   A: Yìfèn zhǐyào jiǔmáo qī. Bú guì.

5. B: _____? (Do you also sell maps of China?) [Use the "ma" question.]
   A: Duì, wǒmen yě mài.

7.5 The New Adverbs "Zhǐ" and "Zài," and Another Use of "yě"

The New Adverbs "Zhǐ" and "Zài"

Subject	Adverb(s)	Verb	Object	
Tāmen	zhǐ	mài	shū.	(They sell only books.)
Wǒ	zài	mǎi	yìběn shū.	(I'll buy another book.)
Nǐmen	yě méi	yǒu	shū.	(You don't have books, either.)

The English word "only" can either precede or follow the verb or even go at the very end of the sentence: "We # sell # Chinese-language books #" (# denotes possible locations for "only" in the sample sentence). Yet since true adverbs in Chinese must precede the verb and come after the subject, the word order allows for only one of those three options, "Wǒmen zhǐ mài Zhōngwén shū," SUBJ + ADV + VERB + OBJ.

"Zài" is the first syllable of "zàijiàn" (see you later; lit., again see). "Zài" usually modifies actions that have not been completed. In the sentence "Zài gěi nǐ shíkuài" (I'll give you another ten yuán), the clerk is getting ready to give the customer another ten yuán in change, but hasn't yet concluded the transaction. Just as the meaning of the adverb "hái" can shift from "still VERB" to "verb another" with certain verbs like "yào" and "yǒu" and with a quantified object, "zài" can mean "another" with the verb "gěi" and a quantified object.

Another Use of "yě"

When "yě" precedes "bù" or "méi" in a negative verb phrase, its meaning is closer to "not VERB either" than to the awkward "also not VERB," as in "Wǒmen yě méiyǒu dìtú" (We don't have maps, either).

Exercises for 7.5: Rearrange the words in each entry to make a correct sentence according to the English meaning given.

1. mài zhǐ zázhì tāmen Yīngwén (They sell only English-language magazines.)

   _____

2. Zhōngwén bàba wǒ bú bàozhǐ kàn yě (My dad doesn't read Chinese-language newspapers, either.)

   _____

3. zài nǐ cídiǎn wǒ yìběn gěi Hànyǔ (I'll give you another Hàn Chinese dictionary.)

   _____

4. péngyou yě māma Měiguó tā méiyǒu (Her mom doesn't have American friends, either.)

   _____

5. háizi yìzhī zài chǒngwù mǎi nèige yào (That child wants to buy another pet.)

   _____

7.6 The Rhetorical Question Pattern, "Búshì . . . ma?"

One way to express doubt about something someone has said or done is to use the rhetorical question pattern, "Búshì . . . ma?" as in "Búshì shíèrkuài wǔmáo ma?" (Is it not 12 yuán 50?). The "búshì" here functions as "It is not a case of . . .", while the "ma" at the end of the sentence turns it into the question "Is it not a case of X?"

***Exercises for 7.6: Complete the following dialogue,
using the cues given.***

1. A: Qǐngwèn, Yīngwén cídiǎn yìběn jǐkuài qián?

2. B: _____ (17 yuán 50 each)

3. A: _____ (I'll buy three.)
    _____ (Here's 60 yuán.)

4. B: Zhǎo nǐ wǔkuài wǔ.

5. A: _____ (Isn't it 52 yuán 50 altogether?)

6. B: Ò, duìbùqǐ, zài gěi nǐ liǎngkuài. Nǐ háiyào mǎi shénme?

7. A: _____. (I also want to buy one English-
    Chinese dictionary [Yīng-Hàn cídiǎn].)

8. B: Wǒmen méiyǒu le. (We don't have [them] anymore.)

9. A: _____. (Isn't that one an English-Chinese
    dictionary?)

10. B: Ò, duìbùqǐ, wǒmen háiyǒu yìběn.

CULTURE NOTES

The PRC's economic reforms first initiated in the Dèng Xiǎopíng era (1978–1995) have made most economic enterprises increasingly mindful of customers' wants and needs, particularly in the growing private sector.

As an American of Chinese descent, Mínglěi's face automatically places him in the category of "Zhōngguórén" (Chinese person), a term that refers to ethnicity as much as nationality. On the other hand, Mínglěi's accent, clothing, and general mannerisms reveal him to be something of an outsider in this society, a "huáqiáo" or "overseas Chinese." Chinese society is more welcoming of visiting outsiders than are many other societies in East Asia, especially when a foreign visitor makes a sincere effort to speak Chinese, however haltingly. Like some other Leninist regimes, however, the PRC government has often tried to prevent foreign visitors from mingling too freely with Chinese locals, especially in the countryside. Fortunately, foreign visitors usually spend most of their time in cities, where such restrictions are far looser and often hardly noticeable. Foreign visitors have felt even more at home in Hong Kong and Taiwan, where an atmosphere of freedom has extended further into the political system and the media.

Because the PRC's borders contain various minority nationalities who speak their own languages, such as Tibetans, Mongolians, and Uighurs, the vastly dominant population of Chinese ethnics distinguish themselves from those minorities with the term "Hànrén" (persons of Hàn, Imperial China's first great and enduring dynasty). Similarly, the traditional term for the Chinese language, "Zhōngwén," which is still the standard term in Táiwān and Hong Kong, has been largely replaced by "Hànyǔ" (the Hàn language) in the PRC.

SUMMARY

"Duōshǎo qián?" is the standard way of asking how much something costs, though it is possible to substitute "Jǐkuài qián?" (How many yuán is it?) for an item in the one-to-20-yuán range. The three measures used for prices are "kuài" for the currency unit, "máo" for the dime unit, and "fēn" for the penny; an example is "Yìběn cídiǎn shíèrkuài wǔmáo qīfēn" (One dictionary is 12 yuán 57). The topic-comment construction is also used to ask how much a certain thing costs: "Yìběn cídiǎn duōshǎo qián?" (How much money is it for one dictionary?).

If you have underpaid somebody and are about to hand over another 20 yuán, use the uncompleted-action adverbial "zài" (again/another): "Wǒ zài gěi nǐ èrshíkuài" (I'm giving you another 20 yuán). In contrast, a shop clerk who is returning to you 15 yuán in change would say, "Zhǎo nǐ shíwǔkuài."

Note that while "Zhōngwén shū" is a Chinese-language book, "Zhōngguó shū" refers to a book in any language that is printed in China. Similarly, "Zhōngwén lǎoshī" is a Chinese-language teacher, while "Zhōngguó rén" means "Chinese person(s)." To make the name of a country, territory, or specific language modify a noun, simply place the modifier before the noun without the *de* particle sandwiched between. Substituting the *de* particle for the noun converts the modifier into a noun phrase, as in "Měiguó de" (an American one), "Zhōngwén de" (a Chinese-language one), "Yīngwén de" (an English-language one), and "Zhōngguó de" (a Chinese one).

CHAPTER 8

NǏMEN YǑU FÁNGJIĀN MA?

(Do you have any rooms?)

CHAPTER OVERVIEW

1. The Honorific Measure "Wèi" and Appositions Such As "Wǒmen liǎngge rén"

2. The Coverb of Accompaniment, "Gēn," and the Adverb "Yìqǐ"

3. "Líng" (Zero), and "Hào" as the Measure for a Room Number, License Number, and so on

4. The Directional Verb Complements "Qù" and "Lái"

5. Adverbial Modifiers of Adjectives Such As "Tài" and "Búgòu"

6. The Pattern PW + Yǒu + NOUN, and the Bound Localizers "Shàng" and "Lǐ"

Do you have any rooms? 91

NEW VOCABULARY

TRACK
17

1. Xiānsheng	sir (an honorific term of address)	NOUN
2. fángjiān	room (esp. at a hotel or dormitory)	NOUN
3. zhíyuán	employee	NOUN
4. wèi	(honorific measure for people)	MEAS
5. wǒmen liǎngge rén	the two of us	NOUN
6. zhù	to stay, to live (temporarily or over the long term)	VERB
7. Lǎo + surname	Ol' [surname], as in "Lǎo Zhāng," Ol' Zhāng	NOUN
8. lǎo	be old	ADJ
9. gēn	with (but a coverb instead of a preposition), and	COV
10. yìqǐ	together	ADV
11. èrlíngjiǔhào	Number 209	NUM
12. líng	zero	NUM
13. hào	(measure for a room number, license number, shoe size, and so on)	MEAS
14. zhāngláng	cockroach	NOUN
15. jiālǐ	in home, at home	PW
16. lǐ	in (bound localizer that must be attached to another word)	LOC/BF
17. yìliǎng + MEAS	one or two of them	NOUN
18. méi guānxi	It doesn't matter.	IDIO
19. búhuì + VERB	won't (likely) verb	AUXV
20. yǎo rén	to bite people	VERB-OBJ
21. yǎo	to bite	VERB
22. jiù	then	CONJ
23. qǐng + VERB	please verb	ADV
24. jìnqù	to go in	VERB
25. jìn	to enter	VERB
26. búgòu + ADJ	be not adjective enough	ADV
27. dà	be big	ADJ

28. yùshì	bathroom	NOUN
29. zhème + ADJ	be so adjective (also read "zèmme")	ADV
30. xiǎo	be small	ADJ
31. chuáng	bed	NOUN
32. tài + ADJ	too adjective	ADV
33. ruǎn	be soft	ADJ
34. āi ya!	yikes! / egads!	EXPL
35. chuángdān	bed sheets	NOUN
36. yǒudiǎn + ADJ	be a bit adjective	ADV
37. zāng	be dirty	ADJ
38. gānjìng	be clean	ADJ
39. háishì + bù + VERB	still don't verb	ADV
40. chūqù	to go out, to get out	VERB
41. chū	to exit (go out or come out)	VERB
42. biéde	another, something else	PRO
43. jìnlái	to come in	VERB
44. duóme + ADJ	How adjective it is!	ADV
45. a	(final particle indicating emphasis)	PART
46. zhuōzi shàng	on the table	PW
47. zhuōzi	table	NOUN
48. shàng	on (bound localizer, such as lǐ, that must be attached)	LOC/ BF
49. diànhuà	telephone (lit., "electric speech")	NOUN
50. diàn	electric, electricity	NOUN
51. huà	speech, spoken words	NOUN
52. zhèr	here ("zhèlǐ" in Taiwan)	PW
53. nàr	there ("nàlǐ" in Taiwan)	PW

DIALOGUE

Bǐdé: Xiānsheng, nǐmen yǒu fángjiān ma?

Zhíyuán (at the hotel):   Yǒu. Jǐwèi?

Bǐdé: Wǒmen liǎngge rén, yào zhù yíge fángjiān.

Zhíyuán (to the bellhop): Lǎo Zhāng, nǐ gēn tāmen yìqǐ qù kànkan èrlíngjiǔhào.

Lìlián: Nǐmen de fángjiān yǒu méiyǒu zhāngláng?

Lǎo Zhāng: Méiyǒu. Wǒmen de fángjiān méiyǒu zhāngláng. Wǒ jiālǐ yǒu yì liǎng zhī zhāngláng. Kěshì, méi guānxi, tāmen búhuì yǎo rén.

Lìlián: Fángjiānlǐ méiyǒu zhāngláng jiù hǎo. Wǒmen bú yào zhāngláng.

(later, just outside Room 209)

Lǎo Zhāng: Qǐng jìnqù kànkan.

Bǐdé: Zhèijiān hǎoxiàng búgòu dà. Yùshì zhème xiǎo.

Lìlián: Chuáng tài ruǎn le. Āi ya! Chuángdān yǒudiǎn zāng.

Lǎo Zhāng: Kěshì zhèige fángjiān hěn gānjìng, yě méiyǒu zhāngláng.

Lìlián: Wǒ háishì búyào. Wǒmen chūqù ba!

Lǎo Zhāng: Nàme, qù kànkan biéde ba!

Lǎo Zhāng (entering Room 312 first): Nǐmen jìnlái kànkan, zhèijiān duóme gānjìng a! Zhuōzi shàng hái yǒu diànhuà.

Bǐdé (to Lìlián): Wǒmen jiù zhù zhèr ba!

DIALOGUE TRANSLATION

Peter: Sir, do you have any rooms?

Employee (at the hotel): Yes. For how many people?

Peter: The two of us, and we want to stay in one room.

Employee (to the bellhop): Ol' Zhāng, go together with them to take a look at Number 209.

Lìlián: Are there cockroaches in your rooms?

Ol' Zhāng: No. There aren't cockroaches in our rooms. There are one or two roaches in my house. But it doesn't matter—they won't bite.

Lìlián: It's good there aren't cockroaches in your rooms. We don't want roaches.

(later, just outside Room 209)

Ol' Zhāng: Please go in and take a look.

Peter: It seems this room isn't big enough. The bathroom is so small.

Lìlián: The beds are too soft. Yikes! The bedsheets are a bit dirty.

Ol' Zhāng: But this room is clean, and it doesn't have cockroaches, either.

Lìlián: I still don't want it. Let's get out of here!

Ol' Zhāng: In that case, let's take a look at another room.

Ol' Zhāng (entering Room 312 first): Come in and take a look—how clean this room is! There's also a telephone on the table.

Peter (to Lìlián): Then let's stay here!

8.1 The Honorific Measure "Wèi" and Appositions Such As "Wǒmen liǎngge rén"

The Honorific Measure "Wèi"

You should never use an honorific such as "wèi" in referring to yourself, but only when showing respect to other people, as in "zhèiwèi lǎoshī" (this teacher) or "sānwèi lǎo xiānsheng" (three old gentlemen). Peter thus refers to Lìlián and himself as "liǎngge rén," not "liǎngwèi rén." When using "wèi" to refer to the listeners, as the hotel desk clerk does in the dialogue, the noun is generally omitted. As a result, the expression "jǐwèi?" is very common among waitresses and hotel clerks who need to know how many customers are in a given party; "jǐwèi rén?" is practically unheard of.

Appositions Such As "Wǒmen liǎngge rén"

Pronoun	Noun	Appositional Phrase
tāmen	sānge rén	the three of them
nǐmen	Zhōngguó rén	you Chinese
wǒmen	nǚrén	we women

When simply placing two different terms with the same referent side by side, as in the "wǒmen" and the "liǎngge rén" of "wǒmen liǎngge rén" (the two of us), an appositional relationship exists between "we" and the "two people." Chinese and English appositions usually have the same word order. As long as the first noun of a Chinese appositional expression is not a pronoun, or the second noun is not a certain number of "rén," the word order is exactly the same as in English: "Wǒ rènshì tāde nǚpéngyou Hán Lìlián" (I'm acquainted with his girlfriend, Hán Lìlián) and "wǒmen Měiguó rén" (we Americans).

The only important exception occurs when the first noun of an appositional expression is a pronoun and the second noun is a certain number of "rén"; in such a case, the English word order reverses, even though the Chinese word order remains consistent, as in "tāmen qīge rén" (the seven of them) and "nǐmen wǔge rén" (the five of you). A basic rule of thumb for Chinese appositions is that the more general noun comes first and the more specific noun comes second.

Exercises for 8.1: Complete the following dialogues.

1. Waitress: Nǐmen jǐwèi?
   Lìlián: _____ (The five of us; we are a party of five.)

2. A: _____ kàn shénme bào? (What newspapers do you Americans read?)
   B: _____ (We Americans) kàn Yīngwén bào.

3. A: Nǐ rènshì _____? (his American friend Hán Mínglěi) [Use a "ma" question.]
   B: Bù, wǒ bú rènshì tā.

4. A: _____? (What's the name of that teacher?)
   [Use the honorific measure.]
   B: Tā jiào Lín Jièfǔ.

5. A: _____? (Do you Chinese also love to chat?)
   [Use a "ma" question.]
   B: Duì, wǒmen yě hěn ài liáo tiān.

8.2 The Coverb of Accompaniment, "Gēn," and the Adverb "Yìqǐ"

The Coverb of Accompaniment

Subject	Coverb	Object 1	(Adverb "yìqǐ"/ "yíkuàir")	Verb	(Object 2)
Wǒ (I drink tea with Mom.)	gēn	māma		hē	chá.
Tā (He comes to my home together with his friends.)	gēn	péngyou	yìqǐ	lái	wǒ jiā.
Nǐ (You go to the airport together with her.)	gēn	tā	yíkuàir	qù	fēijīchǎng.

If the subject of an English sentence accompanies somebody in doing something, the subject verbs "with" somebody. In Chinese, on the other hand, the "with somebody" has to precede the verb, and the Chinese counterpart of "with," "gēn," behaves more like a verb than a preposition, and thus is termed a coverb. "Gēn" is the first of several important coverbs this book will introduce.

The basic pattern for coverbial sentences is SUBJ + COV + OBJ1 + VERB (+ OBJ2). In the case of "gēn," it is SUBJ + gēn + OBJ1 + VERB (+ OBJ2), as in "Lǎo Zhāng gēn tāmen qù" (Ol' Zhāng is going with them) and "Wǒ gēn Sānjiě hē chá" (I'm drinking tea with Third Elder Sister).

The Adverb "Yìqǐ"

The most common adverb in accompaniment coverb sentences is "yìqǐ" (together), which precedes the main verb: SUBJ + COV + OBJ1 + yìqǐ + VERB (+ OBJ2). For example, "Lìlián gēn Bǐdé yìqǐ zhù" (Lìlián is staying together with Peter) and "Wǒ gēn Dìdi yìqǐ yóuyǒng" (I'm swimming together with Younger Brother). Northerners sometimes use another version of "together," "yíkuàir," in place of "yìqǐ."

Exercises for 8.2: Use the following words to fill in blanks— gēn, yìqǐ, lái (come), qù (go). Some words may be used more than once.

1. _____ wǒ _____. (Come with me.)

2. Nǐmen _____ tā _____. (Go with her.)

3. Nǐ _____ shéi _____ hē chá? (With whom do you go drinking tea?)

4. Nǐ _____ nǐ fùmǔ _____ zhù ma? (Do you live together with your parents?)

5. Wǒ yào _____ wǒ jiějie _____
_____. (I want to go together with my elder sister.)

6. Tā _____ tā péngyou _____ wǒde gōngsī. (He comes to my company with his friend.)

Shanghai at night.

8.3 "Líng" (Zero), and "Hào" as the Measure for a Room Number, License Number, and so on

"Líng" (Zero)

"Líng" is especially important in large numbers over 100, "yìbǎi," or 1,000, "yìqiān." If you want to say 107 in Chinese, "yìbǎiqī" will not work, because the listener will probably assume that you are just abbreviating "yìbǎiqīshí" (170); you need to say "yìbǎilíngqī" instead. Similarly, you should say "yìqiānlíng'èr" for 1,002, because "yìqiān'èr" will be interpreted as 1,200. "Líng" is more common still in phone numbers, such as 268-0030 ("èrliùbā línglíngsān-líng"), and the date in years ("nián"), such as 2009 ("èrlínglíngjiǔ nián") and 1980 ("yījiǔbālíng nián").

"Hào" in Specific Numbers

"Líng" also occurs in many specific types of numbers, such as license numbers, house numbers, and room numbers, the vast majority of which take the generic measure "hào." Two-digit numbers (10–99) that precede "hào" are typically read in full form: "liùshíèrhào fángjiān" (Room 62) and "sìshíhào gōngyù" (Apartment 40). In contrast, numbers of three digits or more are read digit by digit like phone numbers and the date in years, as in "bālíng'èrhào" (Number 802) and "yīqīlínghào fángjiān" (Room 170).

Exercises for 8.3: Practice saying the following in Chinese.

1. 309

2. the year 2008

3. the year 2010

4. Room 50

5. Room 160

8.4 The Directional Verb Complements "Qù" and "Lái"

Many coming-and-going verbs are neutral as to whether the motion is coming toward or going away from the speaker. These verbs, such as "jìn" (to enter) and "chū" (to exit), can append the verb complement "qù" or "lái" to indicate that the motion is going away from or coming toward the speaker, respectively. Therefore, one winds up with the possibilities "jìnqù" (go in), "chūqù" (go out), "jìnlái" (come in), and "chūlái" (come out). When Lǎo Zhāng is standing outside Room 209 with Lìlián and Peter, he asks them to "jìnqù." Later, when he is alone inside Room 312, he beckons them to "jìnlái."

Exercises for 8.4: Say the following in Chinese.

1. You are in your room. A visitor knocks on your door. Ask the visitor to please come in.

2. Someone calls your mother, and you tell him that your mother has gone out.

3. You are standing outside your teacher's office with your friend. Your teacher asks you to come in. Tell your friend, "Let's go in."

4. When you are outside the house, you notice there's a fire. You knock on the door and call out to your younger brother, "Hurry up and come out!"

5. Someone is in the restroom. Tell your child, "Don't go in!"

8.5 Adverbial Modifiers of Adjectives Such As "Tài" and "Búgòu"

Subject	Adverb(s)	Adjective	(Particle "le"/"a")	
Zhuōzi	tài	dà	(le).	(The table is too big.)
Fángjiān	búgòu	gānjìng.		(The room is not clean enough.)
Yùshì	yǒudiǎn	zāng.		(The bathroom is a bit dirty.)
Chuáng	duóme	xiǎo	a.	(How small the bed is!)

Chinese adjectives such as "xiǎo," "dà," and "gānjìng" often serve as the verb or predicate of a sentence, and as such already convey the sense of "to be" ("is," "was," "are," "were," and so on). Inserting "shì" before an adjective is thus not only unnecessary, but also wrong. Instead, the standard pattern for a sentence with a predicate adjective is SUBJ + ADV + ADJ. Remember that, if you have no particular adverb in mind, the use of an unstressed "hěn" in the adverbial slot will prevent the adjective from taking on a comparative aspect as "more adjective" or "adj.-er."

"Tài" and "búgòu" are opposites, as in "Fángjiān tài zāng" (The room is too dirty) and "Yùshì búgòu gānjìng" (The bathroom isn't clean enough). The tài + ADJ pattern is somewhat unusual in its variation that concludes with a "le" for added emphasis of the "too-ness": SUBJ + tài + ADJ + le, as in "Chuáng tài xiǎo le" (The bed is too small). Odd English word order in the "not adjective enough" pattern should not lead you to split up the "búgòu" syllables in the orderly "búgòu ADJ" Chinese pattern, as in "Zhuōzi búgòu dà" (The table isn't big enough).

For "so adjective," use "zhème ADJ" for a subject relatively close to the speaker, and "nàme ADJ" for a subject relatively far from the speaker: "Sānyīèrhào zhème gānjìng, èrlíngjiǔhào nàme zāng" (Number 312 is so clean, and Number 209 is so dirty). For "a bit adjective," use "yǒudiǎn ADJ": "Chuáng yǒudiǎn ruǎn" (The bed is a bit soft). To exclaim "how adjective it is!" use the "duóme ADJ" pattern: "Yùshì duóme gānjìng!" (How clean the bathroom is!).

Exercises for 8.5: Translate the following.

1. The bathroom is clean.

_____

2. The sheets are too dirty.

_____

3. The bed is not soft enough.

_____

4. This room is a little small.

_____

5. How big that table is! (The measure word for table is "zhāng.")

_____

6. That bathroom is so small.

_____

8.6 The Pattern PW + Yǒu + NOUN, and the Bound Localizers "Shàng" and "Lǐ"

The Pattern PW + Yǒu + Noun

Place Word	yǒu	Noun	
Tā jiā	yǒu	wǔge fángjiān.	(There are five rooms in her home.)
Fēijīchǎng	yǒu	liùshíge rén.	(There are 60 people in the airport.)

The common indefinite pattern PW + yǒu + NOUN means "There is/are noun(s) in/at/on the place word." For example, in "Zhuōzi shàng yǒu diànhuà" (There is a telephone on the table), the speaker is focusing more on the location of the telephone than on any other aspect of the device.

The Bound Localizers "Shàng" and "Lǐ"

Place Word Unit		
Noun	**Bound Localizer**	
chuáng	shàng	(on the bed)
fángjiān	lǐ	(in the room)

Appending a bound-form localizer such as "shàng" (on) or "lǐ" (in) to an appropriate noun changes the expression to a place word. As bound forms, "shàng" and "lǐ" must be hooked onto some other word; they cannot be used in isolation. Adding a localizer to the noun "zhuōzi" makes it into the place word "zhuōzi shàng" (on the table); similarly, the noun "yùshì" (bathroom) becomes the place word "yùshì lǐ" (in the bathroom).

Exercises for 8.6: Rearrange the words in each entry to make a correct sentence according to the English meaning given.

1. sìge zhèr rén yǒu (There're four people here.)

_____

2. méiyǒu jiālǐ lǎoshǔ yǒu nǐ (Do you have mice in your home?)

_____

3. méiyǒu zhèizhāng diànhuà shàng zhuōzi (There's no telephone on this table.)

_____

4. lǐ zhāngláng yǒu nèijiān yìzhī yùshì (There's a cockroach in that bathroom.)

_____

5. yǒu shū chuáng shúshu sānběn shàng wǒ (There're three books on my uncle's bed.)

_____

Family members periodically gather to offer incense and flowers to the souls of deceased relatives, especially during the Qīngmíng Festival in midspring.

CULTURE NOTES

In reality, Chinese hotels are usually free of sagging mattresses; the Chinese tend to prefer firm mattresses, and often sleep on platform beds at home. At smaller hotels in south China, your bed may have a canopy of mosquito netting, which effectively wards off that region's most ornery insect pest.

Chinese hotels are more likely to provide boiled water (kāi shuǐ) in a thermos bottle than ice in a bucket, especially in provincial areas. Therefore, it is a good idea to carry your favorite tea or instant coffee along with some cocoa mix or malt powder for the children. Though tap water is fine when brushing your teeth, you wouldn't actually want to gulp the stuff down, especially when hygienic *kāi shuǐ* is so close at hand. Ice-cold beverages also tend to make the stomach contract, so your hot drink will better prepare you for the generous portions you should be pleased to find at the dinner table.

SUMMARY

To state that there is a noun at a place, use the PW + yǒu + NOUN pattern, as in "Zhèr yǒu yìzhī zhānglán" (There's a cockroach here). A bound localizer such as "shàng" (on) or "lǐ" (in) is typically appended to a noun to form a place word, as in "Zhuōzi shàng yǒu diànhuà" (There's a telephone on the table) and "Yùshì lǐ yǒu yìtiáo máojīn" (There's a towel in the bathroom).

Numbers used for identification, such as room numbers and license numbers, take the measure "hào." When such numbers consist of three digits or more, they are read digit by digit, and include "líng" for any zero: "Bālíngèrlínghào fángjiān" (Room 8020).

To express the idea of verbing with somebody in Chinese, the coverb "gēn" and its object must precede the main verb: "Lìlián gēn tā dìdi zhù" (Lìlián is staying with her younger brother). The adverb "yìqǐ" (together) is often used in this construction, as in "Lǎo Zhāng gēn tāmen yìqǐ qù" (Ol' Zhāng is going together with them).

Many coming-and-going verbs such as "chū" (to exit) and "jìn" (to enter) take a directional complement that indicates whether the action is coming toward the speaker ("lái") or going away from the speaker ("qù"). Note the resulting verb-complement combinations: "chūlái" (to come out), "chūqù" (to go out), "jìnlái" (to come in), and "jìnqù" (to go in).

Like other honorific phrases, the honorific measure "wèi" should be used only in reference to other people, not oneself. The hotel desk clerk thus says "Jǐwèi?" when asking Peter how many people are in his party, and Peter includes the generic measure "ge" in his reply "Wǒmen liǎngge rén" (The two of us). Pronouns in Chinese appositions always precede the noun equivalent, as in "tāmen qīge rén" (the seven of them).

CHAPTER 9

NǏMEN DǍSUÀN ZHÙ DUŌJIǓ?

(How long do you plan to stay?)

CHAPTER OVERVIEW

1. Calendar Dates and Indicating Age

2. Duration of Verbing, Quasi Measures, and the Number of Times to Verb

3. Verb-Complement Compounds in Resultative and Potential Forms

4. The "Shì . . . de" Pattern for Emphasizing Something Besides the Verb

5. "Shénme Shíhòu" with "When?" Questions

6. Action at a Place with the Coverb "Zài," and the "Show Me" Pattern

7. "Didn't Verb" or "Haven't Verbed" with "Méiyǒu VERB"

8. "SUBJ Zěnme Nàme ADJ" as "How Come the SUBJ Is So ADJ?"

NEW VOCABULARY

1.	jīntiān	today	TW
2.	tiān	day (bound form)	TW/NOUN
3.	qīyuè sìhào	July 4	TW
4.	qīyuè	July (lit., "the seventh month")	TW
5.	yuè	month (bound form)	TW/NOUN
6.	sìhào	fourth day of the month	TW
7.	NUM + hào	the NUMth day of the month	TW
8.	dǎsuàn	to plan	VERB
9.	duōjiǔ	how long (in duration)?	QW
10.	tīngbùdǒng	cannot understand (through listening)	VERB
11.	tīng	to listen	VERB
12.	dǒng	to understand	VERB
13.	qǐng	please; to invite	ADV/VERB
14.	zài shuō yícì	Say it once again./ Say it one more time.	
15.	yícì	once, one time	NOUN
16.	NUM + cì	NUM times	NOUN
17.	jǐtiān	how many days?	QW
18.	jīnnián	this year	TW
19.	nián	year (bound form)	TW
20.	jǐsuì	how many years old? (for fairly young people)	QW
21.	NUM + suì	NUM years old	ADJ
22.	shénme shíhòu	when?	QW
23.	shíhòu	time	NOUN
24.	shēng	to be born	VERB
25.	gěi wǒ kàn	show me	COV-NOUN-VERB
26.	hùzhào	passport	NOUN
27.	něinián	which year?	QW
28.	jiéhūn	to marry	VERB

29. háizi	child(ren)	NOUN
30. hái méiyǒu + VERB	haven't yet verbed	ADV1-ADV2-VERB
31. méiyǒu + VERB	haven't verbed, didn't verb	ADV-VERB
32. zài + PW + VERB	verb at PW	COV-PW-VERB
33. nǎr	where? ("nǎlǐ" in Taiwan)	QW
34. gōngzuò	to work; job	VERB/NOUN
35. jiā	(measure for workplace)	MEAS
36. Yīngguó	England	NOUN
37. yínháng	bank	NOUN
38. niánxīn	annual salary	NOUN
39. wèntí	question, problem	NOUN
40. zěnme nàme ADJ	how come so adjective?	QW
41. duō	be many, be numerous, be much	ADJ
42. hǎole, hǎole	okay, okay	ADJ
43. búwèn le	I won't ask any more.	
44. yàoshi	key	NOUN

DIALOGUE

TRACK 20

Zhíyuán (at the hotel): Jīntiān shì qīyuè sìhào. Nǐmen dǎsuàn zhù duōjiǔ?

Bǐdé: Duìbùqǐ, wǒ tīngbùdǒng. Qǐng nǐ zài shuō yícì.

Zhíyuán: Nǐmen yào zhù jǐtiān?

Bǐdé: Wǔtiān.

Zhíyuán: Nǐ jīnnián jǐsuì? Shì shénme shíhòu shēng de?

Bǐdé: Wǒ èrshísān suì. Shì yījiǔbāliùnián shēng de.

Zhíyuán: Qǐng gěi wǒ kànkan nǐmen de hùzhào. Nǐmen shì něinián jiéhūn de? Yǒu méiyǒu háizi?

Bǐdé: Wǒmen hái méiyǒu jiéhūn.

Zhíyuán: Nǐ zài nǎr gōngzuò?

Bǐdé: Wǒ zài yìjiā Yīngguó yínháng gōngzuò.

Zhíyuán: Nǐ niánxīn duōshǎo?

Bǐdé: Nǐde wèntí zěnme nàme duō?

Zhíyuán: Hǎole, hǎole, búwèn le. Zhè shì nǐmen fángjiān de yàoshi.

DIALOGUE TRANSLATION

Employee (at the hotel): Today is July 4. How long do you plan to stay?

Peter: Sorry, I couldn't understand. Please say it once again.

Employee: How many days are you going to stay here?

Peter: Five days.

Employee: How old are you this year? When were you born?

Peter: I'm 23 years old. I was born in 1986.

Employee: Please show me your passports. Which year did you get married? Do you have any children?

Peter: We haven't yet married.

Employee: Where do you work?

Peter: I work at an English bank.

Employee: How much is your annual salary?

Peter: How come you've got so many questions?

Employee: Okay, okay, I won't ask any more. Here are the keys to your room.

9.1 Calendar Dates and Indicating Age

Calendar Dates

Number 1	nián (year)	Number 2	yuè (month)	Number 3	hào/rì (day)
yījiǔqībā (January 2, 1978)	nián	yī	yuè	èr	hào
èrlínglíngjiǔ (November 22, 2009)	nián	shíyī	yuè	èrshíèr	rì.

Jīntiān	shì	jǐyuè	jǐhào?	(What's the date today?)
Tāde shēngrì	shì	jǐyuè	jǐhào?	(What's the date of her birthday?)

As with other units of time and space in Chinese, for calendar dates you begin with the larger units and move progressively to the smaller units, as in "èrlíngyīlíngnián shíyīyuè èrshíqīhào" (November 27, 2010). The pattern is NUM1 + nián + NUM2 + yuè + NUM3 + hào, where "nián," "yuè," and "hào" are the measures for the year, the month, and the day of the month, respectively. Note that, although the numbers for the month and the day of the month are read as ordinary numbers from 1 to 12 and 1 to 31 respectively, the four-digit number for the year is read as a series of individual digits, as with a phone number.

Of course, it isn't necessary to include all three units; you may want to indicate just two, such as "yījiǔjiǔbānián èryuè (February 1998) or "liùyuè yīhào" (June 1), or refer to only one unit: the day, "sānshíhào" (the thirtieth), the month, "shíèryuè" (December), or the year, "èrlínglíngbānián" (2008). For the last year, èrqiānlíngbānián is also used.

The appropriate question words are "něinián?" (which year?), "jǐyuè" (which month?), and "jǐhào" (which day of the month?). A common question is "Nǐde shēngrì shì jǐyuè jǐhào?" (What's the date of your birthday?).

Indicating Age

Subject	Number	suì	
Nǐ	jǐ	suì?	(How old are you?)
Wǒ	èrshíyī	suì.	(I'm 21 years old.)

To indicate a person's age, the most common pattern is SUBJ + NUM + suì, as in "Xiǎo Hán èrshísuì" (Young Hán is 20 years old). "Suì" functions both as the measure of the actual number of years and as the predicate adjective of the sentence. While it is possible to insert the verb "yǒu" after the subject in this pattern, people rarely do so.

Like the number for the day of the month, the number of years is read as an ordinary number between 1 year old, "yísuì," and 99 years old, "jiǔshíjiǔsuì," or in the exceptional case of a centenarian as "yìbǎilíngwǔsuì" for 105 years old.

To ask the age of someone younger than 30 or so, one usually says, "Nǐ jǐsuì?" (How old are you?). The version of this question for people middle-aged or older is "Nǐ duódà suìshù?"

The 12 Months

The 12 months are as follows:

January	yīyuè	July	qīyuè
February	èryuè	August	bāyuè
March	sānyuè	September	jiǔyuè
April	sìyuè	October	shíyuè
May	wǔyuè	November	shíyīyuè
June	liùyuè	December	shíèryuè

Exercises for 9.1: Complete the following dialogues, using the cues given.

1. A: Nǐ jīnnián jǐsuì?
   B: _____. (I'm 27 years old.)

2. A: Nǐde shēngrì shì jǐyuè jǐhào?
   B: _____. (My birthday is November 30.)

3. A: _____? (Which year is this year?)
   B: Jīnnián shì _____. (2008)

4. A: Nín duódà suìshù?
   B: _____. (I'm 89 years old.)

5. A: Jīntiān shì jǐyuè jǐhào? (What's the date for today?)
   B: _____. (It's February 14 today.)

9.2 Duration of Verbing, Quasi Measures, and the Number of Times to Verb

Duration of Verbing

Duration	
sāntiān	(three days)
sìnián	(four years)
wǔge xīngqī	(five weeks)
liùge yuè	(six months)
yìfēn (zhōng)	(one minute)
yíge zhōngtóu	(one hour)

During the Dragon-boat Festival, some residents hang cuttings of mugwort and reeds over windows and doorways to ward off sickness and evil spirits.

It is important to distinguish between the action's time frame, the time words, which must go somewhere before the verb, and the duration of that action, which must follow the verb in affirmative sentences. To state that you are going to listen to music ("yīnyuè") on December 2 of this year at half-past eight in the morning, you will need to put the time words of the time frame before the verb of the sentence: "Wǒ jīnnián shíèryuè èrhào zǎoshàng bādiǎnbàn yào tīng yīnyuè." However, if you simply want to indicate that you are going to listen to music for the duration of one day ("yìtiān"), the expression of duration follows the verb: "Wǒ yào tīng yìtiān yīnyuè."

Quasi Measures

"Tiān" and "nián" fall into a small category of "quasi measures" because even though they often function as ordinary nouns of the time-word variety, they do not take a measure when numbered; note the absence of "ge" in "liǎngtiān" (two days) and "jiǔnián" (nine years). In contrast, "yuè" and "xīngqī" (week) are ordinary time words that require the measure "ge" when numbered, as in "shíèrge yuè" (12 months) and "yíge xīngqī" (one week).

Number of Times to Verb

Subject	Adverb	Verb	Number	cì	
Tā		tīng	liǎng	cì.	(He heard it twice.)
Qǐng nǐ	zài	shuō	sān	cì.	(Please say it three more times.)

To indicate the number of times or instances you are verbing, use NUM + cì after the verb, much as if indicating duration. Typically, the object of the verb in this pattern is already understood from the context or is otherwise omitted from its standard position after the verb, as in "Qǐng nǐ shuō liǎngcì" (Please say it twice) or "Zài tīng yícì ba" (Better listen to it once again). In these examples, the speakers would know what specific sentence and musical work needed more speaking and listening practice, respectively. On the other hand, if you are introducing new subject matter and want to say something like "There was one time I was doing such and such," use the pattern Yǒu yícì SUBJ + VERB + OBJ, as in "Yǒu yícì, wǒ gēn Wáng Jīnglǐ yìqǐ gōngzuò . . ." (There was one time I was working together with Manager Wáng . . .).

Exercises for 9.2: Translate the following.

1. Three days

_____

2. 45 weeks

_____

3. 12 years

_____

4. Eight months

_____

5. How many days are there in a week?

_____

6. How many months are there in one year?

_____

7. Please say it once again.

_____

8. There are 52 weeks in one year.

_____

9.3 Verb-Complement Compounds in Resultative and Potential Forms

Verb-Complement Compounds in Resultative Form

Subject	Verb	Complement	le	Object
Nǐ	tīng	dǒng	le	Yīngwén.
(You have understood English through listening.)				
Tā	kàn	wán	le	nèiběn shū.
(She has finished reading that book.)				

Two independent verbs are sometimes placed together in a relationship of verb and complement to express a more specific kind of activity than either verb could express alone. In such a compound, the first verb is considered the ordinary verb and generally indicates the major activity being described. The second verb is regarded as the complement of the first verb and states the result of the major activity; for these reasons, it is known as the "resultative complement."

For instance, the act of understanding, "dǒng," can result from either the activity of listening, "tīng," as in "tīngdǒng" (to understand through listening), or the activity of reading, "kàn," as in "kàndǒng" (to understand through reading). The resultative complement "wán" (to finish) is more versatile in its ability to serve as the complement of numerous action verbs, as in "hēwán" (to finish drinking), "tīngwán" (to finish listening), and "shuōwán" (to finish saying something).

Verb-Complement Compounds in Potential Form

Subject	Verb	de	Complement	Object
Nǐ	tīng	de	dǒng	Yīngwén.
(You can understand English through listening.)				
Tā	kàn	de	wán	nèiběn shū.
(She can finish reading that book.)				

Subject	Verb	bù	Complement	Object
Nǐ	tīng	bù	dǒng	Yīngwén.
(You cannot understand English through listening.)				
Tā	kàn	bù	wán	nèiběn shū.
(She cannot finish reading that book.)				

The potential form of the resultative verb pattern expresses either "can VERB + COMP" or "cannot VERB + COMP" depending on whether you sandwich "de" or "bù," respectively, between the verb and complement. Thus we have "tīngdedǒng" (can understand through listening), "tīngbùdǒng" (cannot understand through listening), "kàndewán" (can finish reading), and "kànbùwán" (cannot finish reading). This chapter introduces the resultative verb pattern through its potential form; subsequent chapters will include more variations of the resultative pattern and additional practice exercises.

Exercises for 9.3: Fill in each blank with one of the following potential compounds—tīngdedǒng, tīngbùdǒng, kàndedǒng, kànbùdǒng, kàndewán, kànbùwán.

1. A: Jīntiān nǐ _____ zhèiběn shū ma?

2. B: Bù, jīntiān wǒ _____ zhèiběn shū.

3. A: Nǐ māma _____ Yīngwén ma? (Can your mom understand English through listening?)

4. B: Bù, wǒ māma _____ Yīngwén.

5. Wáng Xiānsheng _____ (can understand through reading) Zhōngwén bào, kěshì tā _____ Yīngwén bào.

9.4 The "Shì . . . de" Pattern for Emphasizing Something Besides the Verb

Subject	shì	Time/Manner of Verbing	Verb	Object	de
Nǐ (Which year were you born?)	shì	něinián	shēng		de?
Wǒ (I was born in 1986.)	shì	yījiǔbāliù nián	shēng		de.
Nǐmen (How did you go to China?)	shì	zěnme	qù	Zhōngguó	de?
Wǒmen (We went by airplane.)	shì	zuò fēijī	qù		de.

In the dialogue, the hotel clerk is not interested in the obvious fact that Bǐdé was born, but rather in the date of his birth. The clerk thus prefaces his "when?" question phrase, "shénme shíhòu," with the verb "shì," much as a curious English speaker might say, "When was it you were born?" The difference in Chinese is that the modification particle "de" must be placed at or near the end of the sentence, and at least after the verb, as in "Tā shì shénme shíhòu jiéhūn de?" (When did she marry?). Aside from emphasizing *when* an action took place, the "shì . . . de" pattern can often indicate *how* an action occurred, as in the particular conveyance by which someone traveled, whether someone verbed alone or together with others, and so on. "Shì . . . de" sentences almost always refer to past actions, though it is worth remembering that the Chinese verb has no tenses, and that the pattern represents an overlap with English past tense, not an equivalency to past tense.

Exercises for 9.4: Use the "Shì . . . de" pattern to complete the following sentences.

1. Nǐde nǚpéngyou _____? (In what year was your girlfriend born?)

2. Tāde zǔfù, zǔmǔ _____. (His grandfather and grandmother got married in 1925.)

3. Nǐ shūshu _____? (How did your uncle come to [lái] America?)

4. Wǒ jiějie de háizi _____. (My elder sister's child
   was born at 2:00 in the afternoon on March 10, 1994.)

5. Wǒmen de jiàoliàn _____. (Our coach didn't go
   to China by airplane [zuò fēijī].)

9.5 "Shénme Shíhòu" with "When?" Questions

Subject	shénme shíhòu (When)/Time Word	Verb	Object
Nǐmen (When are you getting married?)	shénme shíhòu	jié	hūn?
Wǒmen (We're getting married this June.)	jīnnián liùyuè	jié	hūn.
Nǐ (When do you go to work?)	shénme shíhòu	shàng	bān?
Wǒ (I go to work at 7:30.)	qīdiǎn bàn	shàng	bān.

The question phrase "shénme shíhòu" (when?) consists of the
question word "shénme" (what?) and the noun "shíhòu" (time).
In "when?" questions, "shénme shíhòu" needs to go after the
subject and before the verb, as in "Nǐ shénme shíhòu gěi tā fángjiān de yàoshi?" (When did you give her the room key?): SUBJ +
shénme shíhòu + VERB. If the answer to this question were
"today," the response would involve substituting "jīntiān" for
"shénme shíhòu."

***Exercises for 9.5: Rearrange the words in each entry to make
a correct sentence according to the English meaning given.***

1. shíhòu nǐ chūzū yào shénme jiào qìchē (When are you going to
   call a taxicab?)

   _____

2. Zhōngguó shénme nǐ dǎsuàn qù shíhòu (When do you plan to
   go to China?)

   _____

3. zǎoshàng wǒ gěi Xiǎojiě yàoshi jīntiān Lín (Miss Lín gave me the
   key this morning.)

   _____

4. qù dìdi shíèryuè tā Yīngguó yào jīnnián (Her younger brother wants to go to England this December.)

_____

5. Měiguó shénme lái zǔmǔ de shíhòu nǐ shì (When did your grandmother come to America?)

_____

9.6 Action at a Place with the Coverb "Zài," and the "Show Me" Pattern

Action at a Place with the Coverb "Zài"

Subject	(Adverb)	Coverb "zài"	Place Word	Verb	(Object)
Tā (She works at a bank.)		zài	yínháng	gōngzuò.	
Tā (She doesn't work at an airport.)	bú	zài	fēijīchǎng	gōngzuò.	
Wǒ (I teach at a university.)		zài	dàxué	jiāo	shū.

"Zài" can function as an independent verb meaning "to be in or at": "Lín Xiānsheng zài Zhōngguó" (Mr. Lín is in China). Even more common, however, is the use of "zài" as a coverb to indicate where the action denoted by the main verb is taking place: SUBJ + zài + PW + VERB (+ OBJ). To elaborate on the above sentence, one can say, "Lín Xiānsheng zài Zhōngguó gōngzuò" (Mr. Lín is working in China). Note that in negating sentences with coverbs, the negative adverb "bù" precedes the coverb rather than the verb, as in "Lín Tàitài búzài yínháng gōngzuò" (Mrs. Lín doesn't work at a bank).

The "Show Me" Pattern

Subject	(Adverb)	Coverb "gěi"	Object 1	kàn	Object 2
Wǒ (I show him my passport.)		gěi	tā	kàn	hùzhào.
Tā (He doesn't show me his photograph.)	bù	gěi	wǒ	kàn	tāde zhàopiàn.

To express the idea of showing a person something, use "gěi" (to give) as a coverb along with "kàn" (to look at) at the main verb: SUBJ + gěi + person + kàn + OBJ, as in "Bǐdé gěi nèige zhíyuán kàn tā de hùzhào" (Peter is showing that employee his passport), and "Qǐng nǐ gěi wǒ kàn nǐ de lǎoshǔ" (Please show me your mouse). The negative form of a sentence with "gěi" as a coverb works about the same as when "zài" is used in this way: "Wǒ bù gěi nǐ kàn tāmen de hùzhào" (I'm not showing you their passports).

Exercises for 9.6: Answer the following questions in the negative.

1. A: Nǐ māma zài Měiguó zhù ma?
   B: _____.

2. A: Nǐ bàba zài yínháng gōngzuò ma?
   B: _____.

3. A: Nèige rén gěi nǐ kàn tāde hùzhào ma?
   B: _____.

4. A: Nǐ jiějie zài xuéxiào (school) yóuyǒng ma?
   B: _____.

5. A: Nǐ péngyou gěi nǐ kàn tāde zhàopiàn ma?
   B: _____.

9.7 "Didn't Verb" or "Hasn't Verbed" with "Méiyǒu VERB"

Subject	méi(yǒu)	Verb	(Object)	
Wǒmen	méi(yǒu)	hē	chá.	(We didn't drink tea.)
Tāmen	méi(yǒu)	kàn	dìtú.	(They didn't look at the map.)

Instead of indicating the tense of a verb, Chinese focuses on matters related to the "aspect" of a verb, such as whether the action denoted by the verb has or has not started, has or has not been completed, and is or is not ongoing. Admittedly, there is a large overlap between negative English past tense and the Chinese negative completed action form SUBJ + méi(yǒu) + VERB (+ OBJ), which means "subject didn't verb" or "subject hasn't verbed." It is important to remember, however, that the negative completed action form of Chinese is not at all equivalent to the negative English past tense, and that English past tense often does not correlate with Chinese completed action, and vice versa. For instance, past tense is common to virtually all English verbs, but Chinese completed action occurs only with action verbs, not static verbs such as "shì" (to be) or certain "stative" verbs denoting mental states, such as "xǐhuān" (to like).

It is thus possible to say "Tāmen méi yǒu jiéhūn" (They didn't get married), but not "Wǒ méi xǐhuān Mínglěi." If you wanted to say "I didn't like Mínglěi," you would simply say "Wǒ bù xǐhuān Mínglěi." Predicate adjectives such as "gāoxìng" (to be happy) fall under the general category of stative verbs, so "Lìlián bù gāoxìng" can mean either "Lìlián wasn't happy" or "Lìlián isn't happy," depending upon the context; "méiyǒu VERB" is not possible with such a stative verb.

Exercises for 9.7: Use "méiyǒu" in the translation of the following sentences.

1. She did not bear a child.

_____

2. I haven't called a taxicab yet ("hái méiyǒu VERB").

_____

3. Didn't you go to the airport?

_____

4. Peter didn't show that employee his passport.

_____

5. My friend didn't show me his pet's photograph.

_____

9.8 "SUBJ Zěnme Nàme ADJ" as "How Come the SUBJ Is So ADJ?"

Subject	zěnme nàme	Adjective	
Nǐmen jiā	zěnme nàme	dà?	(How come your home is so big?)
Rén	zěnme nàme	duō?	(How come there are so many people?)

More often than not, "subject zěnme VERB?" means "How does the subject verb?" as in "Passport, Zhōngwén zěnme shuō?" (How does one say "passport" in Chinese?). Another important meaning of "subject zěnme VERB" is "How come the subject verbs?" as in "Tā zěnme bù hē chá?" (How come she doesn't drink tea?).

A common variety of the "how come" zěnme usage is SUBJ + zěnme + nàme + ADJ: "How come the subject is so adjective?" Examples are "Nǐ zěnme nàme máng?" (How come you're so busy?) and "Xiǎo Hán zěnme nàme gāoxìng?" (How come Young Hán is so happy?).

Exercises for 9.8: Complete the following sentences, using the cues given.

1. Hotel, Zhōngwén _____? (How does one say "hotel" in Chinese?)

2. Wǒmen _____? (How do we go to the airport?)

3. Nǐ péngyou _____? (How come your friend doesn't come to our home?)

4. Lǐ Jīnglǐ zhèige xīngqī _____? (How come Manager Lǐ is so busy this week?)

5. Nǐ gēge de fángjiān _____? (How come your older brother's room is so dirty?)

Thousands of the Goddess Māzǔ's worshippers annually throng the streets of Běigǎng in Táiwān.

CULTURE NOTES

As this chapter's dialogue indicates, concepts of privacy differ greatly from culture to culture. Many Americans prefer to keep their salaries a secret even from fairly close friends, and would not dare risk offending their friends by inquiring about their incomes; an American's concept of sexual mores is often easier to pin down than his or her salary. On the other hand, a stranger whom you have just met on a Chinese train may casually ask you what your salary is, but show extreme reticence to express his views if the conversation turns to a topic such as sexual practices.

The curiosity of many Chinese people about things foreign is often piqued by the government-run media's spotty and very selective coverage of foreign news. The *Apollo* moon landings of the late 1960s and early 1970s were not reported publicly in the PRC for many years, since that technological feat seemed to reflect poorly upon socialism. While the situation has greatly improved with China's open-door policy after the death of Máo Zédōng, China's party-supervised media reporting still meets with much skepticism among the populace, who depend on grapevines of informal news and conversations to counterbalance the official line.

SUMMARY

In calendar dates, the year (nián) is read as a short series of digits, while the month (yuè) and day (hào) are read as ordinary numbers from one to 12 and one to 31, respectively. Examples are "Yījiǔjiǔjiǔnián shíèryuè sānshíyīhào" (December 31, 1999) and "Èrlínglíngbānián èryuè shíhào" (February 10, 2008). To indicate a person's age, use "suì" instead of "nián" after the number of years: "Tā gēge yǐjīng èrshísuì le" (Her older brother is already 20 years old).

The question phrase "shénme shíhòu" (when?) consists of the question word "shénme" (what?) and the noun "shíhòu" (time): "Nǐ shénme shíhòu chī wǔfàn?" (When do you eat lunch?). Even though Chinese verbs do not have tenses, the use of "shì . . . de" pattern usually frames the action in the past: "Nǐmen liǎngge rén shì shénme shíhòu jiéhūn de?" (When did the two of you get married?). Although the time frame of an action is indicated somewhere before the verb, the actual duration of an action must follow the verb, as in "Zhèige xīngqī wǒmen yào xiūxi liǎngtiān" (This week, we want to rest for two days).

Action verbs may be prefaced by "méiyǒu" to indicate that an action did not take place: "Zǔfù méiyǒu wèn wèntí" (Grandfather didn't ask questions). On the other hand, potential compounds are negated by inserting "bù" between the verb and the complement, as in "Nèige zhíyuán tīngbùdǒng" (That employee can't understand [through listening]), and "Tāmen kànbùdǒng nèiběn shū" (They can't understand [through reading] that book). Substituting "de" for "bù" in those sentences would make them affirmative—in each case, the only change would be from "can't" to "can."

CHAPTER 10

CÈSUǑ ZÀI NǍR?
(Where are the toilets?)

CHAPTER OVERVIEW

1. The Directional Coverbs "Cóng," "Dào," and "Wàng," and the Four Compass Points

2. Asking What You Ought to Do, and Asking for Directions

3. Providing Directions, and the "Xiān + VERB1 + Zài + VERB2" Pattern

4. Expressing Distance with NUM + lǐ + lù

5. The Most Versatile Localizer: "Biān"

6. "Búyòng VERB" as "Needn't Verb"

7. More on Directional and Resultative Complements

NEW VOCABULARY

TRACK
21

1.	shàng cèsuǒ	to use the toilet	VERB-OBJ
2.	cèsuǒ	toilet	NOUN
3.	shàng	to go to, to get on	VERB
4.	cóng	from	COV
5.	wàng	toward, to (pronounced "wǎng" in Taiwan)	COV
6.	běi	north	ADJ
7.	zǒu	to go, to leave, to walk	VERB
8.	dàgài	probably	ADV
9.	lǐ	(measure for distance, currently usually a kilometer)	MEAS
10.	lù	road (and a measure for bus routes)	NOUN
11.	dào	to, arrive	COV/VERB
12.	Dōng Cháng'ān Jiē	East Eternal Peace Street	PW
13.	dōng	east	ADJ
14.	jiē	street	NOUN
15.	nà fùjìn	in that vicinity	PW
16.	fùjìn	in the vicinity	PW
17.	Běijīng Fàndiàn	the Běijīng Hotel	PW
18.	fàndiàn	hotel	PW
19.	fēicháng + ADJ	extremely ADJ	ADV
20.	wèishēng	be sanitary	ADJ
21.	yuǎn	be far, distant	ADJ
22.	zěnme bàn?	What'll I do?/ How does one handle this?	IDIO
23.	bàn	to handle, to do	VERB
24.	bǐjiào	relatively, comparatively	ADV
25.	jìn	be close, near	ADJ
26.	xībiān	the west side	PW
27.	xī	west	ADJ
28.	biān	(bound localizer meaning "side")	LOC/BF
29.	gōngyuán	park	PW
30.	lǐbiān	inside	PW

31. xiān VERB1, zài VERB2	first VERB1, then VERB2	ADV, CONJ
32. yòu	right	ADJ
33. zhuǎn	to turn	VERB
34. kàndào	to see	VERB-COMP
35. hónglǜdēng	traffic light	NOUN
36. hóng	be red	ADJ
37. lǜ	be green	ADJ
38. dēng	light, lamp	NOUN
39. zuǒ	left	ADJ
40. suànle	the heck with it, enough already	IDIO
41. dài	to escort, to lead	VERB
42. wèishēng zhǐ	toilet paper	NOUN
43. zhǐ	paper	NOUN
44. ná	to take, to hand, to hold	VERB
45. yòng	to use	VERB
46. búyòng xiè	Don't mention it./ You needn't thank me.	IDIO
47. búyòng + VERB	no need to VERB	AUXV
48. niánqīngrén	youth, young person	NOUN

DIALOGUE

TRACK 22

Mínglěi: Qǐngwèn, cèsuǒ zài nǎr? Wǒ yào shàng cèsuǒ.

Niánqīngrén: Nǐ cóng zhèr wàng běi zǒu, dàgài bàn lǐ lù, jiù dào Dōng Cháng'ān Jiē. Nà fùjìn yǒu Běijīng Fàndiàn. Tāmen de cèsuǒ fēicháng wèishēng.

Mínglěi: Tài yuǎn le! Zěnme bān? Yǒu méiyǒu bǐjiào jìnde?

Niánqīngrén: Yǒu. Xībiān yǒu ge gōngyuán. Lǐbiān yě yǒu cèsuǒ.

Mínglěi: Zěnme zǒu?

Niánqīngrén: Xiān yòu zhuǎn, kàndào hónglǜdēng zài zuǒ zhuǎn... Suànle, wǒ dài nǐ qù ba!

Mínglěi Cèsuǒ lǐ huì yǒu wèishēng zhǐ ma?

Niánqīngrén: Cèsuǒ lǐ huì yǒu wèishēng zhǐ. Wǒ zhèr yě yǒu. Nǐ ná qù yòng ba!

Mínglěi: Xièxie nǐ!

Niánqīngrén: Búyòng xiè.

DIALOGUE TRANSLATION

Mínglěi: May I ask where the toilets are? I have to use the toilet.

Youth: From here go north about half a kilometer; then you'll get to East Eternal Peace Street. There's the Běijīng Hotel in that vicinity. Their toilets are extremely sanitary.

Mínglěi: It's too far away. What can we do? Is there anything relatively close by?

Youth: Yes. There's a park to the west. There are also some toilets in it.

Mínglěi: How do you get there?

Youth: First turn right. Once you see some traffic lights, then turn left... Ah, the heck with it, I'd better take you there!

Mínglěi: Will there be toilet paper in the toilets?

Youth: There'll be toilet paper in the toilets. I've also got some here. Better take it and use it!

Mínglěi: Thank you!

Youth: Don't mention it.

10.1 The Directional Coverbs "Cóng," "Dào," and "Wàng," and the Four Compass Points

The Three Directional Coverbs

Subject	cóng	Place Word 1	dào	Place Word 2	qù/lái
Tā (She went to China from America.)	cóng	Měiguó	dào	Zhōngguó	qù.
Nǐ (You came to my home from the park.)	cóng	gōngyuán	dào	wǒ jiā	lái.

Subject	wàng	Direction	Verb of Locomotion	
Tā	wàng	dōng	zǒu.	(He went toward the east.)
Qǐng (nǐ)	wàng	yòu	zhuǎn.	(Please turn right.)

In English, you go from PW1 to PW2. In Chinese, you "from PW1 to PW2 go": SUBJ + cóng + PW1 + dào + PW2 + qù. Coming from PW1 to PW2 uses exactly the same pattern, except for the substitution of "lái" in place of "qù." Peter may be going from Young Hán's home to the park (Bǐdé cóng Xiǎo Hán de jiā dào gōngyuán qù), or else coming from Hong Kong to Běijīng (Bǐdé cóng Xiānggǎng dào Běijīng lái). Whatever the case may be, the coverb "cóng" precedes the place word of origination, while "dào" precedes the place word of destination. When "dào" is used as the main verb instead of as a coverb for a main verb like "qù" or "lái," it means "to arrive," as in "Wǒmen shénme shíhòu dào Xī Cháng'ān Jiē?" (When are we arriving at West Eternal Peace Street?)

If you are proceeding in a certain direction, use the same kind of sentence structure as above but with the coverb "wàng," as in "Qǐng nǐ wàng běi zǒu" (Please go toward the north). With a small number of verbs involving direction, such as "zhuǎn" (to turn), the use of the coverb is optional when indicating verbing left or right: "wàng yòu zhuǎn" is the full form for "turn right" or "turn to the right," but the abbreviated form "yòu zhuǎn" is also correct for this verb.

The Four Compass Words

The four directions of the Chinese compass are read in a generally clockwise manner, starting from the east: "dōng, xī, nán, běi" (east, west, south, north). When not appearing in a pattern such as "SUBJ + wàng + direction + verb of locomotion," the four directions of the compass must typically be connected to locale-denoting localizers such as "biān" and "fāng," as in "Yuènán zài nánbiān" (Vietnam is to the south) and "Wáng Jīnglǐ shì běifāngrén" (Manager Wáng is a northerner).

Exercises for 10.1: Use "cóng," "dào," "wàng," "dōng," "xī," "nán," "běi," "zuǒ," "yòu" to fill in the blanks. Some words may be used more than once.

1. _____ zhèr _____
   _____ zǒu. Cèsuǒ zài _____ biān.
   (Go north from here. The toilet is to the east.)

2. Qǐng nǐ _____ _____ zhuǎn, bié
   _____ _____ zhuǎn.
   (Please turn right, don't turn left.)

3. Lìlián _____ Měiguó _____
   Zhōngguó qù. (Lìlián went to China from America.)

4. Bǐdé de bàba shì _____ fāngrén. Tā shì Měiguó
   _____ fāngrén.
   (Peter's father is a westerner. He is a southerner from America.)

5. _____ zhèige gōngyuán _____
   _____zǒu. Yínháng zài _____ biān.
   (Go west from this park. The bank is to the right.)

10.2 Asking What You Ought to Do, and Asking for Directions

Asking What You Ought to Do

Chinese conceptualizes the English query "What is one to do?" as "How is one to handle this (the problem)?" You thus use the question word "zěnme" instead of "shénme," and usually omit the subject if it is understood from the context. The context in which "zěnme bàn?" occurs in the dialogue clearly involves Mínglěi's dilemma, and thus this expression can be translated as "What am I to do?" "What'll I do?" or "How am I to handle this?"

It is not necessary to spell out the idea of "ought" or "should" ("yīnggāi") in this pattern. If, however, you wish to exercise that option, you must include the subject along with "yīnggāi": "Wǒ yīnggāi zěnme bàn?" (What should I do?).

Asking for Directions

(Subject)	cóng	Place Word 1	dào	Place Word 2,	zěnme zǒu/ zěnme qù?
	Cóng	zhèr	dào	gōngyuán,	zěnme zǒu?
	(How do you get from here to the park?)				
	Cóng	nǐ jiā	dào	fēijīchǎng,	zěnme qù?
	(How does one go from your home to the airport?)				

When asking for directions, you are also asking *how* to get somewhere, and thus should again use the adverbial question word "zěnme," this time along with the verb "zǒu": "Zěnme zǒu?" (How does one go? / How do I get there?). To be explicit about your origination point and/or destination, you can preface this question phrase with the "cóng + PW1 + dào PW2" structure: "Cóng zhèr dào nàr, zěnme zǒu?" (How do you get from here to there?).

The question phrase "zěnme zǒu?" asks for directions to somewhere, while "zěnme qù" (How does one go there?) asks about an appropriate mode of conveyance, such as riding the bus ("zuò chē qù") or going on foot ("zǒu lù qù"). This latter pattern of going by conveyance will be introduced in Chapter 15.

Exercises for 10.2: Complete the following dialogue.

1. A: Cóng zhèr dào _____, _____?
   (How do you get from here to the airport?)

2. B: Nǐ cóng zhèr _____. (You go east from here.)

3. B: Nǐ yào _____? (How are you going to go there?)

4. A: _____. (I'm going to ride the bus.)

5. B: Kěshì zhèr méiyǒu chē, nǐ _____? (But there're no buses here. What are you to do?)

6. A: Nàme wǒ zhǐhǎo zǒu lù qù. (In that case I can only go on foot.)

A large stone lion that formerly stood at the gate of a village ancestral temple now adorns a bridge in Southern Ānhuī.

10.3 Providing Directions, and the "Xiān + VERB1 + Zài + VERB2" Pattern

While the coverbial phrase "cóng + PW" (from the place word) can precede many different verbs, its counterpart, "dào + PW" (to the place word) can precede only the main verb "qù" or "lái." Because speakers typically use the main verb "zǒu" when providing directions to someone, it is necessary to use the coverb "wàng" instead of "dào" when indicating where the puzzled visitor should be going: "Nǐ cóng zhèr wàng nèige hónglǜdēng zǒu . . ." (From here, go toward that traffic light . . .).

Subject	xiān	Verb 1	Object 1,	zài	Verb 2	Object 2.
Wǒ	xiān	mǎi	shū,	zài	hē	chá.
(I first bought books, then drank tea.)						

Subject	xiān	wàng	Direction 1	Verb 1	zài	(wàng)	Direction 2	Verb 2.
Nǐ	xiān	wàng	nán	zǒu,	zài	(wàng)	zuǒ	zhuǎn.
(First go toward the south, then turn left.)								

In giving directions, you often have to tell a visitor first to go one way and then go another. A very common Chinese pattern for first doing one thing and then doing another is SUBJ + xiān + VERB1 + OBJ1, zài + VERB2 + OBJ2, as in "Nǐ xiān mǎi wèishēng zhǐ, zài shàng cèsuǒ" (First buy toilet paper, then use the toilet). The character for "then" in this pattern is the same "zài" as in "zàijiàn" (lit., "again see," or "see you later"); in both cases "zài" refers to a subsequent action that has not been completed at the time of utterance.

When helping a lost visitor, you might use this pattern to say something like "Nǐ xiān wàng Běihǎi Gōngyuán zǒu, zài wàng zuǒ zhuǎn" (First go toward Northern Sea Park, then turn left). Note that although "zài" functions as a conjunction, its word order in a clause is that of an adverb such as "xiān": it must precede the verb and follow the subject, if any.

Exercises for 10.3: Complete the following sentences.

1. Nǐ xiān wàng xī zǒu, _____. (First go toward the west, then go toward the north.)

2. Nǐ _____ zǒu, zài _____. (First go toward the Běijīng Hotel, then turn left.)

3. Nǐde jīnglǐ xiān _____, _____ ma?
   (Did your manager first go to the park, then go to his company?)

4. Tāmen _____, _____ ma? (Did they
   first go to the airport, then buy the newspapers?)

5. Qǐng nǐmen _____, _____. (Please
   first turn right, then go toward the east.)

10.4 Expressing Distance with NUM + lǐ + lù

Place Word 1	Coverb "lí"	Place Word 2	yǒu	Number	lǐ	lù
Gōngyuán (The park is three kilometers from my home.)	lí	wǒ jiā	yǒu	sān	lǐ	lù.
Zhèr (It's 12 kilometers from here to there.)	lí	nàr	yòu	shíèr	lǐ	lù.

Place Word 1	Coverb "lí"	Place Word 2	Adverb	Adjective
Zhèr (The toilet is far from here.)	lí	cèsuǒ	hěn	yuǎn.
Nǐ jiā (Your home is close to the Běijīng Hotel.)	lí	Běijīng Fàndiàn	hěn	jìn.

English speakers may express distance with a phrase such as "three kilometers down the road." The Chinese pattern for distance in kilometers is very similar, with "lǐ" (kilometer) functioning as the measure word and "lù" (road) serving as the noun in the NUM + MEAS + NOUN structure, as in "liǎng lǐ lù" (two kilometers). The traditional Chinese "lǐ" was only about half a kilometer or a third of a mile, but in recent decades China has made such progress in adopting the metric system that you can generally assume that "lǐ" refers to kilometers. For shorter units such "mǐ" (meters), "lù" drops out, as in "jiǔshíèr mǐ" (92 meters). When the context of kilometers is very clear, "lù" may be omitted for the sake of brevity, as in "liǎng lǐ" (two kilometers) and "bàn lǐ" (half a kilometer).

To indicate the distance from one place to another, do not use "cóng" for "from," but instead use the "distance from" coverb "lí": PW1 + lí + PW2 + hěn yuǎn, as in "Gōngyuán lí fēijīchǎng hěn yuǎn" (The park is far from the airport). If the two places are near rather than far from one another, simply substitute "jìn" for "yuǎn," as in "Běijīng Fàndiàn lí gōngyuán hěn jìn" (The Běijīng Hotel is close to the park).

To express the distance in kilometers from one place to another, use the pattern PW1 + lí + PW2 + yǒu + NUM + lǐ + lù, as in "Zhèr lí Jiějie de jiā yǒu sì lǐ lù" (It's four kilometers from here to Elder Sister's home). The verb "yǒu" can be omitted from the above pattern during rapid speech.

Exercises for 10.4: Say the following in Chinese.

1. Ask your friend if her home is far from yours.

_____

2. Tell her that your home is close to the park.

_____

3. Tell her that it's two kilometers from here to your home.

_____

4. Ask your manager if his home is very far from the company.

_____

5. Tell him that it's 58 kilometers from your home to the airport.

_____

10.5 The Most Versatile Localizer: "Biān"

gōngyuán	lǐbiān	(inside the park)
yínháng	wàibiān	(outside the bank)
nèitiáo lù	pángbiān	(beside that road)
chēzi	zuǒbiān	(to the left of the car)
fángzi	yòubiān	(to the right of the house)
xuéxiào	dōngbiān	(east of the school)

The original meaning of "biān" is "side." Nevertheless, this word is a bound localizer that must be connected to another word, often another bound form such as "páng" (side), "lǐ" (in), or "xī" (west), in order to form independent semantic unit like the place words "pángbiān" (the side), "lǐbiān" (inside), and "xībiān" (the west). Words such as the four points of the compass ("dōng, xī, nán, běi"), "zuǒ" (left), and "yòu" (right) behave more like adjectives than place words. They can modify nouns, as in "zuǒ shǒu" (left hand), and serve as the object of the coverb "wàng," as in "Wàng yòu zhuǎn" (Turn toward the right), but they cannot fill the place-word slot of a sentence such as "Wǒmen zài fēijīchǎng" (We are at the airport). To become true place words, the four points of the compass, "zuǒ," and "yòu" need to have a localizer like "biān" appended to them. "Zuǒ" and "yòu" actually take no other localizer but "biān," as in "Cèsuǒ zài yòubiān" (The toilet is to the right) and "Shū zài zuǒbiān" (The books are on the left).

Exercises for 10.5: Fill in each blank with an appropriate place word.

1. Zhèizhāng zhàopiàn _____ (in this photo) yǒu sānge rén.

2. Wǒ māma zài wǒ _____ (to my left), wǒ dìdi zài wǒ _____ (to my right).

3. Rìběn zài Zhōngguó _____. (Japan is to the east of China.)

4. Jiānádà (Canada) zài Měiguó _____ (to the north), Mòxīgē (Mexico) zài Měiguó _____ (to the south).

5. Fǎguó (France) zài Déguó (Germany) _____ (to the west).

10.6 "Búyòng VERB" as "Needn't Verb"

(Subject)	búyòng	Verb	(Object)	
Nǐ	búyòng	mǎi	shū.	(You needn't buy books.)
Tāmen	búyòng	qù	gōngyuán.	(They needn't go to the park.)

Like the negative imperative "bié VERB" (don't verb) pattern, "búyòng VERB" recommends that the listener and perhaps some other people refrain from doing something; the subject of such an imperative sentence is usually "nǐ" or "nǐmen," and is often omitted because it is obvious. However, instead of just telling someone not to do something with "bié VERB," you can suggest that the proposed action is unnecessary by using "búyòng VERB": "Nǐ búyòng gěi qián" (You needn't give money).

Exercises for 10.6: Use "bié VERB" or "búyòng VERB" to make one sentence for each of the following situations.

1. You show a young woman how to get to a park. You tell her to go north, not to go east.

   _____

   _____

2. When the young woman and her son thank you, you tell them that they needn't thank you.

   _____

   _____

3. Your mother wants you to go buy some paper. She expressly tells you not to buy books.

   _____

   _____

4. You go to a Chinese bookstore in Chinatown and pick up some newspapers there. They are free local newspapers in Chinese. When you offer to pay for them, the clerk tells you that you needn't give money.

   _____

   _____

5. At the airport ticket counter, the clerk tells you that you needn't show her your passport.

   _____

   _____

10.7 More on Directional and Resultative Complements

Directional Complements

Subject	Verb	Object	Directional Complement	Object
Māma	dài	háizi	qù	gōngyuán.
(The mother took her child to the park.)				
Tā	dài	wǒ	lái	zhèr.
(He brought me here.)				

Some transitive verbs such as "dài" (to take or bring someone or something with you) not only hook up with directional complements such as "qù" or "lái," indicating movement away from or toward the speaker, but also sandwich the direct object between the verb and the complement: SUBJ + VERB + OBJ + COMP, as in "Niánqīngrén dài Mínglěi qù" (The youth is taking Mínglěi there), and "Bǐdé dài Lìlián lái" (Peter is bringing Lìlián here).

Resultative Complements

Subject	Verb	Resultative Complement	Object	
Wǒ	kàn	dào	nǐde māo.	(I see your cat.)
Tā	kàn	jiàn	yìtáo lù.	(He sees one road.)

The verb "kàn" by itself means merely "to look at." If you want to convey the idea of having looked with the result of *seeing* something, attach either "dào" or "jiàn" as a resultative complement (this concept was introduced in Section 9.3) to form the VERB + COMP compound "kàndào" or "kànjiàn." You simply *look* at television ("kàn diànshì"), but you make a left turn ("zuǒ zhuǎn") after *seeing* a particular traffic light ("kàndào hónglǜdēng").

Exercises for 10.7: Rearrange the words in each entry to make a correct sentence according to the English meaning given.

1. háizi dài bàba gōngyuán qù nèige (That papa takes his child to the park.)

   _____

2. hónglǜdēng zài nǐmen zuǒzhuǎn kàndào (When you see the traffic light, then turn left.)

   _____

3. shíèryuè dài mèimei lái tā jīnnián yào Zhōngguó (She is bringing her younger sister to China this December.)

   _____

4. tā kàndào shàng dìdi cèsuǒ qù wǒ dài tā (I saw him taking his younger brother to the toilet.)

   _____

5. zǔfù dài xiǎojiě yínháng zhèige yào wǒ qù
   (This young lady is going to take my grandfather to the bank.)

After tidying up the family tombs, people often place offerings of fresh flowers and fruit at the graveside.

CULTURE NOTES

China has a far more impressive passenger rail system than America's, but its public toilets often come up short, especially for an unprepared traveler such as Mínglěi, who forgot to carry toilet paper with him on his outings. Fortunately, Mínglěi's Chinese was good enough to permit him to enlist the help of a Good Samaritan who happened to be passing by. Such passersby tend to be especially solicitous to visitors who are making an effort to speak Chinese.

A Chinese Song

The Little Mouse That Climbed the Bean-Oil Lampstand

Xiǎo lǎoshǔ,
shàng dēngtái,
tōu yóu chī,
xiàbùlái,
jiào māma,
mā bù lái,
Jīligūlu gǔnxiàlái.

(The little mouse climbed up
the lampstand high,
He sipped lamp-oil on the sly,
But he couldn't get down.
He called for his mama,
but his mama wouldn't come.
With a bang and a clatter,
he came tumbling down.)

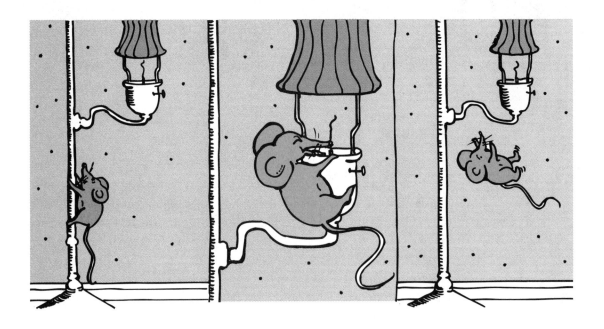

SUMMARY

To indicate coming or going from one place to another, use the pattern SUBJ + cóng + PW1 + dào + PW2 + lái/qù, as in "Nèige niánqīngrén cóng Běijīng Fàndiàn dào gōngyuán lái" (That youth is coming from the Běijīng Hotel to the park). When talking about going in a certain direction to reach a destination, use "wàng" instead of "dào" as the coverb, and "zǒu" instead of "qù" as the verb: "Cóng zhèr zěnme zǒu?" (How do you get there from here?); "Wàng běi zǒu. Dàgài bànlǐ lù jiù dào le" (Go north. In about half a kilometer you'll have gotten there).

Distance in kilometers is expressed by the phrase NUM + lǐ + lù, as in "sì lǐ lù" (four kilometers). Specifying the distance between two places requires the coverb "lí": PW1 + lí + PW2 + yǒu + NUM + lǐ + lù; for example, "Nàr lí Dōng Cháng'ān Jiē yǒu bàn lǐ lù" (It's half a kilometer from there to East Eternal Peace Street). Alternatively, an adjectival verb such as "yuǎn" (far) or "jìn" (near) can be substituted for a numerical distance, as in "Cèsuǒ lí hónglǜdēng hěn jìn" (The toilets are close to the traffic light).

To express the idea of first ("xiān") doing one thing and then ("zài") doing something else, place each of the two adverbs directly before the appropriate coverb or verb, and pause briefly where the comma divides the two clauses: "Nǐ xiān wàng xī zǒu, zài wàng yòu zhuǎn" (First go west, then turn right). If some action need not be taken, use "búyòng" before the relevant verb: "Mèimei búyòng shàng cèsuǒ" (Younger Sister needn't go to the toilet).

WǑ XIĂNG QǏNG NǏMEN CHĪ FÀN.

(I'd like to invite you to dinner.)

CHAPTER OVERVIEW

1. Making a Phone Call ("Dǎ Diànhuà") and Inviting Friends to Dinner

2. SUBJ + Jiù Shì + OBJ as "Subject Is Nothing Other than Object"

3. "Gāng + VERB" as "Just Now Verbed"

4. Indicating Ongoing "Progressive" Action with SUBJ + Zài + VERB or SUBJ + VERB + zhe + OBJ

5. "Guò" in Directional Complements

6. "Kěyǐ" as Verb and as Auxiliary Verb

7. Using Question Words Such As "Shénme" as Indefinites

NEW VOCABULARY

1. tàitai	Mrs. (after surname), a married lady	NOUN
2. wéi	hello (used mainly at start of phone calls)	INTJ
3. zài	to be at, to be there	VERB
4. wǒ jiù shì	It's none other than I./ "Speaking"	IDIO
5. jiù shì	to be none other than	ADV-VERB
6. kòng	free time, leisure time	NOUN
7. xiǎng + VERB	would like to VERB, want to VERB	AUXV
8. qǐng	to invite, to request	VERB
9. chī fàn	to eat (VERB-OBJ compound)	VERB-OBJ
10. chī	to eat something	VERB
11. fàn	cooked rice, food, a meal	NOUN
12. kèqi	be polite, be considerate	ADJ
13. bútài + ADJ	is not very ADJ	ADV
14. fāngbiàn	be convenient	ADJ
15. diànnǎo	computer	NOUN
16. gāng + VERB	has just verbed	ADV
17. huài	be bad, be broken, malfunction	ADJ
18. xiānsheng	husband	NOUN
19. zài + V	is verbing (same "zài" as #3, different "zài" from that in "zàijiàn")	AUXV
20. xiūlǐ	to repair	VERB
21. zuò fàn	to cook (VERB-OBJ compound)	VERB-OBJ
22. zuò	to do, to make	VERB
23. VERB + zhe	is verbing	PART
24. guòlái	to come over	VERB-COMP
25. guò	to cross, to exceed	VERB
26. yíkuàir	together	ADV
27. kěyǐ	to be permitted, to be able, to be okay	VERB/ AUX VERB
28. dāngrán	of course, naturally	MADV

29. zhēn	truly, really	ADV
30. bù hǎo yìsi	to be embarrassed	ADJ
31. yìsi	meaning	NOUN
32. yuánlái	originally	MADV
33. méi shénme	It's nothing to speak of./ It's nothing much.	IDIO
34. děng huǐr jiàn	see you after awhile	IDIO
35. děng	to wait	VERB
36. huǐr (or yìhuǐr)	awhile	NOUN

DIALOGUE

Lín Tàitai (answering the phone in her home): Wéi?

Mínglěi: Qǐngwèn, Lín Tàitai zàibúzài?

Lín Tàitai: Wǒ jiù shì.

Mínglěi: Nǐmen jīntiān yǒu kòng ma? Wǒ xiǎng qǐng nǐmen chī fàn.

Lín Tàitai: Xièxie. Nǐ tài kèqi le. Kěshì jīntiān bútài fāngbiàn.

Mínglěi: Ō, nǐmen xiànzài hěn máng ma?

Lín Tàitai: Wǒmen de diànnǎo gāng huài le, wǒ xiānsheng zài xiūlǐ diànnǎo. Wǒ xiànzài zuòzhe fàn. Nǐ yào búyào guòlái gēn wǒmen yíkuàir chī?

Mínglěi: Kěyǐ ma?

Lín Tàitai: Dāngrán kěyǐ a!

Mínglěi: Nà zhēn bùhǎo yìsi. Wǒ yuánlái xiǎng qǐng nǐ, xiànzài nǐ qǐng wǒ le.

Lín Tàitai: Méi shénme. Děng huǐr jiàn!

DIALOGUE TRANSLATION

Mrs. Lín (answering the phone in her home): Hello?

Mínglěi: May I ask if Mrs. Lín is there?

Mrs. Lín: Speaking.

Mínglěi: Do you have free time today? I'd like to invite you to have a meal.

Mrs. Lín: Thanks. You're too considerate. But it's not very convenient today.

Mínglěi: Oh, are you busy now?

Mrs. Lín: Our computer just went haywire. My husband is fixing the computer, and I'm cooking right now. Do you want to come over and eat together with us?

Mínglěi: Would that be okay?

Mrs. Lín: Of course it would be!

Mínglěi: Well, then I'm really embarrassed. Originally I wanted to invite you, and now you're inviting me.

Mrs. Lín: It isn't anything much. See you after awhile!

11.1 Making a Phone Call ("Dǎ Diànhuà") and Inviting Friends to Dinner

Making a Phone Call

wéi	(Hello. [when answering a phone call])
Lǐ Xiānsheng zài jiā ma?	(Is Mr. Lǐ at home?)
Lín Xiǎojiě zàibúzài?	(Is Miss Lín at home?)
Tā búzài.	(She's not in.)
(Nǐ) shì Hán Lǎoshī ma?	(Is this Teacher Hán?)
Duì, wǒ jiù shì.	(Right, this is she./Speaking.)

After picking up your ringing phone in China, use "wéi" with a rising pitch for "hello." The caller will sometimes respond with a "wèi" like a falling-pitch "hello," but often simply asks straightaway to speak with a particular person, using the verb "zài," as in "Hán Xiǎojiě zàibúzài?" (Is Miss Hán there?) or "Lín Xiānsheng zài jiā ma?" (Is Mr. Lín at home?).

If you are the person to whom the caller wishes to speak, you will reply, "Wǒ jiù shì" (Speaking). In the dialogue, if Hán Mínglěi could have identified Mrs. Lín at once from her voice when she said "wéi," he might have asked, "Shì Lín Tàitai ma?" or "Nǐ shìbúshì Lín Tàitai?" (Is this Mrs. Lín?).

Extending an Invitation

Verb – Object Compounds		
chī	fàn	(eat; "eat food")
hē	shuǐ	(drink; "drink water")
shuō	huà	(talk; "speak words")

Note that Mínglěi invites ("qǐng") the Líns to "chī fàn," not merely to "chī." A number of common transitive verbs such as "chī," "hē," and "shuō" require a direct object to follow; in its absence, the listener will assume that the speaker has such an object in mind, and will interpret the meaning to be "eat it," "drink it," and "say it," respectively.

If you simply want to convey the idea that SUBJ1 eats, SUBJ2 drinks, and SUBJ3 talks, you need to use the appropriate generic or dummy object of the given verb, in these cases "fàn" (food), "shuǐ" (water), and "huà" (speech), respectively: SUBJ1 chī fàn, SUBJ2 hē shuǐ, SUBJ3 shuō huà. These three "verb-object compounds" are generally abbreviated as "VERB-OBJ."

In Mrs. Lín's question to Mínglěi about coming over to join them for dinner, she need not append the object "fàn" to the verb "chī." Since she had just uttered "fàn" in the preceding sentence, it became the understood object of the following sentence.

Exercises for 11.1: Make up phone conversations using the cues given.

1. Bǐdé called Lìlián. He identified her at once from her voice when she said "Wéi." He asked immediately, "Is this Lìlián?" She said, "Yes." He asked her whether she had free time on that day. She said, "Yes, I do." He invited her to have a meal. She accepted the invitation, saying, "It's wonderful" ["tài hǎo le"], and thanked him.

_____

_____

_____

_____

2. Mínglěi called Manager Lǐ at home. When someone answered the phone, Mínglěi asked whether Manager Lǐ was there. This person said he was none other than Manager Lǐ. Mínglěi said he would like to invite Manager Lǐ to his home to have tea. Manager Lǐ said Mínglěi was too considerate, but it was not very convenient on that day. Mínglěi asked whether Manager Lǐ was busy at that time. Manager Lǐ said, "Yes, I'm very busy. I'm truly sorry."

_____

_____

11.2 SUBJ + Jiù Shì + OBJ as "Subject Is Nothing Other than Object"

Subject	jiù shì	Object	
Tā	jiù shì	Hán Jiàoshòu.	(He is none other than Professor Hán.)
Nèige nánrén	jiùshì	wǒ shúshu.	(That man is none other than my uncle.)

Although the most common function of "jiù" is as a conjunction meaning "then," it behaves rather like an adverb in having to precede the verb and follow the subject, if any. When "jiù" precedes the verb "shì," it is wholly adverbial and means something like "precisely" or "none other than," as in "Tā jiù shì wǒ bàba" (He is none other than my dad).

Exercises for 11.2: Use "jiù shì" to complete the following dialogues.

1. A: Nèige nǔlǎoshī shì nǐ jiějie ma?
   B: Duì, _____. (She is none other than my elder sister.)

2. A: Qǐngwèn, Lín Xiānsheng zàibúzài?
   Lín Xiānsheng: _____. (Speaking.)

3. A: Něizhī gǒu shì nǐde chǒngwù? (Which dog is your pet?)
   B: _____. (It is none other than this one.)

4. A: Qǐngwèn, nín shì búshì Wèi Jiàoshòu (Professor Wèi)?
   B: Duì, _____. (I am none other than Professor Wèi.)

5. A: Něige rén shì nǐmen de jiàoliàn?
   B: _____. (It is none other than that young lady.)

11.3 "Gāng + VERB" as "Just Now Verbed"

Subject	gāng	Verb	(le)	(Object)	
Tā	gāng	lái.			(She just arrived.)
Nǐmen	gāng	chī	le	fàn.	(You just ate.)

To recount an action that has just now occurred, use the adverb "gāng" in its normal position after the subject and before the verb, as in "Hán Xiǎojiě gāng zǒu" (Miss Hán just left). Because a situation in which something has just happened tends to imply completed action or a change of circumstances, the particle "le" is often used in this pattern.

Exercises for 11.3: Translate the following sentences.

1. I just bought ("mǎi le") a book.

_____

2. Miss Lǐ just came to my home.

_____

3. Manager Wáng just went to China.

_____

4. He just sold ("mài le") his car ("chē").

_____

5. My child just went to ("shàng le") the toilet.

_____

6. Her younger brother's telephone has just malfunctioned.

_____

7. My husband just fixed the computer.

_____

11.4 Indicating Ongoing "Progressive" Action with SUBJ + Zài + VERB or SUBJ + VERB + zhe + OBJ

Subject	zài	Verb	(Object)	
Tā jiějie	zài	kàn	shū.	(His older sister is reading a book.)
Wǒ	zài	zuò	fàn.	(I'm cooking.)

The easiest way of emphasizing that an action is ongoing is to place the verb "zài" (to be at) directly before the verb. In this usage, "zài" works like an auxiliary verb: SUBJ + zài + VERB (+ OBJ), or "subject is verbing the object"; for example, "Lìlián zài yóuyǒng" (Lìlián is swimming), and "Bǐdé zài xiūlǐ chē" (Peter is fixing the car).

Subject	Verb	zhe	(Object)	
Nèige rén	zhàn	zhe.		(That person is standing.)
Tā	ná	zhe	yìzhāng zhàopiàn.	(He's holding a photograph.)

Another way of indicating progressive action, especially for many single-syllable action verbs, is to add the particle "zhe" directly after the verb: SUBJ + VERB + zhe, as in "Nèige xuéshēng názhe hùzhào" (That student is holding a passport), and "Mínglěi de lù zhànzhe" (Mínglěi's deer is standing). These two patterns are not totally interchangeable, but the subtle differences between them are beyond the scope of this book.

Exercises for 11.4:

I. Use the cues given to make sentences with the SUBJ + zài + VERB pattern.

1. You knock on your younger sister's door to tell her that Father is calling her.

   _____

2. You ask your friend whether she and her husband are eating. (Use a "ma" question.)

   _____

3. Someone asks to see your elder brother, and you reply that your elder brother is fixing the computer.

   _____

4. Someone calls you on the phone, and you tell him that you are reading books now.

   _____

II. Use the cues given to make sentences with the SUBJ + VERB + zhe + (OBJ) pattern.

1. Your boyfriend is late for a date. You call him and tell him that you are waiting for him.

2. You and your friend go to the concert too late. All the seats are taken. You suggest to your friend, "Let's be standing (remain standing)."

3. You ask your friend why ("zěnme") that young woman ("xiǎojiě") is holding newspapers.

4. You call your mother from school, asking her what she is doing. She says, "I'm cooking right now."

11.5 "Guò" in Directional Complements

guòqù	(go over)
zǒuguòqù	(walk over there)
guòlái	(come over)
zǒuguòlái	(walk over here)

"Guò jiē" is to cross the street, and the sense of crossing *over* something applies to verb compounds in which the directional complements "qù" and "lái" are appended to "guò," as in "guòqù" (go over) and "guòlái" (come over). Two examples are "Qǐng nǐ guòqù gēn jīnglǐ shuō" (Please go over and talk about it with the manager), and "Nǐmen guòlái kànkan diànnǎo ba" (Better come over and take a look at the computer).

"Guòqù" and "guòlái" can also be used as compound directional complements for action verbs such as "ná" (take/bring) and "zǒu" (walk), as in "náguòqù" (take it over), "náguòlái" (bring it over), "zǒuguòlái" (walk over here), and "zǒuguòqù" (walk over there).

Exercises for 11.5: Translate the following, using appropriate directional complements.

1. Why don't you come over to eat with us?

_____

2. She wants to go over and talk about it ("shuō") with her coach.

_____

3. Please (you [plural]) walk over here.

_____

4. He walks over there to look at that cat ("māo").

_____

5. Are we going to go over and swim with them? [Use a "ma" question.]

_____

11.6 "Kěyǐ" as Verb and as Auxiliary Verb

Subject	Adverb	kěyǐ	Verb	(Object)	
Nǐmen		kěyǐ	hē	chá.	(You are permitted to drink tea.)
Tā	bù	kěyǐ	kàn	bào.	(He is not permitted to read newspapers.)

As a verb, "kěyǐ" means "to be okay," in the sense of "to be permitted" or "to be permissable," as when a bookstore clerk asks a customer, "Zhōngwén shū kěyǐ ma?" (Are Chinese-language books okay?). Most frequently, however, "kěyǐ" conveys the same meaning as an auxiliary verb, as in "Wǒmen kěyǐ hē jiǔ ma?" (May we drink alcohol?) and "Wǒ kěyǐ bùkěyǐ zài zhèr chōu yān?" (Am I permitted to smoke cigarettes here?)

Characteristic lamasery architecture at the giant Tibetan Buddhist temple Tǎ'ěrsì in Qīnghǎi, the far western province bordering Tibet (Xīzàng).

In affirmative sentences only, "kěyǐ" may alternatively mean "can" (circumstances permitting), as in "Wǒmen kěyǐ xiān chī fàn, zài zǒu" (We can eat first and then leave). By way of contrast, negative sentences with "kěyǐ" always convey the sense of not being permitted to do something: "Nǐ bùkěyǐ kāi chē" (You're not permitted to drive a car).

Exercises for 11.6: Use "kěyǐ" to make the indicated sentences.

1. Your friend asks to borrow a dictionary of yours, and you happen to have a dictionary on your desk. Ask her whether this dictionary is okay.

_____

_____

2. You show your friend the pool near your house and tell him that he can swim there.

_____

_____

3. Your friend asks you whether he is permitted to smoke ("chōu yān") here.

   _____

   _____

4. After your friend drinks some wine, he asks to leave. But you warn him that he is not permitted to drive a car now.

   _____

   _____

5. Tell a child that she is permitted to play with your dog (gǒu).

   _____

   _____

11.7 Using Question Words Such As "Shénme" as Indefinites

Subject	bù/méi	Verb	Question Words	(Object)
Wǒ (I'm not going anywhere to speak of.)	bú	qù	nǎr.	
Tā bàba (Her papa barely has a few friends.)	méi	yǒu	jǐge	péngyou.
Wǒmen (We didn't eat anything to speak of.)	méi	chī	shénme.	

Subject	yào	Verb	yìdiǎn	shénme
Tā (He wants to drink a little something.)	yào	hē	yìdiǎn	shénme.

Sometimes a question word such as "shéi," "shénme," "nǎr," or "jǐ" comes somewhere after the verb, but the speaker doesn't seem to be asking a question. In that case the question word is probably functioning as an indefinite noun in declarative sentence, and means "much of anyone," "anything to speak of," "anywhere to speak of," or "but a few," respectively.

The use of question words as indefinites is most common in the negative mode, as in "Wǒ bù qǐng shéi" (I'm not inviting much of anyone), "Lìlián bù mǎi shénme" (Lìlián isn't buying anything to speak of), "Dìdi bú qù nǎr" (Younger Brother isn't going anywhere to speak of), and "Wáng Jīnglǐ méiyǒu jǐge Měiguó péngyou" (Manager Wáng barely has a few American friends). The most common question word used as an indefinite in the positive mode is "shénme" (something), as in "Wǒmen yào chī yìdiǎn shénme" (We want to eat a little something).

Exercises for 11.7: Use "shénme" in the following sentences.

1. Ask your friend if she wants to drink a little something.

_____

2. When someone asks you how many students Teacher Lǐ has, you tell her that Teacher Lǐ barely has a few students.

_____

3. Ask your son whether he wants to eat a little something.

_____

4. Tell your friend that your dad has but a few photographs.

_____

5. Tell your mom that you didn't buy anything to speak of.

_____

CULTURE NOTES

Chinese legal codes and business contracts can be written with as much hair-splitting precision as can be found in such documents in English. On the other hand, vagueness and ambiguity can often smooth over the rough edges of social interactions, and the Chinese language makes it quite easy to be vague when that is what you desire. To say "four or five kilometers" and "two or three yuán," you don't even need the Chinese equivalent of "or," but instead should simply say "sì-wǔ lǐ lù" and "liǎng-sānkuài qián." Using question words as indefinites in the manner of Mrs. Lín's "méi shénme" is another common way of being vague in Chinese.

The most widely used terms for "husband" and "wife" are "zhàngfū" and "qīzi," as in "nǐ zhàngfū" (your husband) and "wǒ qīzi" (my wife). Among some older Chinese in the PRC, "àirén" (lover) may refer to either the wife or the husband, but this usage should generally be avoided in Taiwan, Hong Kong, Singapore, and among overseas Chinese. Chinese speakers from the latter

Puppeteers often enact engaging folk tales, as in this performance in Táiwān.

four groups typically use either "zhàngfū" or "xiānsheng" for "husband," and either "qīzi" or "tàitai" for "wife." The latter phraseology has also become common among younger PRC residents.

If you are being introduced to Mr. and Mrs. Wáng, you would never address either of them as "Wáng Àirén." You may call the husband "Wáng Xiānsheng" anywhere, but to address the wife as "Wáng Tàitai" is completely proper only in Hong Kong, Singapore, Taiwan, and among most overseas Chinese.

In the PRC, the term "tàitai" was long avoided as "bourgeois" and thus incorrect, and a married woman was often referred to instead by her maiden surname followed by "Comrade" (tóngzhì), as in "Lǐ Tóngzhì" (Comrade Lǐ). This politicized form of address has greatly waned in popularity, however, since the passing of Máo's generation of hard-core Communist leaders, though you still occasionally hear it today in some circles and during certain formal occasions.

The term of address for women that is neutral as to marital status, "nǚshì," is more stiffly formal than its closest English equivalent, "Ms.," and is seldom appropriate except for such occasions as formal banquets and conferences. Often, the best policy is to avoid addressing a married woman in the PRC directly until you can determine what form others are using, then follow suit.

If either of the Wángs has a high-status position, you can alternatively use the honorific term "fūrén" (Madam), that is, "Wáng Fūrén" (Madam Wáng). Please be sure, though, not to use the honorific term "fūrén" in reference to your own wife; there are many jokes about a thick-headed husband who refers to his own wife as "Wǒ fūrén" (My madam).

SUMMARY

If the subject just now verbed, use "gāng" in the adverbial position right before the verb: "Lín Xiānsheng gāng zǒu" (Mr. Lín just now left). Ongoing or progressive action may be indicated by placing "zài" in the adverbial position: "Māma zài xiūlǐ diànnǎo" (Mom is fixing the computer). Moreover, the particle "zhe" may be suffixed to many monosyllabic action verbs to mark progressive action: "Lín Tàitai xiànzài zuòzhe fàn" (Mrs. Lín is cooking right now).

When Mínglěi made a phone call ("dǎ diànhuà") to Mrs. Lín, she said "Wéi" (Hello) after picking up the receiver. Not recognizing her voice, he asked whether Mrs. Lín was there ("Lín Tàitài zài búzài?"). Her response, "Wǒ jiù shì" (Speaking), literally means "I am none other than [she]." Another example of this common pattern is "Nèige nánrén jiù shì wǒde jiàoliàn" (That man is none other than my coach).

To ask whether something is permitted, use the auxiliary verb "kěyǐ": "Wǒmen kěyǐ guòqù kàn nǐmen ma?" (Is it okay if we go over to see you?). A likely reply would be "Dāngrán kěyǐ" (Of course it's okay).

"Shénme" and other question words sometimes function as indefinite nouns or modifiers within a declarative sentence. Three examples are "Jiějie xiǎng chī yìdiǎn shénme" (Elder Sister would like to eat a little *something*), "Shúshu méi yǒu shénme qián" (Uncle doesn't have *any* money *to speak of*), and "Wǒ bù zhǎo shéi" (I'm not looking for *anyone in particular*).

CHAPTER 12

QǏNG NǏ BǍ CÙ NÁGĚI WǑ.
(Please pass me the vinegar.)

CHAPTER OVERVIEW

1. "Kuài" and Sentence-end "le" as "About to Verb (the Object)"

2. VERB + hǎo as "to Finish Verbing," and the Completed-action "le"

3. The Plural Measure "Xiē"

4. Huì + VERB as "Know How to VERB"

5. Subjectless Sentences Such As "Xià Yǔ" (It's Raining)

6. Pulling the Object Up Before the Verb with the "Bǎ" Construction

7. The Versatile Adverb "Cái" and Verb "Kāi"

NEW VOCABULARY

1.	huānyíng nǐ lái	welcome, We welcome your visit ("having come").	IDIO
2.	huānyíng	welcome	VERB
3.	qǐng zuò	Please have a seat.	IDIO
4.	zuò	to sit, to ride a conveyance (such as a bus)	VERB
5.	jiǎozi	dumplings (a mostly northern specialty)	NOUN
6.	kuài bāo hǎo le	about to finish wrapping	ADV-VERB-COMP-PART
7.	kuài	be fast	ADJ
8.	kuài + VERB + le	about to VERB, on the verge of verbing	ADV-VERB-PART
9.	bāo	to wrap	VERB
10.	VERB + hǎo	to finish verbing	VERB-COMP
11.	wǒ dùzi è le	My stomach's (I've) gotten hungry.	
12.	dùzi	stomach	NOUN
13.	è	be hungry	ADJ
14.	ADJ + le	have gotten ADJ	ADJ-PART
15.	bāng	to help	VERB
16.	yìxiē	some (of them)	NUM-MEAS
17.	xiē	(plural measure that goes with any noun)	MEAS
18.	nánfāngrén	southerner	NOUN
19.	nánfāng	the South (of a country), southern	NOUN
20.	huì	to know how to, can (do something one has learned)	AUXV
21.	tīng	to listen	VERB
22.	xià yǔ le	It's now raining (changed situation).	VERB-OBJ-PART
23.	xià	to get off (bus), to fall (rain, snow), below	VERB
24.	yǔ	rain	NOUN
25.	xià yǔ	It's raining.	VERB-OBJ

TRACK 25

26. bú yàojǐn	It doesn't matter (like "méi guānxi").	IDIO
27. yàojǐn	be important	ADJ
28. bǎ	(coverb for prestating the object—see Section 12.6)	COV
29. yǔsǎn	umbrella	NOUN
30. jiègěi	to lend to somebody	VERB-COMP
31. jiè	to borrow, to lend	VERB
32. cù	vinegar	NOUN
33. nágěi	to hand to somebody, to pass	VERB-COMP
34. nàme xǐhuān	to like so much, to be so fond of	ADV-VERB
35. xǐhuān	to like, to be fond of	VERB
36. chī cù	to taste vinegar, to be jealous of your spouse's lover	VERB-OBJ
37. Ō	oh	PART
38. a	(particle used in various exclamations and questions)	PART
39. nǎlǐ	where? (in rhetorical questions, "How could that be?")	QW
40. cái	only then, only (narrower usage than "zhǐ")	ADV
41. ne	(end particle indicating something contrary to expectation)	PART
42. kāi wánxiào	to crack a joke	VERB-OBJ
43. kāi	to open, to turn on, to wisecrack, to drive, to convene (see Section 12.7)	VERB
44. wán	to play	VERB
45. xiào	to laugh	VERB
46. wánxiào	joke (used mostly after "kāi")	NOUN

DIALOGUE

TRACK
26

Lín Tàitai	(opening the front door of her home): Qǐng jìn. Huānyíng nǐ lái! Qǐng zuò.
Mínglěi:	Xièxie.
Lín Tàitai:	Jiǎozi kuài bāohǎo le.
Mínglěi:	Wǒ dùzi è le. Wǒ bāng nǐ bāo yìxiē.
Lín Tàitai:	Ō, nánfāng rén yě huì bāo jiǎozi ma?
Mínglěi:	Dāngrán huì. (Pricking up his ears at the sound of raindrops falling) Nǐ tīng—xià yǔ le.
Lín Tàitai:	Bú yàojǐn. Wǒ huì bǎ yǔsǎn jiègěi nǐ.

(After all the dumplings are wrapped and boiled, they finally start eating.)

Lín Tàitai:	Qǐng nǐ bǎ cù nágěi wǒ.
Mínglěi:	Ō, nǐ nàme xǐhuān chī cù a? [See vocabulary list for the double entendre.]
Lín Tàitai:	Nǎlǐ, wǒ xiānsheng cái xǐhuān ne!
Lín Xiānsheng:	Nǐmen zhēn huì kāi wánxiào.

DIALOGUE TRANSLATION

Mrs. Lín	(opening the front door of her home): Please come in. Welcome! Please have a seat.
Mínglěi:	Thanks.
Mrs. Lín:	We're about to finish wrapping the dumplings.
Mínglěi:	I've gotten hungry. I'll help you wrap some of them.
Mrs. Lín:	Oh, do southerners also know how to wrap dumplings?
Mínglěi:	Of course we do. (Pricking up his ears at the sound of raindrops falling) Listen—it's raining now.
Mrs. Lín:	That doesn't matter. I'll lend you the umbrella.

(After all the dumplings are wrapped and boiled, they finally start eating.)

Mrs. Lín:	Please pass me the vinegar.
Mínglěi:	Oh, you're so fond of tasting vinegar, then? (See vocabulary list for the double entendre.)
Mrs. Lín:	How could that be? Actually, it's only my husband who's so fond of that!
Mr. Lín:	You two really know how to crack jokes.

Two of the well over 20 million Chinese Muslims stand beside a commemorative stone stele inside a great mosque in Xī'ān, the ancient Táng imperial capital and nowadays the provincial capital of Shǎnxī.

12.1 "Kuài" and Sentence-end "le" as "About to Verb (the Object)"

Subject	kuài	Verb	(Object)	le
Tāmen (They are about to arrive.)	kuài	lái		le.
Wǒ dìdi (My younger brother is about to get on the plane.)	kuài	shàng	fēijī	le.

Chinese has various structures that allow an ordinary adjective to modify the verb and thus function adverbially. An adjective is especially likely to be functioning adverbially if it is placed right before the verb, as "kuài" is in this pattern. However, this particular pattern stresses the imminence, rather than the rapidity, of the action: SUBJ + kuài + VERB (+ OBJ) + le, meaning "The subject is about to verb the object." Note that the change-of-situation "le" appears at the end of the sentence rather than being appended to the verb phrase, as in "Tāmen kuài chī zǎofàn le" (They're about to eat breakfast).

Exercises for 12.1: Use the SUBJ + kuài + VERB (+ OBJ) + le pattern to transform the following into correct sentences according to the English meaning given.

1. Wǒ zǔmǔ zǒu. (My grandmother is about to leave.)

_____

2. Fēijī qǐfēi. (The plane is about to take off.)

_____

3. Gēge chī wǔfàn. (Elder Brother is about to eat lunch.)

_____

4. Nèige xuéshēng qù Zhōngguó. (That student is about to go to China.)

_____

5. Wǒmen dào gōngyuán. (We are about to arrive at the park.)

_____

12.2 VERB + hǎo as "to Finish Verbing," and the Completed-action "le"

Subject	Verb	hǎo/wán	le	(Object)
Wǒ zǔfù	zuò	hǎo	le	èrshíge jiǎozi.
(My grandfather has finished cooking 20 dumplings.)				
Tā māma	mǎi	hǎo	le	yìzhāng fēijī piào.
(His mom has finished buying a plane ticket.)				
Tā	hē	wán	le	yìbēi chá.
(She has finished drinking a cup of tea.)				
Nǐ	kàn	wán	le	liǎngběn shū.
(You finished reading two books.)				

When used as a verb complement, "hǎo" is very similar to "wán" ("to finish"): both "zuòhǎo" and "zuòwán" mean "to finish doing." Because finishing the action amounts to completion, the completed-action "le" is often attached to the end of the VERB + hǎo (+ OBJ) or VERB + wán (+ OBJ) phrase, as in "Lín Xiānsheng zuòhǎo le sìshíge jiǎozi" (Mr. Lín finished cooking 40 dumplings).

Although the completed-action "le" pattern overlaps with the English past tense, the two structures are completely different in conceptual terms. There are many instances in which the completed-action "le" appears in sentences that would be in the future tense in English, and many English verbs in the past tense whose Chinese equivalents do not take the completed-action "le."

The most important thing to remember at this point is that the completed-action "le" is attached to the end of the verb phrase and indicates completion of the verbing. The change-of-situation "le" on the other hand, appears at the end of the sentence and emphasizes the newness of the situation.

Exercises for 12.2: Use the cues given to complete the following dialogues.

1. A: _____? (Did your mother finish cooking [zuò . . . fàn]?)
   B: Duì, tā zuòhǎo le.

2. A: _____? (Did your uncle finish reading newspapers [kàn . . . bào]?)
   B: Bù, tā hái méiyǒu kànwán. (No, he hasn't yet finished reading the newspapers.)

3. A: Nǐ bāohǎole jǐge jiǎozi? (How many dumplings did you finish wrapping?)
   B: _____. (I finished wrapping 24 dumplings.)

4. A: _____? (How many books has your older brother finished reading?)
   B: Tā kànwán le liǎngběn shū.

5. A: _____? (Have you [plural] all finished handling the matter [shì]?) [Use a "ma" question.]
   B: Duì, wǒmen dōu zuòhǎo le.

12.3 The Plural Measure "Xiē"

yìxiē/zhèixiē/nèixiē/něixiē	Noun	
yìxiē	chē	(several cars)
zhèixiē	shū	(these books)
nèixiē	rén	(those people)
něixiē	cídiǎn	(which dictionaries?)

Measures are usually neutral as to the number of nouns under discussion. Whether we are speaking of one table, "yìzhāng zhuōzi," or 12 tables, "shí'èrzhāng zhuōzi," the measure "zhāng" does not change. Nor is there any way of marking ordinary nouns for singular or plural; the same "zhuōzi" means "table" in the first example, and "tables" in the second. The pluralizing suffix "men" is almost always reserved for pronouns such as "wǒ," which becomes "wǒmen" in the plural.

The closest that Chinese comes to pluralizing ordinary nouns is through the plural measure "xiē," as in "yìxiē rén" (several people), "yìxiē jiǎozi" (some dumplings), "nèixiē jiàoliàn" (those coaches), "zhèixiē fēijī" (these airplanes), and "něixiē fángjiān?" (which rooms?). The only number that can precede "xiē" in the NUM + xiē + NOUN pattern is one; "yìxiē NOUN" means "some nouns" or "several nouns," depending on the context.

Exercises for 12.3: Translate the following phrases.

1. a few tables

_____

2. those dumplings

_____

3. which airplanes?

_____

4. some taxicabs

_____

5. these books

_____

6. which umbrellas?

_____

12.4 Huì + VERB as "Know How to VERB"

Subject	Adverb(s)	huì	Verb	Object
Nǐ māma (Your mom knows how to speak Chinese.)		huì	shuō	Zhōngwén.
Nèige rén (That person doesn't know how to cook.)	bú	huì	zuò	fàn.
Wǒ gēge (My older brother knows how to drive very well.)	hěn	huì	kāi	chē.

Chapter 8 explained how the auxiliary verb "huì" often means "will likely verb," as in "Jīntiān búhuì xià yǔ" (It will not likely rain today). The other important meaning of "huì + VERB" is "know how to verb," as in "Lìlián huì shuō Zhōngwén" (Lìlián knows how to speak Chinese), and "Bǐdé búhuì bāo jiǎozi" (Peter doesn't know how to wrap dumplings).

Note that "huì" refers to the presence or absence of a learned ability. This auxiliary verb is not used when an ability or inability to do something is connected with physical factors such as a laryngitis sufferer's inability to sing, constraining circumstances like an insufficient amount of money to eat at your favorite fancy restaurant, or prohibitions against smoking in an airplane and other forbidden activities.

Exercises for 12.4: Use "huì," "hěn huì," "búhuì," or "huì búhuì" to translate the following sentences.

1. Does your younger sister know how to swim?

_____

2. My husband knows how to wrap dumplings.

_____

3. That coach doesn't know how to speak Chinese.

_____

4. These teachers know how to read English newspapers.

_____

5. Does your child know how to go to the toilet?

_____

6. Her boyfriend is very easily made jealous.

_____

12.5 Subjectless Sentences Such As "Xìa Yǔ" (It's Raining)

Compared with speakers of English, Chinese speakers are more likely to leave out a sentence's subject when it is clear from the overall context. Many Chinese sentences simply have no place for the subject. Such sentences may be impersonal descriptions of natural phenomena, such as "Xià yǔ" (It's raining), "Jīntiān guā dà fēng" (There are strong winds blowing today), and "Bú xià xuě le (It's not snowing anymore). Many sentences with the topic-comment structure have no subject; examples are those in the unmarked passive mode such as "Dēng kāi le" (The lights have now been turned on), "Mén kāi le" (The door has now been opened), and "Qián dōu náqù le" (The money's all been taken away).

12.6 Pulling the Object Up Before the Verb with the "Bǎ" Construction

	Subject	bǎ	Object 1	Verb	Complement	(Object 2)
	Tā	bǎ	háizi	dài	guòlái.	
	(She brought the child over here.)					
	Nǐ	bǎ	shū	jiè	gěi	shéi?
	(Whom did you lend the book to?)					
Qǐng	nǐ	bǎ	bàozhǐ	ná	gěi	lǎoshī.
	(Please hand the teacher the newspapers.)					

The importance of coverbs and verb complements may be observed in the way that the verb "jiè" can mean either "borrow" or "lend," depending on whether you use this verb with the coverb "gēn" or with the verb complement "gěi." Compare "Mínglěi gēn Lín Tàitai jiè yǔsǎn" (Mínglěi borrows the umbrella from Mrs. Lín) with "Lín Tàitai bǎ yǔsǎn jiègěi Mínglěi (Mrs. Lín lends the umbrella to Mínglěi).

Note that in the latter sentence the indirect object (Mínglěi) of the verb-complement phrase "jìegěi" must directly follow that verb phrase, so the direct object "yǔsǎn" would have to come after the indirect object in order to appear in its standard place after the verb. However, to place both the indirect object and the direct object together after a compound verb might confuse the listener and create the linguistic equivalent of traffic congestion after the main verb.

To clear up some of this congestion, Chinese speakers often place the coverb "bǎ" after the subject and use it to transfer the direct object from the congested area after the verb to the less cramped area between the subject and the main verb. Instead of SUBJ + VERB + COMP (+ indirect object) + OBJ, you have SUBJ + bǎ + OBJ + VERB + COMP (+ indirect object), as in "Nèige niánqīngrén bǎ bàozhǐ nágěi Mínglěi" (That youth handed Mínglěi the newspaper).

In classical Chinese, "bǎ" once meant grabbing or taking something; and while you are getting used to "bǎ" it is a good idea of think informally of "bǎ-ing," taking the direct object and disposing of it in the manner described by the main verb. Therefore, in the sentence above, your initial interpretation would be that of the youth taking the newspaper out and handing it to Mínglěi.

Note that the direct object in the "bǎ" construction must be a specific, concrete thing in the speaker's mind rather than an abstract concept such as "hope" or "encouragement." Almost any action verb that is hooked to a complement can take the "bǎ" construction. However, most verbs expressive of mental states, such as "xǐhuān" and "xiǎngniàn" (to miss someone), are ineligible, as are all potential compounds like "tīngdedǒng" and "tīngbùdǒng" (can/cannot understand through listening).

Exercises for 12.6: Rearrange the words in each entry to make a correct sentence according to the English meaning given.

1. wǒ jiègěi bǎ qǐng yǔsǎn nǐ (Please lend me the umbrella.)

   _____

2. nǐ yán māma qǐng bǎ wǒ nágěi (Please pass my mom the salt.)

   _____

3. Tàitai bǎ nèige Lín fúwùyuán nágěi dìtú (That shop clerk hands Mrs. Lín the map.)

   _____

4. xuéshēng Wáng bǎ Zhōngguó nèixiē dàiqù Lǎoshī (Teacher Wáng took those students to China.)

   _____

5. chē jiègěi wǒ bù háizi bǎ nèixiē bàba (My father doesn't lend the car to those children.)

   _____

12.7 The Versatile Adverb "Cái" and Verb "Kāi"

The Adverb "Cái"

(Subject)	Time Word	cái	Verb	(Object)
Wú Jīnglǐ (Manager Wú is coming only next week./ is not coming until next week.)	xiàge xīngqī	cái	lái.	
Tā tàitai (His wife is only now cooking./ hasn't been cooking until now.)	xiànzài	cái	zuò	fàn.
	Zǎoshàng bādiǎn (It didn't rain until 8 A.M.)	cái	xià	yǔ.

The basic meaning of the adverb "cái" is "only then"; however, depending on the context in which "cái" appears, its meaning and function vary considerably. For instance, if you had originally expected some good friends to visit you last week but they won't actually arrive until tomorrow, you might say, "Tāmen míngtiān cái dào" (They're arriving only tomorrow). In other words, they're not arriving until tomorrow, and *only then* will begin their visit.

In Mrs. Lín's last sentence in the dialogue, her use of "cái" underlines her jocular contention that any jealousy she and Mr. Lín might feel toward the spouse's real or imagined lovers ("chī cù") comes *only* from her husband, not from her. If her husband indulges in such jealous imaginings, *only then* do such preoccupations exist in their marital life. Note that "cái" is an adverb, and thus must come before the verb and after any time word.

The Verb "Kāi"

The meaning of the verb "kāi" shifts according to the direct object that follows it. "Kāi wánxiào" is to crack or tell a joke; "kāi mén" refers to opening a door; "kāi dēng" indicates turning on a lamp or some other light. Other common usages are "kāi chē" (drive a car) and "kāi huì" (convene a meeting).

Most Chinese verbs have narrower ranges of meaning than "kāi," but this verb is an instructive example of how important the context can be to the proper understanding of a Chinese sentence. Furthermore, any introductory textbook's English gloss for a given Chinese word should not be assumed to be an exhaustive or complete definition—for that you must consult a good dictionary.

Exercises for 12.7

I. Use "cái" when translating the following sentences into Chinese.

1. Those managers are only arriving tomorrow. (Those managers are not arriving until tomorrow.)

   _____

2. Her son ["érzi"] wasn't born until 1995. (Her son was only born in 1995.)

   _____

3. Mr. Hán is only fixing the computer now. (Mr. Hán isn't fixing the computer until now.)

   _____

4. It didn't start raining until 2:00 P.M.

_____

5. That Chinese coach won't come to America until next year
["míngnián"].

_____

II. Use "kāi" when translating the following sentences into Chinese.

1. Please open the door. I want to go in.

_____

2. Do you know how to drive a car?

_____

3. Those teachers won't convene a meeting until tomorrow.
[. . . cái . . .]

_____

4. Dad first turns on the light, then reads the newspapers.

_____

5. Manager Lǐ doesn't know how to crack jokes.

_____

CULTURE NOTES

Without any doubt, Chinese food is one of the world's finest and most nutritious cuisines. Its excellence has something to do with the fact that most Chinese families allot a generous portion of their spare time and budgets to buying and preparing fresh food.

Innumerable business transactions, family get-togethers, and public gatherings take place over tables laden with steaming dishes that everybody samples in a spirit of communal sharing. In informal situations among good friends or relatives, diners may even share in the preparation of the meal, as when Mínglěi helps the Líns wrap dollops of seasoned ground pork and finely chopped vegetables inside circles of thin dough to form "jiǎozi" (dumplings) ready for boiling or steaming. The fact that jiǎozi enthusiasts will often dip a steaming dumpling into a dainty sauce receptacle containing soy sauce and vinegar reminds Mínglěi of a joke that adds to the conviviality of the evening.

SUMMARY

If the subject is *about to* verb, place "kuài" in the adverbial position right before the verb, and complete the sentence with "le" at the very end: "Zhèige xuéshēng kuài qù Zhōngguó le" (This student is about to go to China). If, on the other hand, the subject has finished verbing, append "hǎo" or "wán" as a complement of the verb, and add the completed-action "le" to the complement: "Nèige nánfāngrén bāohǎo le èrshíwǔge jiǎozi" (That southerner finished wrapping 25 dumplings).

Ordinary Chinese nouns are not marked for singular or plural, but the plural measure "xiē" can convert just about any countable noun into a *de facto* plural. Compare "nèibǎ yǔsǎn" (that umbrella) with "nèixiē yǔsǎn" (those umbrellas); "yíge běifāngrén" (one northerner) with "yìxiē běifāngrén" (several northerners); and "něizhāng zhàopiàn?" (which photograph?) with "něixiē zhàopiàn?" (which photographs?).

When verbs are followed by complements, it can be inconvenient or sometimes even impossible to place the direct object in its normal slot after the verb. In such cases, tangible and specific direct objects are often pulled up before the verb with the "bǎ" coverbial construction, as in "Qǐng nǐ bǎ jiàngyóu nágěi wǒ" (Please pass me the soy sauce), "Lǎoshī bǎ qián názǒu le" (The teacher took the money away).

"Huì" is an auxiliary verb that usually refers to a learned ability, for example, "Tāmen zhǐ huì shuō yìdiǎn Zhōngwén" (They only know how to speak a little Chinese), and "Mínglěi yě huì yóuyǒng" (Mínglěi also knows how to swim).

CHAPTER 13

NǏ WÈISHÉNME GĚI TĀ XIĚ XÌN?

(Why are you writing him a letter?)

CHAPTER OVERVIEW

1. More Examples of "Méi (yǒu) + VERB"

2. The Coverb "Yòng" as an Instrumental "With"

3. "Gěi" as a Coverb with a Verb Such As "Xiě"

4. The VERB + zài + PW Pattern

5. "Why" Questions with "Wèishénme"

6. Responding to "Why" Questions with "Yīnwèi A, suǒyǐ B"

7. Placing Duration of Verbing Before the Verb in Negative Sentences

---

NEW VOCABULARY

TRACK
27

1.	méi xiǎngdào	didn't realize . . .	ADV-VERB-COMP
2.	xiǎng	to think, to miss somebody	VERB
3.	xiǎngdào	to realize (literally, "to think to . . .")	VERB-COMP
4.	yòng	(instrumental "with")	COV
5.	shǒu	hand	NOUN
6.	xiě zì	to write (when no object is specified)	VERB-OBJ
7.	xiě	to write (something in particular)	VERB
8.	zì	Chinese character, word	NOUN
9.	duì	be correct, "that's right . . ."	ADJ
10.	ná	to hold, to take or bring	VERB
11.	kuàizi	chopsticks	NOUN
12.	xíguàn	to be accustomed, to be used to; habit, custom	AUXV/VERB/NOUN
13.	dāochā	knife and fork	NOUN
14.	xìn	letter; to believe	NOUN/VERB
15.	zhùzài + PW	to live at PW	VERB-COMP
16.	Xiānggǎng	Hong Kong	PW
17.	Xiānggǎngrén	Hong Kong person(s), someone from Hong Kong	NOUN
18.	Měiguórén	American person(s), an American	NOUN
19.	Niǔyuē	New York	PW
20.	zuò shēngyì	to do business	VERB-OBJ
21.	shēngyì	business, commerce	NOUN
22.	wèishénme	why?	QW
23.	gěi P xiě xìn	to write P a letter	COV-NOUN-VERB-OBJ
24.	yīnwèi	because	CONJ
25.	hěn jiǔ	a long time ("a very . . ." if "hěn" is stressed)	ADV-TW
26.	jiǔ	a long time	TW/ADJ
27.	méi jiàn miàn	haven't met in person	ADV-VERB-OBJ

28. jiàn miàn	to meet somebody familiar in person (lit., "see a face")	VERB-OBJ
29. hěn xiǎng tā	miss him very much	ADV-VERB-OBJ
30. yīnwèi A, suǒyǐ B	because A, . . . B	
31. suǒyǐ	therefore	ADV
32. dǎ diànhuà	to make a phone call	VERB-OBJ
33. dǎ	to hit, to manipulate by hand	VERB

DIALOGUE

Ānnà (entering Lìlián's room): Ō, wǒ méi xiǎngdào, nǐ yòng zuǒshǒu xiě zì.

Lìlián (looking up from her seat behind the desk): Duì, kěshì wǒ yòng yòushǒu ná kuàizi.

Ānnà: Nǐ xíguàn yòng kuàizi chī fàn ma?

Lìlián: Duì, kěshì wǒ yě huì yòng dāochā.

Ānnà: Nǐ zài gěi shéi xiě xìn?

Lìlián: Wǒ gěi wǒde nánpéngyou xiě xìn.

Ānnà: Tā zhùzài nǎr?

Lìlián: Tā zhùzài Xiānggǎng.

Ānnà: Tā shì Xiānggǎngrén ma?

Lìlián: Bù, tā shì Měiguórén. Tā shì cóng Niǔyuē lái de.

Ānnà: Tā zài Xiānggǎng zuò shénme?

Lìlián: Tā zài zuò shēngyì.

Ānnà: Nǐ wèishénme gěi tā xiě xìn?

Lìlián: Yīnwèi wǒmen hěn jiǔ méi jiàn miàn, wǒ hěn xiǎng tā, suǒyǐ gěi tā xiě xìn.

Ānnà: Nǐ wèishénme bù gěi tā dǎ diànhuà?

Lìlián: Yīnwèi wǒ bǐjiào xǐhuān gěi wǒ nánpéngyǒu xiě xìn. Wǒmen yě dǎ diànhuà. Kěshì, tā yě hěn xǐhuān gěi wǒ xiě xìn.

DIALOGUE TRANSLATION

Ānnà (entering Lìlián's room): Oh, I didn't realize you write with your left hand.

Lìlián (looking up from her seat behind the desk): That's right, but I hold chopsticks with my right hand.

Ānnà: Are you accustomed to eating with chopsticks?

Lìlián: Right, but I can also eat with a knife and fork.

Ānnà: To whom are you writing a letter?

Lìlián: I'm writing to my boyfriend.
Ānnà: Where does he live?
Lìlián: He's living in Hong Kong.
Ānnà: Is he from Hong Kong?
Lìlián: No, he's an American. He comes from New York City.
Ānnà: What does he do in Hong Kong?
Lìlián: He's doing business.
Ānnà: Why are you writing him a letter?
Lìlián: Because we haven't met in person for a long time, and I miss him very much, I'm writing him a letter.
Ānnà: Why don't you give him a phone call?
Lìlián: Because I'm relatively fond of writing letters to my boyfriend. We also have telephone calls. However, he also likes to write me letters.

13.1 More Examples of "Méi (yǒu) + VERB"

Subject (Time Word)	méi (yǒu)	Verb	(Complement)	(Object)
Tā (She didn't come.)	méi	lái.		
Nǐ (You didn't read books.)	méi	kàn		shū.
Wǒ (I didn't see you.)	méi	kàn	dào	nǐ.
(It didn't rain today.)	Jīntiān	méi	xià	yǔ.
Wǒ (I didn't realize that you know how to swim.)	méi	xiǎng	dào	nǐ huì yóuyǒng.

Although the full form of "didn't verb" or "haven't verbed" is "méiyǒu VERB," the "yǒu" drops out more often than not. Ānnà thus "méi xiǎngdào" (didn't realize that) Lìlián writes with her left hand, and Lìlián "méi jiàn miàn" (didn't meet in person) with Peter for a long time. "Méi xiǎngdào" (lit., "didn't arrive in my thinking at the fact that") is one of a relative handful of verbal units that take an entire sentence as their object; "Nǐ yòng zuǒshǒu xiě zì" (You write with your left hand) is simultaneously an independent sentence and the object of the aforesaid verbal unit.

Exercises for 13.1: Use the Méi (yǒu) + VERB pattern when translating the following sentences into Chinese.

1. She didn't use a knife and fork.

_____

2. Miss Lín didn't go to Hong Kong.

_____

3. Those youths didn't play with (wán) the computer.

_____

4. This student didn't wrap 30 dumplings.

_____

5. I didn't realize that you know how to speak Chinese.

_____

6. His mom didn't realize that he knows how to drive a car.

_____

13.2 The Coverb "Yòng" as an Instrumental "With"

Subject	(Adverbs)	(Auxiliary Verb)	yòng	Object 1	Verb	(Object 2)
Tā			yòng	diànnǎo	xiě	shū.
(She writes books with a computer.)						
Nǐ	bú		yòng	kuàizi	chī	fàn.
(You don't eat with chopsticks.)						
Wǒ	hěn	huì	yòng	zuǒshǒu	ná	chāzi.
(I know how to hold a fork with my left hand very well.)						

When "gēn" is a coverb, it most commonly functions as an accompaniment "with," as in "Wáng Jīnglǐ gēn Mínglěi yìqǐ gōngzuò" (Manager Wáng works together with Mínglěi). You must use a different coverb, usually "yòng," however, when expressing an instrumental "with," as in "Ānnà yě yòng yòushǒu ná kuàizi" (Ānnà also holds chopsticks with her right hand). Although "yòng" can function elsewhere as a main verb meaning "to use," it is clumsy and somewhat inaccurate to translate the above sentence as "Ānnà also uses her right hand to hold chopsticks with."

The closest English equivalent to a Chinese coverb such as "gēn" or "yòng" is an adverbial preposition such as "with." You must be able to distinguish, though, between the "accompaniment with" (gēn) and the "instrumental with" (yòng).

Exercises for 13.2: Use either "gēn" or "yòng" to fill in the blanks and then translate the sentences into English.

1. Bǐdé hěn huì _____ kuàizi chī fàn.

    _____

    _____

2. Ānnà yě _____ wǒmen yìqǐ qù mǎi cídiǎn.

    _____

    _____

3. Lín Xiānsheng _____ yòushǒu xiězì, kěshì tā _____ zuǒshǒu ná chāzi.

    _____

    _____

4. Tā xǐhuān _____ tāde gǒu yíkuàir yóuyǒng.

    _____

    _____

5. Wǒ zǔfù bú _____ diànnǎo xiě xìn.

    _____

    _____

6. _____ dāochā chī fàn shì Měiguórén de xíguàn.

    _____

    _____

13.3 "Gěi" as a Coverb with a Verb Such As "Xiě"

Subject	(Time Word)	(Adverb)	gěi	Object 1	Verb	(Object 2)
Tā (He is making a phone call to me.)			gěi	wǒ	dǎ	diànhuà.
Māma (Mom is not cooking for us today.)	jīntiān	bù	gěi	wǒmen	zuò	fàn.

A list of coverbs that fits into the pattern SUBJ + COV + OBJ1 + VERB (+ OBJ2), in which a place word can be substituted for an ordinary noun object on occasion, includes "cóng" (from), "dào" (to), "wàng" (toward/to), "gēn" (with [accompaniment]), "yòng" (with [instrumental]), "zài" (at/in/on), and "lí" ([distance] from). "Gěi" is another common coverb, and can mean either "for" or "to," depending on the context. "Gěi" expresses the idea of doing something *for* or on behalf of someone else in a sentence such as "Bǐdé jīntiān gěi Lìlián zuò fàn" (Peter is cooking for Lìlián today). In sentences about communication, the initiator sends a message *to* the recipient: "Lìlián gěi Bǐdé xiě xìn" (Lìlián is writing a letter to Peter), and "Mínglěi gěi tā jiějie dǎ diànhuà" (Mínglěi is making a phone call to his elder sister).

Exercises for 13.3: Rearrange the words in each entry to make a correct sentence according to the English meaning given.

1. wǒ kāi tā gěi mén jiějie (He opens the door for my elder sister.)

   _____

2. xǐhuān háizi māma zuòfàn gěi nèige tā hěn (That mom likes very much to cook for her children.)

   _____

3. gěi Zhōngguó wǒ xìn jīnnián méi péngyou xiě wǒde (My Chinese friend didn't write letters to me this year.)

   _____

4. bādiǎnbàn gěi diànhuà wǒ huì jiàoliàn wǎnshàng dǎ jīntiān (I will make a phone call to the coach at 8:30 tonight.)

   _____

5. péngyou gěi sānshíliùge nǐ bāohǎole yǐjīng nǐ jiǎozi (Your friend has already finished wrapping 36 dumplings for you.)

   _____

13.4 The VERB + zài + PW Pattern

Subject	(Adverb)	zài	Place Word	Verb	(Object)
Bàba		zài	fángjiān(lǐ)	kàn	shū.
(Dad is reading a book in the room.)					
Tā	bú	zài	gōngsī	gōngzuò.	
(She doesn't work at a company.)					

You have a lot of latitude in indicating action at a place with the standard pattern SUBJ + zài + PW + VERB (+ OBJ). Virtually any action verb can be plugged into this pattern, as in "Lín Xiānsheng zài jiālǐ xiūlǐ diànnǎo" (Mr. Lín is fixing the computer at home).

Subject	(Adverb)	Verb	zài	Place Word
Nǐ (You live in New York.)		zhù	zài	Niǔyuē.
Tā (He's not sitting on the bed.)	bú	zuò	zài	chuángshàng.

For certain single-syllable verbs of a relatively stationary nature such as "zuò" (sit), "zhàn" (stand), "zhù" (stay, live), "tǎng" (lie supine), and "pā" (lie prone), however, it is more common to convert "zài" from a coverb into a complement, and to move both it and its attached place word to a position directly after the verb: SUBJ + VERB + zài + PW. Examples are "Lǐ Lǎoshī zhùzài Běijīng" (Teacher Lǐ lives in Běijīng), "Lìlián zuòzài yǐzishàng" (Lìlián is sitting on the chair), and "Mínglěi tǎngzài chuángshàng" (Mínglěi is lying supine on the bed).

Exercises for 13.4

I. Use the SUBJ + zài + PW + VERB (+ OBJ) pattern to complete the following sentences.

1. Nèige zhíyuán _____. (That clerk works at a bank.)

2. Nǐ bàba, māma _____ ma? (Are your mom and dad fixing the car at home?)

3. Nèige māma gēn tā sānsuì nǚér (daughter) _____. (That mom and her three-year-old daughter play in the park.)

4. Wǒmen bú _____. (We don't eat dumplings at the airport.)

II. Use the SUBJ + VERB + zài + PW pattern to complete the following sentences.

1. Nèizhī māo _____. (That cat is lying prone on the chair.)

2. Qǐng bié _____. (Please do not stand on the bed.)

Crowded processions often pass by temples during festivals, such as this one in celebration of the Goddess Māzǔ's birthday in Táiwān.

3. Wáng Jiàoliàn bāyuè huì _____ ma? (Will Coach Wáng be staying in the Běijīng Hotel in August?)

4. Zhèi liǎngge háizi _____. (These two children are not permitted to sit on the table.)

13.5 "Why" Questions with "Wèishénme"

"Zěnme" is neutral and free of prejudgment in its primary function of asking *how* something verbs. In its secondary usage of inquiring *why* or *how come* something verbs, however, this word usually carries an undertone of impatience or puzzlement.

Subject	wèishénme	Clause	
Nǐ	wèishénme	yào qù tā jiā?	(Why do you want to go to her home?)

Wèishénme	Subject	Clause	
Wèishénme	nǐmen	bù tīng māma de huà?	(Why wouldn't you listen to your mom?)

"Wèishénme" (why?) is both a more common and a relatively neutral way of asking why something verbs. "Wèishénme" is not restricted to an adverb slot, as is "zěnme," but behaves like a moveable adverb that must precede the verb, yet can either precede or follow the subject. Compare "Nǐ wèishénme bāng Lín Tàitai bāo jiǎozi?" (Why are you helping Mrs. Lín wrap dumplings?) and "Wèishénme Měiguórén yòng dāochā chī fàn?" (Why do Americans eat with a knife and fork?)

Exercises for 13.5: Use "Wèishénme" to ask questions that will elicit the indicated answers.

1. A: _____? (Why do you ride his car to the park?)
   B: Yīnwèi wǒ méiyǒu chē.

2. A: _____? (Why does that person eat salad ["shālā"] with chopsticks?)
   B: Yīnwèi nèige rén shì Zhōngguó rén.

3. A: _____? (Why does your mom help Miss Lǐ cook?)
   B: Yīnwèi wǒ māma hěn xǐhuān Lǐ Xiǎojiě.

4. A: _____? (Why doesn't your grandfather type ["dǎ zì"]?)
   B: Yīnwèi tā zhǐ huì yòng bǐ ("pen") xiě zì. (Because he knows only how to write with a pen.)

5. A: _____? (Why are you laughing?)
   B: Yīnwèi zhèiběn shū hěn hǎowán. (Because this book is fun.)

13.6 Responding to "Why" Questions with "Yīnwèi A, suǒyǐ B"

Subject	yīnwèi	Clause A,	suǒyǐ	(Subject)	Clause B
Wǒ bàba	yīnwèi	hěn máng,	suǒyǐ	(tā)	bù chī wǎnfàn.
(Because my dad is very busy, he doesn't eat dinner.)					

Yīnwèi	Subject	Clause A,	suǒyǐ	Subject	Clause B
Yīnwèi	wǒ bàba	hěn máng,	suǒyǐ	tā	bù chī wǎnfàn.
(Because my dad is very busy, he doesn't eat dinner.					
Yīnwèi	nǐ	nàme hǎo,	suǒyǐ	wǒmen	dōu ài nǐ.
(Because you are so nice, we all love you.)					

By itself, "suǒyǐ" means "therefore," and would at first glance seem unnecessary or redundant in the Chinese version of "because A, B," in which Clause A provides the reason for Clause B. However, "suǒyǐ" must be at the very start of Clause B: "Yīnwèi Lín Tàitai nàme máng, suǒyǐ wǒ bāng tā bāo jiǎozi" (Because Mrs. Lín is so busy, I'm helping her wrap dumplings). Like "wèishénme," "yīnwèi" behaves rather like a moveable adverb, and can optionally follow the subject of Clause A if that subject also governs Clause B, as in "Měiguórén yīnwèi búhuì ná kuàizi, suǒyǐ yòng dāochā chī fàn" (Because Americans don't know how to hold chopsticks, they eat with a knife and fork).

Exercises for 13.6: Use the cues given to respond to "why?" questions with "Yīnwèi A, suǒyǐ B."

1. A: Nǐ wèishénme bù lái wǒ jiā yóuyǒng?
   B: (Because your home is very far away, I don't go to your home to swim.)

   _____

   _____

2. A: Lín Jīnglǐ wèishénme yào jiào chūzū qìchē?
   B: (Because he is going to the airport, he must call a taxicab.)

   _____

   _____

3. A: Nǐ wèishénme bāng nǐ péngyou xiūlǐ diànnǎo?
   B: (Because she is so busy, I'm helping her fix the computer.)

   _____

   _____

4. A: Nǐ wèishénme yào gǎnkuài gěi nǐ jiějie zuòfàn?
   B: (Because she just delivered ["shēng le"] a child, I want to hurry to cook for her.)

   _____

   _____

5. A: Nǐ wèishénme yào gěi nèige zhíyuán kàn nǐde hùzhào?
   B: (Because I would like to stay at that hotel [nèijiā fàndiàn], I want to show that clerk my passport.)

   _____

   _____

13.7 Placing Duration of Verbing Before the Verb in Negative Sentences

Subject	Time Duration	méi (you)	Verb	(Object)	(le)
Nǐmen	sānge yuè	méi	xué	Zhōngwén.	
(You have not studied Chinese for three months.)					
Wǒmen	hěn jiǔ	méi	jiàn	miàn	le.
(We haven't seen each other for a long time.)					
Tā	liǎngge xīngqī	méi	yóu	yǒng	le.
(She hasn't been swimming for two weeks.)					

For sentences in the affirmative, expressions of time duration must follow the verb, as in "Tāmen yào zhù liǎng tiān" (They want to stay two days). However, if the verb is negative, the time duration must precede the verb and any adverb prefacing it: "Tāmen liǎng tiān méi chī fàn" (They didn't eat for two days).

If you want to express the idea of "a long time," use the expression "hěn jiǔ," because "jiǔ" is a bound form that must be attached to another word: "Nǐmen hěn jiǔ méi kāi wánxiào" (You haven't cracked a joke for a long time). Sometimes a sentence-end "le" is added to indicate a change of situation in a sentence using this pattern.

Exercises for 13.7: Complete the following sentences.

1. Tāmen _____. (They haven't talked [shuō huà] for two months.)

2. Nǐ nǚ'ér (daughter) _____ le. (Your daughter hasn't been swimming for one year.)

3. Tā _____ le. (He hasn't been typing at the computer [dǎ diànnǎo] for four days.)

4. Yīnwèi wǒ gēn wǒ māma _____, _____. (Because I haven't seen my mother for a long time, I am giving her a phone call.)

5. Nèige xiǎo háizi _____ le. (That little child hasn't been drinking milk [niúnǎi] for two days.)

CULTURE NOTES

Many Chinese people "xǐhuān shàngwǎng" (like to go on the Web), and younger persons who particularly enjoy the "hùliánwǎng" (Internet) often "qù wǎngbā" (go to an Internet bar). When telephoning, many Chinese prefer using a "shǒujī" (cell phone) over a traditional wire-based telephone.

If Peter's "shēngrì" (birthday) were approaching and Lìlián wanted to send him her best wishes for that special day, she would write, "Zhù nǐ shēngrì kuàilè" (I wish you a happy birthday), which is a subjectless sentence of the pattern zhù + nǐ + NOUN + ADJ. The pattern's structure is much like the title of the song, "We Wish You a Merry Christmas," except for the deletion of the understood subject "we" and the inversion of the noun and adjective; that is, the word order is switched from "wish you a merry Christmas" in English to "wish you Christmas merry" (Shèngdànjié kuàilè) in Chinese: "Zhù nǐmen Shèngdànjié kuàilè." If no holiday or other special occasion lay ahead, Lìlián still would probably resort to the zhù + nǐ + NOUN + ADJ pattern near the end of her letter with a sentence such as "Zhù nǐ shēntǐ jiànkāng" (I wish you a healthy physique).

Traditionally, Chinese people would often celebrate a birthday by eating "zhū jiǎo shòu miàn" (pig's feet and longevity noodles). The long noodles in this tasty dish symbolize long life, while pork has served for centuries as the main type of meat in the Chinese diet, and pig's feet are suggestive of vitality and abundance. The feet are boiled and braised until quite tender with star anise, ginger, rice wine, crystallized sugar, vinegar, and soy sauce.

In recent times, pig's feet and noodles have increasingly given way to the birthday cake common in the West. The illustration depicts celebrants gathering around a birthday boy and his cake to sing "Zhù nǐ shēngrì kuàilè."

SUMMARY

Chapter 8 introduced the coverb "gēn" as the accompaniment "with." This chapter introduces the coverb "yòng" as the instrumental "with"; for example, "Zhōngguórén yòng kuàizi chīfàn" (Chinese people eat with chopsticks), "Lìlián yòng zuǒshǒu xiě zì" (Lìlián writes with her left hand), and "Nǐ xíguàn yòng dāochā chī fàn ma?" (Are you accustomed to eating with a knife and fork?).

Strings of light bulbs add to the festive atmosphere of a temple after nightfall.

As a coverb, "gěi" often expresses the idea that something is being done *for* someone else, as in "Lín Xiānsheng jīntiān gěi tā tàitai zuò fàn" (Mr. Lín is cooking for his wife today). In sentences about communication, however, the coverb "gěi" typically means "to," and takes the recipient of the communication as its object. For example, "Mínglěi gěi tāde nǚpéngyou xiě xín" (Mínglěi is writing a letter to his girlfriend), and "Wǒ yào gěi Wáng Jīnglǐ dǎ diànhuà" (I have to make a phone call to Manager Wáng).

The standard pattern for action at a place is SUBJ + zài + PW + VERB, as in "Bǐdé zài Xiānggǎng gōngzuò" (Peter works in Hong Kong). However, another pattern works for some monosyllabic verbs of a static nature: SUBJ + VERB + zài + PW. Two examples are "Bǐdé zhùzài Xiānggǎng" (Peter lives in Hong Kong), and "Zhèige háizi zuòzài chuáng shàng" (This child sits on the bed).

Use the question word "wèishénme" to ask why, and the "yīnwèi A, suǒyǐ B" pattern to explain the reason for something. You would say, for example, "Nǐ wèishénme yào xué Zhōngwén?" (Why do you want to study Chinese?) and "Yīnwèi wǒ nánpéngyou shì cóng Zhōngguó lái de, suǒyǐ wǒ yào xué Zhōngwén" (Because my boyfriend came from China, I want to study Chinese).

CHAPTER 14

DÀGÀI LIǍNG SĀN JĪN JIÙ GÒU LE.

(About two or three *jīn* would be enough.)

CHAPTER OVERVIEW

1. Adverbs of Approximation (Dàgài), Entirety (Dōu), and Particularity (Yóuqíshi)

2. Expressing "Don't Know Whether the Noun Verbs or Not" with "Bù Zhīdào"

3. "Bǎ" as a Measure for "Grabbable" Things

4. Distinguishing "Xǐhuān VERB" (Like to Verb) from "Xiǎng VERB" (Would Like to Verb)

5. "When" Clauses with " . . . de shíhòu"

6. Expressing "Both VERB1 and VERB2" with Yòu + VERB1 + Yòu + VERB2

NEW VOCABULARY

TRACK
29

1.	shīfu	sir, ma'am, master (honorific address common in PRC)	NOUN
2.	yīfu	clothing	NOUN
3.	piàoliàng	be pretty	ADJ
4.	zhūròu	pork	NOUN
5.	zhū	pig	NOUN
6.	ròu	meat	NOUN
7.	jīn	(weight measure equal to 0.5 kilogram or 1.1 pounds)	MEAS
8.	dàgài	probably, approximately, about	ADV
9.	liǎng sān jīn	two or three *jīn*	NUM1-NUM2-MEAS
10.	jiù gòu le	would (then) be enough	ADV-ADJ-PART
11.	bù zhīdào	don't know (whether noun verbs or not)	ADV-VERB
12.	zhīdào	to know (something)	VERB
13.	shēngcài	lettuce (nearly always leaf lettuce, not a head of iceberg lettuce)	NOUN
14.	bǎ	(measure for "grabbable" things like chairs and bunches of vegetables)	MEAS
15.	yǎng	to raise (children, pets, livestock, and so on)	VERB
16.	yā	duck	NOUN
17.	dōu	all, both	ADV
18.	yóuqíshi	especially	ADV
19.	tiānqì rè de shíhòu	when the weather is hot	
20.	tiānqì	weather	NOUN
21.	rè	be hot	ADJ
22.	A . . . de shíhòu,	when A . . .	CONJ
23.	xiàtiān	summer	TW/NOUN
24.	xīguā	watermelon	NOUN

25. yòu VERB1	both VERB1 and VERB2	ADV-VERB1-
yòu VERB2		ADV-VERB2
26. piányi	be cheap	ADJ
27. hǎochī	be tasty	ADJ
28. xíng	okay, all right	ADJ

DIALOGUE

Shīfu (standing behind tables stacked with vegetables and meat):
Xiǎojiě, nǐde yīfu zhēn piàoliàng!

Lìlián (politely declining the compliment while shopping at the open-air vegetable market): Nǎlǐ, nǎlǐ. Shīfu, wǒ xiǎng mǎi yìdiǎnr zhūròu. Duōshǎoqián yìjīn?

Shīfu: Shíliù kuài yìjīn. Nǐ yào jǐjīn?

Lìlián: Dàgài liǎng sān jīn jiù gòu le.

Shīfu: Háiyào shénme?

Lìlián: Wǒ bù zhīdào nǐmen mài búmài shēngcài. Wǒ hái yào wǔbǎ shēngcài.

Shīfu: Yào zhènme duō a? Nǐmen yǎng yā ma?

Lìlián: Búshì. Kěshì wǒmen dōu xǐhuān chī shēngcài, yóuqíshi tiānqì rè de shíhòu.

Shīfu: Xiànzài xiàtiān xīguā hěn duō, yòu piányi, yòu hǎochī. Nǐ yào búyào mǎi?

Lìlián: Xíng, wǒ mǎi yíge.

DIALOGUE TRANSLATION

Shīfu (standing behind tables stacked with vegetables and meat):
Young lady, your clothes are really pretty!

Lìlián (politely declining the compliment while shopping at the open-air vegetable market): How could *that* be? Sir, I'd like to buy a little pork. How much is it per *jīn*?

Shīfu: Sixteen *yuán* per *jīn*. How many *jīn* do you want?

Lìlián: About two or three *jīn* would be enough.

Shīfu: What else do you want?

Lìlián: I don't know whether you sell lettuce or not. I also want five bunches of lettuce.

Shīfu: You want so much? Do you raise ducks?

Lìlián: No. But we all like to eat lettuce, especially when the weather's hot.

Shīfu: Now, in the summertime, there are a lot of watermelons, and they're both cheap and tasty. Do you want to buy any?

Lìlián: Okay, I'll buy one.

14.1 Adverbs of Approximation (Dàgài), Entirety (Dōu), and Particularity (Yóuqíshi)

The Adverb "Dàgài"

Subject	dàgài	(Adverb)	Verb	Object
Wǔge xīguā (Five watermelons are approximately 64 yuán.)	dàgài			liùshísì kuài.
Tāmen (They probably aren't going to the park.)	dàgài	bú	qù	gōngyuán.

Dàgài	Subject	(Adverb)	Verb	Object	(le)
Dàgài (About two of three [of these] would be enough.)	liǎng sān ge	jiù	gòu		le.

When placed directly before a verb or another adverb, "dàgài" means "probably," as in "Lín Tàitai dàgài zǒu le" (Mrs. Lín has probably left) and "Tāde nǔpéngyou dàgài bú qù yínháng" (His girlfriend is probably not going to the bank). However, if "dàgài" precedes a number, its meaning changes slightly to "approximately": "Sān jīn zhūròu dàgài sìshíbā kuài" (Three *jīn* of pork is approximately 48 *yuán).*

The Adverb "Dōu"

Subject(s)	dōu	Verb	Object
Nǐ gēn wǒ (Both you and I are men.)	dōu	shì	nánrén.
Shēngcài, xīguā, hé zhūròu (Lettuce, watermelon, and pork are all expensive.)	dōu	hěn guì.	

Subject	bǎ	Object	dōu	Verb	Complement	(le)
Wǒ (I finished reading all the books.)	bǎ	shū	dōu	kàn	wán	le.

The basic meaning of the adverb "dōu" is "in all cases." When "dōu" refers to just two things or categories, it means "both," as in "Xīguā gēn shēngcài dōu nàme piányi a!" (Both watermelons and lettuce are so cheap!). On the other hand, if "dōu" refers to three or more things or categories, it means "all," as in "Wáng Jīnglǐ, Lǐ Lǎoshī, hé Lín Xiānsheng dōu shì Zhōngguó rén" (Manager Wáng, Teacher Lǐ, and Mr. Lín are all Chinese persons), and "Wǒmen bǎ jiǎozi dōu bāohǎo le" (We've finished wrapping all of the dumplings). Note that whereas there is some flexibility and variation in word order for the English words "both" and "all," "dōu" is a standard Chinese adverb that must be placed before the verb it modifies.

A shaven-headed Buddhist monk leads a group of lay worshippers in a ritual offering.

The Adverb "Yóuqíshi"

	Subject	yóuqí	Adverb	Verb		Object
	Tā mèimei	yóuqí		ài		hóng chē.
	(Her younger sister especially loves red cars.)					
	Wǒ dìdi	yóuqí	bù	xǐhuān	chī	ròu.
	(My younger brother especially dislikes eating meat.)					
Xiàtiān	xīguā	yóuqí		piányi.		
(In the summer, watermelons are especially cheap.)						

Clause A,	yóuqíshi	Noun
Nàr cài dōu hěn guì,	yóuqí shi	shūcài.
(All groceries are expensive there, especially vegetables.)		
Zhèixiē shū dōu hěn hǎo,	yóuqí shi	zhèiběn.
(All these books are good, especially this one.)		

The adverb "yóuqí" (especially) directly precedes the verb or predicate adjective that it modifies, as in "Nǚ xuéshēng yóuqí xǐhuān piàoliàng de yīfu" (Female students especially like pretty clothes), and "Lìlián jīntiān yóuqí máng" (Lìlián is especially busy today). If you want to use "yóuqí" to modify some other type of word, such as a noun, you must append a neutral-tone "shì" (to be) to this adverb, as in "Nèixiē chǒngwù nàme kě'ài, yóuqíshi Mínglěi de lù" (Those pets are so cute, especially Mínglěi's deer).

Exercises for 14.1: Use "dàgài," "dōu," "yóuqí," or "yóuqíshi" in generating the following sentences.

1. Her elder brother probably won't go to China this year.

_____

2. That room is especially clean.

_____

3. Both pork and lettuce are very expensive.

_____

4. She likes to drink tea, especially Chinese tea.

_____

5. We are all Americans.

_____

6. These children especially like to swim.

_____

7. Those teachers probably have already arrived.

_____

8. My mom has finished writing all the letters. (Use a "bǎ" construction.)

_____

14.2 Expressing "Don't Know Whether the Noun Verbs or Not" with "Bù Zhīdào"

(Subject)	bù zhīdào	Noun	Verb-bù-Verb		(Object)
(Wǒ)	bù zhīdào	nèige lǎoshī	hǎo bùhǎo.		
(I don't know whether that teacher is good or not.)					
Tā	bù zhīdào	nèixiē háizi	chī bùchī		shēngcài.
(He doesn't know whether those children eat lettuce or not.)					
Nǐmen	bù zhīdào	wǒ bàba	huì búhuì	yòng	diànnǎo.
(You don't know whether my dad knows how to use the computer or not.)					

Question words and interrogative structures can sometimes appear in declarative sentences, as we have seen with question words used as indefinites (such as "méi shémme). Although the VERB-bù-VERB pattern usually appears in questions, it is sometimes part of a larger declarative sentence with the pattern (SUBJ +) bù zhīdào + NOUN + VERB-bù-VERB (+ OBJ). Examples are "Wǒ bù zhīdào nèige fúwùyuán yào búyào gōngzuò" (I don't know whether that clerk wants to work or not), and "Wǒmen bù zhīdào zhūròu gòu búgòu" (We don't know whether there's enough pork or not).

Because the subject of a sentence in this pattern is usually "wǒ" or "wǒmen," the listener will assume there is a first-person subject if you leave out the subject altogether, as in "Bù zhīdào Bǐdé yǒu méiyǒu háizi" (I don't know whether Peter has children or not). Note also that the "yǒu-méiyǒu" question pattern is merely a variation of the VERB-bù-VERB pattern; the two question patterns are structurally equivalent.

Exercises for 14.2: Translate the following.

1. I don't know whether those people are Japanese [Rìběnrén] or not.

_____

2. We don't know whether that child knows how to swim or not.

_____

3. Mrs. Lín doesn't know whether you like to drink tea or not.

_____

4. Mom doesn't know whether you have pretty clothes or not.

_____

5. My elder sister doesn't know whether these dumplings are enough or not.

_____

6. That employee doesn't know whether Manager Wáng is at home or not.

_____

14.3 "Bǎ" as a Measure for "Grabbable" Things

The same "bǎ" that can be so useful in pulling direct objects back before the verb also functions as a measure for a variety of objects that are easily grabbed with one hand. Some examples are "něibǎ yǐzi?" (which chair?), "yìbǎ dāozi" (one knife), "liǎngbǎ yǔsǎn" (two umbrellas), "zhèibǎ shēngcài" (this bunch of lettuce), and "nèibǎ cōng" (that bunch of green onions).

14.4 Distinguishing "Xǐhuān VERB" (Like to Verb) from "Xiǎng VERB" (Would Like to Verb)

Subject	Adverb(s)	xǐhuān	Verb	Object
Měiguórén (Americans like to eat lettuce very much.)	hěn	xǐhuān	chī	shēngcài.
Zhōngguórén (The Chinese don't like to eat lettuce very much.)	bú tài	xǐhuān	chī	shēngcài.

Subject	Adverb(s)	xiǎng	Verb	Object
Tā (She would like to drink green tea.)		xiǎng	hē	lǜ chá.
Nèige háizi (That child would very much like to eat duck.)	hěn	xiǎng	chī	yāròu.
Wǒ (I would not like to read newspapers.)	bù	xiǎng	kàn	bàozhǐ.

Many learners of Chinese whose native language is English confuse "xǐhuān VERB" with "xiǎng VERB," since "like" commonly appears in both of the glosses for these terms, and either auxiliary verb can be modified by an adverb such as "hěn." They are more easily distinguished if you remember that "xǐhuān VERB" (like to verb) expresses the subject's general enjoyment of verbing, while "xiǎng VERB" indicates the speaker's specific desire to verb.

The person who says "Wǒ hěn xǐhuān chī jiǎozi" (I very much like to eat dumplings) is expressing a general fondness for dumplings. However, she may not be as eager to sit down and start helping the cook wrap the dumplings as the salivating fellow who says, "Wǒ hěn xiǎng chī jiǎozi" (I would very much like to eat dumplings).

Exercises for 14.4: Use either "xǐhuān" or "xiǎng" in the following situations.

1. Ask your guest if she would like to drink a little tea.

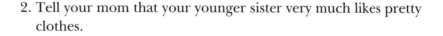

2. Tell your mom that your younger sister very much likes pretty clothes.

3. Today's your friend's birthday, and you would very much like to give him a phone call.

_____

4. Ask your friend if he very much likes to write letters with a computer.

_____

5. Tell your dad that you would not like to eat those dumplings.

_____

14.5 "When" Clauses with " . . . de shíhòu"

Subject		Verb	(Object)	de shíhòu,	Clause B
Tiānqì		rè		de shíhòu,	tā xǐhuān hē hóng chá.
(When the weather is hot, he likes to drink black tea.)					
Nǐ	qù	mǎi	cài	de shíhòu,	wǒ bǎ shū kànwán le.
(When you went out to buy groceries, I finished reading the book.)					
Jiàoliàn	gěi wǒ	dǎ	diànhuà	de shíhòu,	wǒ bú zài jiā.
(When the coach made a phone call to me, I was not at home.)					

In English "when" clauses, "when" goes at the beginning of the clause, as in "When the weather is hot, we all like to eat watermelon." But this word's Chinese equivalent, "de shíhòu," goes at the very end of the "when" clause in the sentence: "Tiānqì rè de shíhòu, wǒmen dōu xǐhuān chī xīguā."

The usual pattern is SUBJ + VERB (+ OBJ) + de shíhòu, [clause] B, though it is possible to invert the A and B clauses by inserting "yóuqíshi" (especially) at the beginning of the A or "when" clause, as in the dialogue. Another example of the usual pattern is "Wǒ gěi Mínglěi dǎ diànhuà de shíhòu, tā bú zài jiā" (When I made a phone call to Mínglěi, he wasn't at home).

**Exercises for 14.5: Use " . . . de shíhòu" to complete the following sentences.**

1. _____, wǒ zǔmǔ _____. (When the weather is cold ["lěng"], my grandmother especially likes to drink soup ["tāng"].)

2. Wǒ zài _____, chángcháng _____.
   (When I was in China, I often ate pork dumplings.)

3. Wú Lǎoshī _____, _____? (When
   Teacher Wú made a phone call to you, what were you doing?)

4. Bàba _____, māma bǎ _____ le.
   (When Dad went out to buy watermelon, Mom finished
   cooking.)

5. Lín Tàitai gēn Mínglěi _____,
   _____. (When Mrs. Lín and Mínglěi go out to-
   gether, her husband is very unhappy [bù gāoxìng].)

14.6 Expressing "Both VERB1 and VERB2" with Yòu + VERB1 + Yòu + VERB2

Subject	yòu	Verb 1	yòu	Verb 2
Zhèixiē xīguā	yòu	dà	yòu	piányi.
Tā	yòu	xiǎng mǎi chē	yòu	xiǎng mǎi diànnǎo.
(He would like to buy both a car and a computer.)				

Conjunctions such as "gēn" and "hé" can join nouns, but not verbs
or verb clauses. You can use either of the two conjunctions to say
"Both Ol' Tāng and I read newspapers" (Lǎo Tāng hé wǒ dōu kàn
bàozhǐ), but neither will be of any avail if you want to say that Ol'
Tāng is both busy and anxious. In the latter sentence, "and" joins
two adjectives, which function as predicate adjectives or verbs in
the Chinese construction, and thus cannot be joined by "gēn" or
"hé"; nor does "dōu" (in all cases) apply here.

The correct Chinese sentence is "Lǎo Tāng yòu máng yòu jí,"
and the pattern being used is SUBJ + yòu + VERB1 + yòu + VERB2.
Here VERB1 and VERB2 can be either verbs or entire verb clauses,
as in "Zhèixiē xuéshēng yòu xiě xìn, yòu kàn bào" (These students
are both writing letters and reading newspapers).

***Exercises for 14.6: Use the yòu + VERB1 + yòu + VERB2
pattern when translating the following sentences into
Chinese.***

1. These clothes are both pretty and cheap.

_____

2. She both eats (chī fàn) and makes phone calls.

_____

3. That room is both small and dirty.

_____

4. Teacher Lín would like to both cook and fix the computer.

_____

5. This cat is both clean and cute.

_____

6. Those youths buy both dictionaries and maps.

_____

7. He raises both children and ducks.

_____

The myriad reddish lanterns displayed during the Ghost Festival in late summer are thought to help guide the spirits of the dead during their annual nocturnal visit to the realm of the living.

CULTURE NOTES

Chinese people seldom eat raw vegetables other than cucumbers and tomatoes; and, as the produce seller's question to Lìlián in the dialogue indicates, they often consider lettuce primarily a type of feed for domestic fowl such as geese and ducks. During the heat of summer (xiàtiān), watermelons are especially prized for their cooling nature. The "tiān" of "jīntiān" (today) is also used for the other three seasons, "qiūtiān" (autumn), "dōngtiān" (winter), and "chūntiān" (spring).

When you speak about the red meat of mammalian livestock, you must append the word "ròu" (meat) to the name of an animal such as "niú" (a cow), as in "zhūròu," "niúròu" (beef), and "yángròu" (mutton). Appending "ròu" to the name of a given type of fish or fowl is optional and, in the case of fish, rare; thus a restaurant menu will include items such as "jī" (chicken), "yā" (duck), "yóuyú" (squid), and "qiūyú" (catfish).

SUMMARY

When used as conjunctions, "gēn" and "hé" mean "and," but they can join only nouns or noun phrases, not verbs or verbal clauses. To communicate the idea of "both VERB1 and VERB2," use the pattern SUBJ + yòu + VERB1 + yòu + VERB2. Examples are "Lǎo Zhāng yòu zuò jiǎozi, yòu xiūlǐ diànnǎo" (Ol' Zhāng both cooks dumplings and fixes computers), and "Zhèige fángjiān yòu dà, yòu gānjìng" (This room is both large and clean).

In English "when" clauses, "when" goes at the front of the clause, as in "When the weather is hot, we all like to eat watermelon." But this word's functional Chinese equivalent, "de shíhòu," goes at the very end of the "when" clause in the sample sentence: "Tiānqì rè de shíhòu, wǒmen dōu xǐhuān chī xīguā."

"Xǐhuān VERB" (like to verb) expresses the subject's general enjoyment of verbing, while "xiǎng VERB" (would like to verb) indicates the speaker's specific desire to verb. Compare the general comment "Jiějie xǐhuān mǎi piàoliàng de yīfu" (Elder Sister likes to buy pretty clothes) with the specific intent in "Wǒ xiǎng mǎi liǎng sān jīn zhūròu" (I would like to buy two or three *jīn* of pork).

Use "bù zhīdào" along with a noun and the VERB-bù-VERB pattern to express the sense of "not knowing whether the noun verbs or not." Examples are "Wǒ bù zhīdào shēngcài hǎochī bùhǎochī" (I don't know whether lettuce is tasty or not), and "Lìlián bù zhīdào Bǐdé xǐhuān bùxǐhuān tāde yínháng" (Lìlián doesn't know whether Peter likes his bank or not).

CHAPTER 15

WǑ YÀO ZUÒ JǏLÙ CHĒ?
(What bus route number must I take?)

CHAPTER OVERVIEW

1. Riding Conveyances with "Zuò" (Sit) as Coverb or Verb

2. "Děi + VERB" as "Must Verb"

3. Indicating Location with Independent Localizers Such As "Lǐtou," "Wàitou," "Duìmiàn," and "Hòumiàn"

4. "Either-or" Questions with "A Háishi B?"

5. Longer Modifying Phrases Before the Particle "de" and the Modified Noun

6. Accepting the Only Viable Course of Action with SUBJ + Zhǐhǎo + VERB

NEW VOCABULARY

1. Chángchéng	Great Wall of China (lit., "the Long Wall")	PW/NOUN
2. cháng	be long	ADJ
3. chéng	wall, city wall, city	NOUN
4. zuò	to ride a conveyance, to sit	VERB/COV
5. děi + VERB	must VERB, have to VERB	AUXV
6. lǎorén	old person	NOUN
7. huǒchēzhàn	train station	PW/NOUN
8. huǒchē	train	NOUN
9. shíjiān	time (duration, not a point in time)	NOUN
10. Gùgōng	Old Imperial Palace (now a museum in Běijīng)	PW/NOUN
11. chéng lǐtou	inside the city	PW
12. lǐtou	inside	PW/LOC
13. háishi	or (in "either-or" questions)	QW
14. wàitou	outside	PW/LOC
15. lí	distance from	COV
16. hǎokàn	be nice looking	ADJ
17. yīnggāi	should	AUXV
18. duìmiàn	the opposite side, across the way	PW
19. shísānlù chē	a Route 13 bus	NOUN
20. chēshàng de rén	people on the bus	PW-PART-NOUN
21. chēshàng	on the bus	PW
22. hěn duō	be many, be much ("very" only if "hěn" is stressed)	ADV-ADJ
23. duō	be many, be numerous, be much (a bound form)	ADJ/BF
24. jǐ	be crowded	ADJ
25. zuòwèi	seat, place to sit	NOUN
26. SUBJ + zhǐhǎo + VERB	the only thing SUBJ can do is VERB	ADV
27. zhànzhe	to be standing, to remain standing	VERB-PART
28. zhàn	to stand	VERB

29. yǒu rén (as SUBJ) . . .	There's somebody . . .	VERB-NOUN
30. zhuā	to pinch, to grab	VERB
31. tuǐ	leg	NOUN
32. hòumiàn	behind	PW
33. dàizi lǐ	in the bag	PW
34. dàizi	bag (here a mesh shopping bag)	NOUN
35. pángxiè	crab (usually bought live)	NOUN

DIALOGUE

TRACK
32

Lìlián   (asking an elderly bystander for directions): Qǐngwèn, dào Chángchéng qù yào zuò jǐlù chē?

Lǎorén: Nǐ děi qù huǒchēzhàn zuò huǒchē.

Lìlián   (to Bǐdé): Nà tài yuǎn le. Wǒmen jīntiān méiyǒu shíjiān qù. (To Lǎorén) Qǐngwèn, Gùgōng zài chéng lǐtou háishi zài chéng wàitou?

Lǎorén: Zài chéng lǐtou. Lí zhèr bù yuǎn. Gùgōng fēicháng hǎokàn, nǐmen yīnggāi qù kànkan.

Lìlián: Cóng zhèr zěnme zǒu?

Lǎorén: Nǐ dào duìmiàn qù děng shísānlù chē.

Lìlián: Xièxie.

Lǎorén: Búyòng kèqi.

Lìlián   (awhile later, just after they squeeze onto the Route 13 bus): Chēshàng de rén hěn duō.

Bǐdé: Zhēn jǐ. Méiyǒu zuòwèi. Wǒmen zhǐhǎo zhànzhe.

Lìlián: Hǎoxiàng yǒu rén zài zhuā wǒde tuǐ.

Bǐdé: Búshì. Shì hòumiàn nèige rén dàizi lǐ de pángxiè.

DIALOGUE TRANSLATION

Lìlián   (asking an elderly bystander for directions): May I ask, what bus route number must I take to go to the Great Wall?

Elder: You've got to go to the train station and take a train there.

Lìlián   (to Peter): In that case, it's too far away. We don't have time to go there today. (To Elder) May I ask, is the Old Imperial Palace inside the city or outside the city?

Elder: It's inside the city, and not far from here. The Old Imperial Palace is extremely nice looking. You should go take a look.

Lìlián: How do you get there from here?

Elder: Go to the opposite side of the street to wait for the Route 13 bus.

Lìlián: Thanks.

Elder: Don't mention it.

Lìlián (awhile later, just after they squeeze onto the Route 13 bus): There are a lot of people on the bus.

Peter: It's really crowded; there aren't any seats. The only thing we can do is to keep standing.

Lìlián: There seems to be somebody pinching my leg.

Peter: No, it's the crab in the mesh bag of that guy behind you.

The Old Imperial Palace in Beijing.

15.1 Riding Conveyances with "Zuò" (Sit) as Coverb or Verb

Subject	(shì)	zuò	Conveyance	qù/lái	Place Word	(de)
Lǐ Xiǎojiě (Miss Lǐ went to China by plane.)		zuò	fēijī	qù	Zhōngguó.	
Tā (He came to my home by car/bus.)		zuò	chē	lái	wǒ jiā.	
Nǐ (You went to the bank by bus.)		zuò	gōnggòng qìchē	qù	yínháng.	
Lín Jīnglǐ (Manager Lín came to New York by train; it was by train that he came to New York.)	shì	zuò	huǒchē	lái	Niǔyuē	de.

The verb "zuò" often means simply "to sit," especially if "zài + PW" is attached as a verb complement or a coverbial phrase, as in "Bǐdé zuòzài chuáng shàng" (Peter is sitting on the bed), and "Qǐng nǐ zài yǐzi shàng zuòzhe" (Please keep sitting on the chair). However, "zuò" may also take a direct object of conveyance such as "fēijī" (plane) or "huǒchē" (train), and in this case means "to ride" or "to take," as in "Lìlián hěn xǐhuān zuò huǒchē" (Lìlián very much likes to ride trains), and "Mínglěi xiǎng zuò fēijī" (Mínglěi would like to take a plane).

To express the idea of going or coming by conveyance, simply use "zuò" as a coverb: SUBJ + zuò + conveyance + qù/lái. Examples are "Mínglěi zuò chūzū qìchē qù" (Mínglěi is going by taxicab), and "Ānnà shì zuò chē lái de," or "Ānnà shì zuò gōnggòng qìchē lái de" (Ānnà came by bus).

Exercises for 15.1: Answer the following questions according to the cues given.

1. A: Nǐ jiějie xiǎng zuò shénme chē qù fēijīchǎng?
   B: _____ (by taxicab)

2. A: Nèige rén shì zěnme dào Měiguó lái de?
   B: _____ (by airplane)

3. A: Nèixiē jīnglǐ shì zuò fēijī qù Niǔyuē de ma?
   B: Bù, _____ (by train)

4. A: Nǐmen shì zěnme lái wǒ jiā de?
   B: _____. (We first take a bus, then walk ["zǒu lù"].)

5. A: Nǐ shúshu shì zěnme qù Mòxīgē wán de?
   B: _____. (by car [zuò chē])

15.2 "Děi + VERB" as "Must Verb"

Subject	děi	(Adverb)	Verb	Object
Nǐ (You must listen to the teacher.)	děi		tīng	lǎoshī de huà.
Tāmen (They must hurry up and board the plane.)	děi	gǎnkuài	shàng	fēijī.

While the auxiliary verb "yào" sometimes means "must verb," in many contexts it means "want to verb" or "is going to verb." For an auxiliary verb that always means "must verb," use "děi": "Wǒmen děi xiān chī fàn, zài qù Gùgōng" (We must first eat and then go the Old Imperial Palace), and "Tā děi zǒu le" (She must leave now).

Exercises for 15.2: Use "děi" in the following situations.

1. You and your boyfriend say good-bye to your hostess. Thank her and say you must leave now.

   _____

2. You are chatting with a friend at school, then you realize that it's time to go home by bus. Tell your friend that you're sorry, but you must take the bus and go back home ("huí jiā").

   _____

3. Your Chinese friend will come to visit America soon. Suggest to her that she must hurry up and learn ("xué") English.

   _____

4. A group of Chinese tourists ask the way to the park. Tell them that they must go toward the south first, then turn right.

   _____

5. Tell your child that she must first wash hands (xǐ shǒu), then eat fruit (shuǐguǒ).

   _____

15.3 Indicating Location with Independent Localizers Such As "Lǐtou," "Wàitou," "Duìmiàn," and "Hòumiàn"

Two-Syllable Forms of the Bound Localizers "Lǐ" and "Shàng"

lǐbiān	lǐtou	lǐmiàn	(in[side])
wàibiān	wàitou	wàimiàn	(out[side])
shàngbiān	shàngtou	shàngmiàn	(on [top])
xiàbiān	xiàtou	xiàmiàn	(below)
qiánbiān	qiántou	qiánmiàn	(in front)
hòubiān	hòutou	hòumiàn	(behind)
		duìmiàn	(opposite side)
pángbiān			(beside)
zuǒbiān			(to the left of)
yòubiān			(to the right of)
xībiān			(to the west of)

Subject	zài	Modifying Noun	Localizer
Tā (She is in the park.)	zài	gōngyuán	lǐ (tou).
Ānnà jiā (Anna's home is opposite mine.)	zài	wǒ jiā	duìmiàn.
Nǐ de gǒu (Your dog is behind the car.)	zài	chēzi	hòumiàn.

The bound localizers "lǐ" and "shàng" are somewhat unusual in the frequency with which they appear in their single-syllable forms instead of their full two-syllable forms: "lǐtou" or "lǐbiān" (in[side]), and "shàngtou" or "shàngbiān" (on [top]). To express simply the idea of "inside" or "on top," as opposed to the idea of inside *something* or on *something*, you must use the full two-syllable forms, as in "Háizi zài lǐtou" (The children are inside), and "Shàngtou de shū shì gēge de" (The books on top are Elder Brother's).

Independent Localizers Containing "Tou" and "Miàn"

Section 10.5 introduced "biān," the versatile bound localizer indicating "side," and this lesson introduces the other two most common localizers with the same function as "biān": "tou" and "miàn." Unlike "biān," "tou" and "miàn" cannot hook onto "zuǒ" and "yòu," nor are they ordinarily appended to the four directions of the compass. However, they can hook onto a number of directional words to form "lǐtou" and "lǐmiàn" (in[side]), "wàitou" and "wàimiàn" (outside), "shàngtou" and "shàngmiàn" (on [top]), "xiàtou" and "xiàmiàn" (below), "hòutou" and "hòumiàn" (behind), and "qiántou" and "qiánmiàn" (in front). "Duìmiàn" refers to the opposite side, while "pángbiān" (beside) may indicate either side of the point of reference.

Unlike the bound localizers "lǐ" and "shàng," all of the localizers mentioned in the preceding two sentences are independent semantic units, and any of them can be used either alone or following a modifying noun. In the latter case, since the word order is opposite to that normally found in English, you can approximate Chinese word order by transforming the expression into an apostrophe-"s" ('s) form as follows:

• "behind the car" becomes "the car's behind," or "qìchē hòumiàn";
• "in front of the room" becomes "the room's front," or "fángjiān qiántou";

- "opposite the park" or "across from the park" becomes "the park's opposite side," or "gōngyuán duìmiàn";
- "beside the old person" becomes "the old person's side," or "lǎorén pángbiān";
- "on top of the table" becomes "the table's top (side)," or "zhuōzi shàngtou";
- "inside the cup" becomes "the cup's inside," or "bēizi lǐtou."

The word order is consistently "modifying noun + localizer."

Exercises for 15.3: Use "lǐtou," "wàitou," "shàngmiàn," "xiàmiàn," "duìmiàn," "qiánmiàn," and "hòumiàn" in the following sentences.

1. My mom's letters are on top of the table.

   _____

2. There is a cockroach inside the cup.

   _____

3. Her company is behind the train station.

   _____

4. That child's clothes are not under the newspapers.

   _____

5. This young man keeps standing ("zhànzhe") in front of the car.

   _____

6. Which (Něijiā) bank is opposite the park?

   _____

7. Are you waiting for your younger brother outside the bathroom?

   _____

Many people offer incense as a show of respect to deceased ancestors during the springtime Qīngmíng Festival.

15.4 "Either-or" Questions with "A Háishi B?"

Subject	(Verb)	Noun/Verb Clause	háishi	Noun/Verb Clause?
Nèige rén (Is that person a male or a female?)	shì	nánde	háishi	nǚde?
Nǐ (Would you like to take a train or a plane?)	xiǎng	zuò huǒchē	háishi	zuò fēijī?

If you want your listener to choose just one of two alternatives you are presenting, either A or B, use the pattern "A háishi B?". A and B may be either verb clauses or nouns: "Tāmen yào děng chē háishi jiào chūzū qìchē?" (Are they going to wait for a bus or call a taxi-cab?), or "Nǐ shì Zhōngguórén háishi Měiguórén?" (Are you a Chinese or an American?).

Exercises for 15.4: Use "háishi" in asking the following "either-or" questions.

1. Are you surnamed Lǐ or Lín?

_____

2. Do you like dogs or cats?

_____

3. Are they going to take a train or an airplane?

_____

4. Are you Japanese or Chinese?

_____

5. Are those crabs inside the bag or outside the bag?

_____

15.5 Longer Modifying Phrases Before the Particle "de" and the Modified Noun

Longer Adjectival Modifiers with "de"

Modifying Phrase		Modified Word		
Subject	Verb	de	Object	
xuéshēng	kàn	de	shū	(the books that students read)
lǎoshī	yòng	de	cídiǎn	(the dictionaries that the teacher uses)

Modifying Phrase		Modified Word		
Verb	Object	de	Subject	
kàn	shū	de	xuéshēng	(the students who read books)
yòng	cídiǎn	de	lǎoshī	(the teacher who uses dictionaries)

An adjectival modifier precedes the modified noun in both English and Chinese, as in "piàoliàng de xiǎojiě" (pretty young lady) and "zāng yīfu" (dirty clothes). In Chinese, though, you will almost always need to sandwich the modification particle "de" between the adjective and the noun it modifies unless the adjective is monosyllabic and has no adverbial modifiers of its own. The adverb "fēicháng" adds two syllables to the modifying phrase in "fēicháng zāng de yīfu" (extremely dirty clothes), so the three-syllable phrase requires "de" before the modified noun.

Relative Clauses with "de"

Word order in Chinese really departs greatly from English with longer modifiers of the noun known as relative clauses, which in English begin with relative pronouns such as "which," "that," "whom," and "who," and follow the modified noun. In contrast, Chinese treats relative clauses just like longer adjectival modifiers that precede the modifying noun and have "de" sandwiched between the modifying phrase and the modified word; there are no relative pronouns to worry about.

Consider the ordinary sentence "Yā chī shēngcài" (Ducks eat lettuce). If we want to transform this sentence into a fragment consisting of a noun and a modifier, English requires us to put the modified noun first, follow it with a relative pronoun ("that" in this case), and then conclude with the modifying phrase, as in "lettuce that ducks eat" or "ducks that eat lettuce."

Chinese begins instead with the modifying phrase, sandwiches the modification particle "de" after it, and concludes by placing the modified noun at the end of the phrase, just as would be the case with an adjectival modifier. The two fragments above would thus read "yā chī de shēngcài" (SUBJ + VERB + de + OBJ) and "chī shēngcài de yā" (VERB + OBJ + de + SUBJ). Some other examples are "kāi wánxiào de péngyou" (friends who crack jokes), "lǎoshī zuò de chē" (the bus that the teacher rides), and "Mínglěi xǐhuān de jīnglǐ" (the manager whom Mínglěi likes).

Subject	Verb	Modifying Phrase	Modified Word
Wǒ	rènshì	nèige kàn shū de	xuéshēng.
(I know that student who is reading a book.)			
Tā	xiǎng mǎi	lǎoshī yòng de	cídiǎn.
(He would like to buy the dictionaries that teachers use.)			

Modifying Phrase	Modified Word		Verb	(Object)	
Xuéshēng kàn de (Are the books that students read expensive?)	shū	hěn	guì		ma?
Nèixiē yòng cídiǎn de (Those teachers who use dictionaries like books.)	lǎoshī		xǐhuān	shū.	

Sometimes you will encounter something like Peter's concluding sentence in the dialog, in which there is a chain of modifiers and modifying words: "Shì hòumiàn nèige rén dàizi lǐ de pángxiè." This is a subjectless sentence, though the context suggests that the leg-pinching culprit is a crab, or "it" in English. Nine of the eleven syllables after the verb "shì" make up the modifying phrase, while only the final two syllables, "pángxiè," represent the modified noun.

"Hòumiàn" situates the action as being behind Lìlián, while modifying the specifier-measure-noun unit "nèige rén," and means "that person who is behind (you)." "Nèige rén" modifies the following word, "dàizi," resulting in "that person's bag." "Dàizi" in turn modifies the bound form "lǐ" in a way that you can approximate with an apostrophe-"s" as "the bag's interior" and translate more naturally as "inside of the bag." The latter phrase in turn modifies "pángxiè," resulting in "the inside-the-bag crab" or, more naturally, "the crab inside the bag." Putting all of the pieces together and basically reading backwards from Chinese to English, you wind up with "the crab inside the bag of that person who is behind you."

You may not wish to follow Peter in creating such a long chain of modifiers during your initial study of Chinese modification. However, if you can remember that "de" functions a bit like apostrophe-"s" (rather than "of"), and that a modifying word almost always precedes the modified word, you will be well on the way to mastering the word order of modification in Chinese.

Exercises for 15.5: Use longer modifying phrases before the particle "de" when translating the following sentences into Chinese.

1. The bank that she likes is very far away.

_____

2. The train that I ride is extremely clean.

_____

3. Those children are looking at (zài kàn) the ducks that eat lettuce.

_____

4. The students who know how to speak Chinese can (kěyǐ) go to China.

_____

5. My husband would like to eat the crabs in your bag.

_____

6. The computer that my dad is fixing is mine.

_____

7. Are the clothes that Miss Wáng lent you nice looking? (Use VERB + bù + VERB question.)

_____

15.6 Accepting the Only Viable Course of Action with SUBJ + Zhǐhǎo + VERB

(Clause A)	Subject	zhǐhǎo	Verb	(Object)
Zhèr méiyǒu pángxiè. (There are no crabs here. The only thing we can do is eat fish.)	Wǒmen	zhǐhǎo	chī	yú.
Xiànzài xià yǔ le. (It's raining now. The only thing you can do is to take a taxicab.)	Nǐ	zhǐhǎo	zuò	chūzū qìchē.

If a particular course of action is rather unpalatable and yet the only viable choice under the circumstances, you will probably want to use the adverbial "zhǐhǎo" as follows: SUBJ + zhǐhǎo + VERB (+ OBJ), "The only thing SUBJ can do is to VERB (the OBJ)." Examples are "Xīguā tài guì le; wǒmen zhǐhǎo mǎi biéde" (Watermelons have become too expensive; the only thing we can do is buy something else), and "Chēshàng de rén nàme duō; nǐmen zhǐhǎo jiào chūzū qìchē" (There are so many people on the bus; the only thing you can do is to call a taxicab).

Exercises for 15.6: Use "zhǐhǎo" to complete the following dialogue.

1. A: Yā tài guì le. Zěnme bàn?
   B: _____. (Well, then the only thing we can do is buy pork.)

2. A: Jīntiān rén hěn duō. Chēshàng méiyǒu zuòwèi le.
   B: _____ (The only thing we can do is to keep waiting here.)

Dragon-boat races represent such a high point of the Duānwǔ Festival that the celebration is usually called the "Dragon-boat Festival" outside of China.

3. A: Nǐ wèishénme yào xué (learn) Zhōngwén?

   B: _____ (Because my husband can speak only
   [zhǐ huì shuō] Chinese, the only thing I can do is to learn
   Chinese.)

4. A: Nǐ wèishénme yào kàn zhème duō shū?

   B: _____. (Because I'm going to take an examination [kǎoshì] next month [xiàge yuè], the only thing I can do is
   to hurry up and read them [the books].)

5. A: Nǐ zěnme zhǐ chī shēngcài?

   B: _____. (Because I'm too fat [pàng], and
   must be on a diet [jiǎnféi], the only thing I can do is to eat
   lettuce.)

CULTURE NOTES

Although the Great Wall is China's most famous attraction and
carries much symbolic weight, visitors can learn much more
about Chinese culture by visiting the relatively accessible Old Imperial Palace and the museum it houses in central Běijīng. Because
practically all of Běijīng's magnificent old city walls were torn down
in the 1950s, however, the most impressive city walls still standing
in China are in the ancient capital city of Xī'ān, located in Shǎnxī
province to the west.

Because Chinese cuisine is greatly enhanced by the freshness of
the ingredients, most Chinese would rather take a live crab home
in a mesh bag than tote a dead crab packed in cellophane. When
shoppers carrying live crabs squeeze onto a crowded public bus, a
comical situation resembling that portrayed in the dialogue may occasionally result.

SUMMARY

Use "zuò" (sit) as either the coverb or the verb of riding conveyances, as in "Zhèige
lǎorén xiǎng zuò huǒchē" (This old person wants to ride a train), "Tāmen zuò gōnggòng qìchē qù" (They're going by bus), and "Bǐdé shì zuò fēijī lái de" (Peter came by
airplane). The verb "kāi" is used for driving a car ("kāi chē"), as well as for turning on
the light ("kāi dēng") and opening a door ("kāi mén").

For an auxiliary verb that always means "must," use "děi." Two examples are "Nǐ
děi xiān xǐ shǒu, zài chī wǎnfàn" (You must first wash your hands, and then eat dinner), and "Wǒmen děi děng shísānlù chē" (We must wait for a Route 13 bus).

"Háishi" functions as a question word in "either-or" interrogatives, in which the listener is expected to choose one of the questioner's two alternatives when answering. For example, if Lìlián were asked the question "Nǐ shì nánháizi háishi nǚháizi?" (Are you a boy or a girl?), she would reply, "Wǒ shì nǚháizi" (I'm a girl).

Unless an adjective is monosyllabic and has no adverbial modifiers of its own, it is almost always necessary to sandwich the modification particle "de" between the adjectival modifier and the noun it modifies, as in "piàoliàng de háizi" (pretty child) and "fēicháng zāng de fángjiān" (extremely dirty room). Chinese sentence structure handles relative clauses about the same as these adjectival modifiers, and dispenses with relative pronouns such as "that," "which," and "who." Some examples of relative clauses are "yā chī de shēngcài" (lettuce that ducks eat), "chī shēngcài de yā" (ducks that eat lettuce), "xiě Zhōngguó zì de xuésheng" (students who write Chinese characters), and "Jiékè gài de fángzi" (the house that Jack built).

CHAPTER 16

QÌSHUǏ HUÒZHĚ PÍJIǓ DŌU KĚYǏ.

(Either soda pop or beer is okay.)

CHAPTER OVERVIEW

1. Ordering Food at a Restaurant (Fànguǎn)

2. Some Abbreviated Bisyllabic Verbs in the VERB-bù-VERB Question Pattern

3. Contrasting the Nonexclusive "Or" (Huòzhě) with the Exclusive "Or" QW (Háishi)

4. VERB-VERB-kàn as "Try Verbing (It)"

5. VERB-bù-VERB and Yǒu-méiyǒu Question Patterns After "Wèn" and "Zhīdào"

6. Mistaken Assumptions with "Yǐwéi"

NEW VOCABULARY

TRACK
33

1. fànguǎn	restaurant	NOUN
2. càidān	menu	NOUN
3. diǎn	to order (from a menu)	VERB
4. xiē	some (short form of yìxiē)	MEAS
5. yào	to order ("We'll have . . ." in this context)	VERB
6. suānlà tāng	hot-and-sour soup	NOUN
7. suān	be sour, be tart	ADJ
8. là	be hot, be spicy	ADJ
9. tāng	soup	NOUN
10. tángcù yú	sweet-and-sour fish (lit., "sugar and vinegar fish")	NOUN
11. táng	sugar	NOUN
12. wǎn	bowl	MEAS/ NOUN
13. báifàn	cooked white rice	NOUN
14. bái	be white	ADJ
15. chǎo qīngcài	sautéed green vegetables	NOUN
16. chǎo	to sauté	VERB
17. qīng	be green, be blue (depending on context)	ADJ
18. cài	vegetable, cooked dish, national cuisine	NOUN
19. kě	be thirsty	ADJ
20. qìshuǐ	soda pop	NOUN
21. qì	vapor	NOUN
22. shuǐ	water	NOUN
23. píjiǔ	beer	NOUN
24. jiǔ	liquor, alcoholic beverage	NOUN
25. huòzhě	or (nonexclusive, and not a QW)	CONJ
26. lái	bring (imperative form in this context)	VERB
27. píng	(measure for a bottle of something)	MEAS
28. Gǎn'ēnjié	Thanksgiving	TW/NOUN
29. jié	festival, holiday (appended to a term indicating specifics)	NOUN

30. wènwen kàn	to try asking about something	VERB-VERB-COMP
31. kǎo huǒjī	roast turkey	NOUN
32. kǎo	to roast	VERB
33. huǒjī	turkey	NOUN
34. zhīdào	to know	VERB
35. yǐwéi	to have mistakenly thought that	VERB
36. huǒjì	waiter (fúwùyuán in PRC)	NOUN
37. jīròu	chicken	NOUN

DIALOGUE

TRACK 34

Mínglěi (at a restaurant): Wǒmen kě(yǐ) bùkěyǐ kànkan càidān?

Fúwùyuán: Dāngrán kěyǐ. Càidān zài zhèr.

(A few moments later)

Fúwùyuán: Xiānsheng, xiǎojiě, nǐmen yào diǎn xiē shénme cài?

Mínglěi: Wǒmen yào yíge suānlà tāng, yíge tángcù yú, liǎngwǎn báifàn.

Fúwùyuán: Háiyào biéde ma?

Lìlián: Háiyào yíge chǎo qīngcài.

Mínglěi (to Lìlián): Nǐ kě bùkě? Nǐ yào hē qìshuǐ háishi píjiǔ?

Lìlián: Qìshuǐ huòzhě píjiǔ dōu kěyǐ.

Mínglěi (to the Fúwùyuán): Lái liǎngpíng qìshuǐ.

Lìlián (whispering to Mínglěi): Jīntiān shì Gǎn'ēnjié. Wǒmen wènwen kàn tāmen yǒu méiyǒu kǎo huǒjī.

Fúwùyuán (having overheard the last two syllables): Nǐmen zài jiào wǒ ma?

Lìlián: Bù, wǒmen méiyǒu jiào nǐ. Wǒmen xiǎng zhīdào nǐmen yǒu méiyǒu kǎo huǒjī.

Fúwùyuán: Ō, wǒ yǐwéi nǐmen shuō "huǒjì." Duìbùqǐ, wǒmen méiyǒu huǒjì. Nǐmen yào búyào lái yíge jīròu?

Mínglěi: Búyòng le. Wǒmen de cài gòu le.

DIALOGUE TRANSLATION

Mínglěi (at a restaurant): Could we take a look at the menu?

Waiter: Of course you can. Here are the menus.

(A few moments later)

Waiter: Sir, Miss, what dishes do you want to order?

Mínglěi: We want a hot-and-sour soup, a sweet-and-sour fish, and two bowls of white rice.

Waiter: What else do you want?

Lìlián:	We also want a sautéed green vegetable.
Mínglěi	(to Lìlián): Are you thirsty? Do you want to drink soda pop or beer?
Lìlián:	Either soda pop or beer would be okay.
Mínglěi	(to the Fúwùyuán): Bring us two bottles of soda pop.
Lìlián	(whispering to Mínglěi): Today is the Thanksgiving holiday. Let's try asking them whether they have roast turkey or not.
Waiter	(having overheard the last two syllables): Were you calling for me?
Lìlián:	No, we weren't calling for you. We'd like to know whether you have roast turkey or not.
Waiter:	Oh, I thought you said "waiter." Sorry, we don't have turkey. Do you want a chicken dish brought out?
Mínglěi:	There's no need to. We've got enough dishes.

16.1 Ordering Food at a Restaurant (Fànguǎn)

Wǒmen yào diǎn zhèige cài.	(We want to order this dish.)
Wǒmen hái yào yíge tāng.	(We also want a soup.)
Nǐmen yǒu méiyǒu qìshuǐ?	(Do you have soda pop?)
Zhèige cài tài là le.	(This dish is too spicy.)
Yígòng duōshǎo qián?	(How much is it altogether?)

Just as with family meals at Chinese homes, restaurant meals in China typically encourage the sharing of dishes (cài) by placing them on common platters in the middle of the table for everyone to sample according to personal preference. The soup (tāng) is put into a big tureen on the table and then ladled into small individual bowls; Chinese soups typically have a thin broth and are "drunk" ("hē") with a spoon rather than eaten (chī). If you enjoy soup or any other thing to drink, you describe it as "hǎohē" (tasty), not as "hǎochī." The major choices for starchy carbohydrates are "mántou" (steamed bread), "miàntiáo" (noodles), "chǎo fàn" (fried white rice), and "báifàn" (boiled white rice), which is usually the preferred carbohydrate staple.

Shortly after restaurant-goers sit down at a table, they may discuss how much they should order in terms of the two key categories, "cài" and "tāng," as in "Wǒmen yīnggāi jiào jǐge cài, jǐge tāng?" (How many dishes and soups should we order?). Note that the five major divisions of the sense of taste are suān, tián (sweet), kǔ (bitter), là, xián (salty).

Exercises for 16.1: Make up a conversation in Chinese, using the situation given.

You got very good grades at school, so your parents took you to a Chinese restaurant to celebrate. Your mom asked you what you would like to eat. You said you would very much like to eat lobster (lóngxiā), but it's too expensive. Your mom said, "It doesn't matter. Let's order one." Turning to your dad, your mom said, "You love (ài) to eat duck meat so much. Let's order a duck dish. I don't know whether they have Peking duck (Běijīng kǎoyā) or not."

Your mom called the waiter and asked him to come over. "We'd like to order a few dishes and we also want a soup." The waiter asked which dishes you wanted to order. Your mom said, "We want sautéed lobster, Peking duck, spinach (bōcài), and seafood soup (hǎixiāntāng)." The waiter asked whether you wanted anything else. Your dad said, "These dishes are enough. Please also give us a few glasses of water (jǐbēi shuǐ)."

After eating, you said, "The lobster they made was extremely tasty." Your mom added, "The soup is also very tasty (hǎohē)." Your dad commented, "Their Peking duck is a little salty but still not bad (búcuò)." You told your parents, "I like this restaurant very much. Thank you for bringing me here."

16.2 Some Abbreviated Bisyllabic Verbs in the VERB-bù-VERB Question Pattern

Subject	Verb-bù-Verb					(Object)
Subject	First Syllable	(Second Syllable)	bù	First Syllable	Second Syllable	(Object)
Nǐ (Do you know?)	zhī	(dào)	bù	zhī	dào?	
Tā (Does he like flowers?)	xǐ	(huān)	bù	xǐ	huān	huā?

During rapid speech, a limited number of bisyllabic verbs and auxiliary verbs may drop the second syllable in their first occurrence in the VERB-bù-VERB pattern. Compare the full form, 1st syllable + 2nd syllable + bù + 1st syllable + 2nd syllable, as in "Tā xǐhuān bùxǐhuān háizi?" (Does he like children?), with the abbreviated form, 1st syllable + bù + 1st syllable + 2nd syllable: "Tā xǐ bùxǐhuān háizi?".

In asking whether the listener knows the price ("jiàqián") of something, the full form is "Nǐ zhīdào bùzhīdào jiàqián?"; the abbreviated version is "Nǐ zhī bùzhīdào jiàqián?". In similar fashion, you can transform the full-form sentence "Wǒmen kěyǐ bùkěyǐ hē píjiǔ?" (May we drink beer?) to the abbreviated "Wǒmen kě bùkěyǐ hē píjiǔ?".

Exercises for 16.2: Use abbreviated bisyllabic verbs in the VERB-bù-VERB question pattern when translating the following questions into Chinese.

1. Do you like to eat roast turkey?

_____

2. Does your mom know that you drink beer?

_____

3. Is that young lady permitted to smoke (chōu yān) in the room?

_____

4. Should those boys (nánháizi) play at the computers?

_____

5. Do you know where he is?

_____

16.3 Contrasting the Nonexclusive "Or" (Huòzhě) with the Exclusive "Or" QW (Háishi)

Subject	Verb	Alternative A	háishi	Alternative B?
Nǐ (Are you a boy or a girl?)	shì	nánháizi	háishi	nǚháizi?
Nǐmen (Do you drink tea or coffee?)	hē	chá	háishi	kāfēi?

To use the exclusive "or" that asks an "either-or" question, use the question word "háishi" between the A and B terms, as in a waiter's common question, "Nǐ yào báifàn háishi chǎofàn?" (Do you want boiled rice or fried rice?). In English, the pitch of the questioner's voice dips near the end of the question to indicate his or her ex-

On many of China's upgraded roads, the formerly omnipresent bicycle has largely given way to an ever-increasing stream of automobiles.

pectation that the listener will choose one or the other alternative in reply; in Chinese, the A háishi B? pattern itself indicates that this is a question that expects a reply of one alternative to the exclusion of the other.

Alternative A	huòzhě	Alternative B	(Subject)	dōu	Verb
Hóng chá (Either black tea or green tea is okay.)	huòzhě	lǜchá		dōu	kěyǐ.
Zhōngwén shū (She reads either Chinese-language or English-language books.)	huòzhě	Yīngwén shū	tā	dōu	kàn.

Most listeners will reply to the above question in one of two ways: those who prefer boiled rice will say "Wǒ yào báifàn," while those who prefer fried rice will say, "Wǒ yào chǎo fàn." On the other hand, a less decisive person such as Lìlián may very well offer a noncommittal answer that uses a completely different "or," "huòzhě," that neither functions as a question word nor establishes an exclusive relationship between the A and B terms on either side of it: "Báifàn huòzhě chǎo fàn dōu kěyǐ" (Either boiled rice or fried rice is okay), that is, "A huòzhě B dōu kěyǐ" (Either A or B is okay).

If a wife isn't too particular about what sort of meat her husband buys at the market, she may tell him, "Nǐ mǎi yìxiē zhūròu huòzhě yángròu ba" (Better buy some pork or mutton). Though "huòzhě" is not a question word, it may appear in questions that include some sort of question pattern or question word. For example, when you order a hamburger, the waiter will probably ask, "Nǐ yào búyào yángcōng huòzhě suān huángguā?" (Do you want onions or pickles?)

Exercises for 16.3: Use either "huòzhě" or "háishi" in formulating the following questions and statements.

1. Are you a male or female student? (Use "háishi.")

_____

2. Either chicken meat or turkey meat is fine. (Use "huòzhě.")

_____

3. Is Ānnà an American or Chinese? (Use "háishi.")

_____

4. My child likes to drink either water or soda pop. (Use "huòzhě.")

_____

5. Do you want to drink tea or coffee (kāfēi)? (Use "háishi.")

_____

16.4 VERB-VERB-kàn as "Try Verbing (It)"

	(Subject)	Verb	Verb	kàn	
Qǐng	nǐ	chī	chī	kàn.	(Please try eating it.)
	Nǐmen	hē	hē	kàn.	(Try drinking it.)

By reduplicating certain monosyllabic action verbs and appending "kàn" in the imperative structure (SUBJ) + VERB + VERB + kàn, you wind up with the equivalent of "verb and see (what happens)," or "try verbing (it)." Some examples are "Nǐ shuō-shuō-kàn" (Try saying it), "Wǒmen hē-hē-kàn" (Let's try drinking it), and "Nǐmen wèn-wèn-kàn" (Try asking about it). The generic way of urging

someone to try something or "give it a try" is "Nǐ shì-shì-kàn"—this
is a different "shì" from the one for "to be."

Exercises for 16.4: Use the VERB + VERB + kàn pattern in the following situations.

1. You open a can of Qīngdǎo beer, which your friend has not tried
   before. You ask her whether she would like to try drinking it.

   _____

   _____

2. At the airport, a man asks you about ground transportation.
   You point to the information booth, and tell him to go there
   and try asking about it.

   _____

   _____

3. At your Chinese friends' house, you see them eating a kind of
   green vegetable that you have never seen before. They ask you
   whether you want to try eating it.

   _____

   _____

4. You just bought a new car. When your uncle came over to visit
   you, you asked him whether he would like to try driving (kāi) it.

   _____

   _____

5. You are teaching a friend how to say a sentence in Chinese. Tell
   him to try saying it.

   _____

   _____

16.5 VERB-bù-VERB and Yǒu-méiyǒu Question Patterns After "Wèn" and "Zhīdào"

Subject 1	(Adverb)	(Auxiliary Verb)	zhīdào	Subject 2	Verb-bù/méi-Verb	(Object)
Wǒ	bù		zhīdào	nǐmen	yào búyào	fàn.
(I don't know whether you want cooked rice or not.)						
Tā		xiǎng	zhīdào	wǒmen	yǒu méiyǒu	chē.
(She would like to know whether we have a car or not.)						

A declarative sentence usually results from the unit "SUBJ + bùzhīdào" followed by a "VERB-bù-VERB" or "yǒu-méiyǒu" question, as in "Wǒ bùzhīdào zhèijiā fànguǎn de cài hǎochī bùhǎochī" (I don't know whether this restaurant's dishes are tasty or not). The verbs "wèn" and "zhīdào" can be plugged in for "bùzhīdào" in this pattern, as in the following examples: "Nǐ wèn huǒjì suānlàtāng hǎohē bùhǎohē" (Ask the waiter whether hot-and-sour soup is tasty or not), and "Wǒ xiǎng zhīdào tāmen yǒu méiyǒu tángcùyú" (I'd like to know whether they have sweet-and-sour fish or not).

Exercises for 16.5: Use the VERB-bù-VERB and yǒu-méiyǒu question patterns in the following declarative sentences.

1. Mom knows whether that restaurant is good or not.

_____

2. Ask whether they have hot-and-sour soup or not.

_____

3. Dad doesn't know whether you have a computer or not.

_____

4. We'd like to know whether you know how to speak Chinese.

_____

5. Teacher Lǐ asks me whether roast turkey is tasty or not.

_____

16.6 Mistaken Assumptions with "Yǐwéi"

Whether a speaker's original judgment about a situation is correct or mistaken, English uses the same verb, "thought." Compare "I thought that restaurant wouldn't have roast turkey" (and indeed the restaurant does not have turkey on the menu) with "I thought Confucius was Japanese," a view that the speaker soon discovers is mistaken.

In contrast, Chinese uses the verb "xiǎng" for having thought something that is not mistaken, and "yǐwéi" for having thought something that proves to be mistaken, even though the notion may initially have seemed reasonable to the speaker. Contrast "Wǒ xiǎng tāmen méi yǒu kǎo huǒjī; tāmen díquè méi yǒu" (I thought they didn't have roast turkey, and they indeed don't have it), and "Lìlián yǐwéi zhèijiā fànguǎn yǒu kǎo huǒjī" (Lìlián mistakenly thought that this restaurant has roast turkey [when in fact it doesn't]).

Exercises for 16.6: Use "yǐwéi" to express the following mistaken assumptions.

1. She thought that manager was an American [when in fact he's not].

   _____

2. Mom thought those children were bad (huài) [when in fact they are not].

   _____

3. Did you think that I know how to drive [when in fact I cannot]?

   _____

4. Dad thought that bank was behind the train station [when in fact it is not].

   _____

5. Did your uncle think that my room was very clean [when in fact it was not]?

   _____

Visitors to China are often impressed by the artistry of painted carvings such as the dragon above.

CULTURE NOTES

Just as Americans usually enjoy turkey during the Thanksgiving and Christmas (Shèngdànjié) holidays, Chinese have traditionally favored special foods during key festivals. For instance, New Year's Eve (Chúxì) falls on the last day of the year according to the old agricultural lunar calendar. During this evening, Chinese people typically get together with relatives to eat a huge New Year's Eve dinner (niányèfàn). A practically mandatory dish on this evening is a fish (yú) cooked whole, because the Chinese word for fish sounds exactly like the lucky word "abundance" (yú), which is every family's hope for the coming year. The famous saying "Niánnián yǒu yú" (Every year there's a fish) is simultaneously understood as "Every year there's abundance" due to the double entendre effect with the word "yú."

Because some parts of northern and northwestern China are too arid or impoverished to allow for a fresh steamed fish on New Year's Eve, they often make do with dumplings (jiǎozi) as a substitute with similarly auspicious symbolism. What makes dumplings lucky is that their crescent shape resembles the shape of the traditional 55-ounce silver or gold ingots (yuánbǎo) that were commonly used in commercial transactions in traditional China by wealthy individuals and businesses. This happy coincidence reflects the sort of prosperity and abundance that most families hope the new year will bring. When platters of steaming dumplings are set on the table, somebody may intone an auspicious classical four-character phrase like "Zhāo cái jìn bǎo" (We're inviting wealth and ushering in ingots.)

Southerners may also prepare and eat dumplings on New Year's Eve, though it is primarily a northern specialty. Another southern New Year's Eve dish that promises good luck in the coming year is a kind of stringy black vegetable called "hair vegetable" (fǎ cài), which sounds very much like "get rich" (fā cái). A common New Year's Day greeting is "Gōngxǐ fā cái!" (Congratulations and get rich)!

SUMMARY

During rapid speech, a limited number of bisyllabic verbs and auxiliary verbs may drop the second syllable in their first occurrence in the VERB-bù-VERB question pattern. Examples are "Huǒjì zhī bùzhīdào jiàqián?" (Does the waiter know the price?), "Nǐ xǐ bùxǐhuān chī qīngcài?" (Do you like to eat green vegetables?), and "Wǒmen kě bùkěyǐ hē jiǔ?" (Is it okay for us to drink liquor?).

"Huòzhě" means "or," but it neither functions as a question word nor implies that an exclusive choice should be made between two things. An example of its usage is "Báifàn huòzhě chǎo fàn dōu kěyì" (Either boiled or fried rice is okay).

"VERB-VERB-kàn" expresses the idea of "try verbing it," and always refers to an action that has not yet taken place. Two examples are "Nǐ wèn-wèn-kàn" (Try asking about it) and "Wǒmen hē-hē-kàn" (Let's try drinking it). The generic way of urging someone to "Give it a try" is "Nǐ shì-shì-kàn."

To convey the idea that someone had a mistaken assumption, use the verb "yǐwéi" (to have mistakenly thought that); this verb, like "wèn" (ask) and "zhīdào" (know), often takes a complete sentence as its object, as in "Zhèige fúwùyuán yǐwéi wǒmen méiyǒu fànwǎn" (This clerk mistakenly thought that we didn't have rice bowls). In this situation, the speaker could go on to say, "Kěshì, wǒ jiějie zhīdào wǒmen yǒu fànwǎn" (However, my elder sister knows that we have rice bowls).

CHAPTER 17

NǏ KÉSÒU KÉ LE DUŌJIǓ LE?

(How long have you been coughing so far?)

CHAPTER OVERVIEW

1. Indicating Days of the Week ("Xīngqī"), Last Week, and Next Week

2. Describing Symptoms and Using "Ránhòu" to Indicate Subsequent Action

3. Completed-action "le" with Duration Continuing through to the Present

4. Indicating Who Grants or Denies Permission with "Ràng" (Allow)

5. Expressing the "Type" or "Kind" of Thing with the Measure "Zhǒng"

6. "Duì" as a Coverb in Phrases Such As "Duì nǐ shēntǐ hěn hǎo" (Good for Your Health)

7. "Duō VERB OBJ" as "Verb More of the Object"

NEW VOCABULARY

TRACK
35

1.	yīshēng	medical doctor	NOUN
2.	shēng bìng le	have fallen ill, have gotten sick	VERB-OBJ-PART
3.	bìng	sickness; be sick	NOUN/ADJ
4.	shàng xīngqīyī	last Monday	TW
5.	xīngqīyī	Monday	TW
6.	xīngqī	week (xīngqí in Taiwan)	TW
7.	kāishǐ	to start, to begin	AUXV/VERB
8.	fāshāo	to run a fever	VERB
9.	tóu tòng	to have a headache	topic-comment
10.	tóu	head (of a person or animal)	NOUN
11.	tòng	to ache, to hurt	VERB
12.	liú bíshuǐ	to have a runny nose	VERB-OBJ
13.	liú	to flow	VERB
14.	bíshuǐ	nasal discharge	NOUN
15.	ránhòu	afterward, later	CONJ
16.	hóulóng	throat	NOUN
17.	késòu	to cough	VERB-OBJ
18.	ké	to cough	VERB
19.	zhāngkāi	to open (certain objects such as the mouth)	VERB
20.	zuǐba	mouth	NOUN
21.	ràng	to permit, to let	VERB
22.	tán	phlegm, coughed-up mucus	NOUN
23.	yánsè	color	NOUN
24.	lǜ de	green, a green one ("de" makes an ADJ into a NOUN)	NOUN
25.	lǜ	be green	ADJ
26.	dé	to contract, to get	VERB
27.	qìguǎnyán	bronchitis (bronchial tube inflammation)	NOUN
28.	qìguǎn	bronchial tubes	NOUN

29. fú	to take (medicine or vitamins)	VERB
30. kàngshēngsù	antibiotic(s)	NOUN
31. gāncǎo wán	licorice root pills	NOUN-NOUN
32. gāncǎo	licorice root (a traditional Chinese medicine, not candy)	NOUN
33. wán	pill	NOUN
34. SUBJ búshì OBJ ma?	Isn't the subject an object?	SUBJ-ADV-VERB-OBJ-PART
35. yìzhǒng NOUN	a kind of noun	NUM-MEAS
36. zhǒng	(measure meaning "kind" or "type" of any noun)	MEAS
37. Zhōng yào	Chinese medicine (traditional)	NOUN
38. yào	medicine	NOUN
39. duì NOUN hěn hǎo	be good for the noun	COV-NOUN-ADV-ADJ
40. duō VERB OBJ	verb more of the object	ADV-VERB-OBJ
41. xiūxi	to rest	VERB

DIALOGUE

Lìlián (sitting on the examination table in a room at the medical clinic): Yīshēng, wǒ shēng bìng le (she coughs). Wǒ shàng xīngqīyī kāishǐ fāshāo, tóu tòng, liú bíshuǐ, ránhòu hóulóng tòng.

Yīshēng: Nǐ késòu ké le duōjiǔ le?

Lìlián: Yǐjīng ké le yíge xīngqī le.

Yīshēng: Zhāngkāi zǔiba ràng wǒ kànkan. Tán shì shénme yánsè de?

Lìlián: Shì lǜ de.

Yīshēng: Nǐ dé le qìguǎn yán. Nǐ yào fú kàngshēngsù gēn gāncǎo wán.

Lìlián: Gāncǎo búshì yìzhǒng táng ma?

Yīshēng: Bù, zhè shì Zhōng yào. Duì nǐde hóulóng hěn hǎo. Nǐ yě yào duō hē shuǐ, duō xiūxi.

DIALOGUE TRANSLATION

Lìlián   (sitting on the examination table in a room at the medical clinic): Doctor, I've gotten sick (she coughs). I started to run a fever last Monday, and had a headache and a runny nose. Later, I had a sore throat.

Doctor: How long have you been coughing so far?

Lìlián: I've already been coughing for a week.

Doctor: Open your mouth and let me take a look. What color has your phlegm been?

Lìlián: It's been green.

Doctor: You've contracted bronchitis. You have to take an antibiotic and licorice root pills.

Lìlián: Isn't licorice a kind of candy?

Doctor: No, this is Chinese medicine. It's good for your throat. You also must drink more water and get more rest.

17.1 Indicating Days of the Week ("Xīngqī"), Last Week, and Next Week

xīngqīyī	(Monday)
xīngqītiān/xīngqīrì	(Sunday)
zhèi(ge) xīngqī	(this week)
shàng(ge) xīngqī	(last week)
xià(ge) xīngqī	(next week)
shàng(ge) xīngqīwǔ	(last Friday)
xià(ge) xīngqīliù	(next Saturday)
zhèige yuè	(this month)
shàngge yuè	(last month)
xiàge yuè	(next month)
zuótiān	(yesterday)
jīntiān	(today)
míngtiān	(tomorrow)
qùnián	(last year)
jīnnián	(this year)
míngnián	(next year)

Starting at "xīngqīyī" (Monday) and counting from one to six in the number slot that directly follows the word "xīngqī," you can easily learn the names of the days from Monday to Saturday (xīngqīliù), namely, "xīngqī'èr" (Tuesday), "xīngqīsān" (Wednesday), "xīngqīsì" (Thursday), and "xīngqīwǔ" (Friday). Sunday is the only day that departs from this numerical structure; either "tiān" (xīngqītiān) or "rì" (xīngqīrì) can be inserted into the number slot.

Traditional Chinese culture has typically represented the flow of time in spatial terms as a downward movement, causing the past to be higher than the present, which in turn is higher than the future. Last week is thus "shàng(ge) xīngqi," next week is "xià(ge) xīngqī," and last month and next month are "shàngge yuè" and "xiàge yuè," respectively. This week and this month both use "zhèige TW," as "zhèige xīngqī" and "zhèige yuè," respectively.

We must follow an analogous but different system when going backward and forward by the day and the year: "jīntiān" (today) matches "jīnnián" (this year), and "míngtiān" (tomorrow) matches "míngnián" (next year). The irregular forms fall in the past as "zuótiān" (yesterday) and "qùnián" (last year).

Exercises for 17.1: Fill in the blanks with appropriate time words.

1. Qián Xiānsheng _____, _____ yǒu yóuyǒng kè. (Mr. Qián has swimming lessons on Tuesdays and Thursdays.)

2. _____ shì Gǎn'ēnjié, nèixiē xuéshēng búyòng qù shàng kè. (Tomorrow is Thanksgiving; those students need not go to classes.)

3. Wú Jīnglǐ _____ dào _____ dōu qù tāde gōngsī gōngzuò. (Manager Wú goes to his company to work from Monday to Friday.)

4. _____ tā méi qù Zhōngguó wán, _____ tā yě méi qù. _____ tā dǎsuàn dài tā zǔmǔ qù. (She didn't go on vacation to China last year, nor did she go this year. She plans to take her grandmother there next year.)

5. _____ wǒmen mài le hěn duō yīfu,
   _____ wǒmen yào kāishǐ mài shū hé cídiǎn.
   (Last month we sold many clothes; next week we're going to start selling books and dictionaries.)

6. Yīnwèi māma _____ kāishǐ shēng bìng, suǒyǐ
   _____ tā qù kàn yīshēng. (Because Mom started to get sick last Sunday, she went to see a doctor yesterday.)

17.2 Describing Symptoms and Using "Ránhòu" to Indicate Subsequent Action

Describing Symptoms

Subject	Time Word	kāishǐ	Symptom 1	Symptom 2	Symptom 3
Māma	shàng xīngqī	kāishǐ	tóu tòng	fāshāo,	liú bíshuǐ.
(Last week Mom started having a headache, a fever, and a runny nose.)					

A doctor will ordinarily want to know what the patient's symptoms are and when they started. Symptoms in Chinese tend to be expressed as verbs or verb clauses: note that "fāshāo," "tòng," and "liú" are all verbs, so that all the symptoms can be prefaced with the auxiliary verb "kāishǐ" (started to VERB): SUBJ + TW + kāishǐ + sympt1 + sympt2 + sympt3.

Using Ránhòu to Indicate Subsequent Action

Clause of Earlier Action,	ránhòu	Clause of Later Action
Tā shàng xīngqī'èr qù Niǔyuē,	ránhòu	tā zài nàr dé le bìng.
(He went to New York last Tuesday; afterwards, he contracted a disease there.)		
Wǒ zuótiān kāishǐ chī (or fú) yào,	ránhòu	wǒ jīntiān jiù hǎo le.
(I started taking medicine yesterday; afterwards, I got well today.)		

Lìlián's sore throat or "throat hurting" ("hóulóng tòng") occurred at a later time than the other symptoms, and thus is preceded by the conjunction "ránhòu" (afterwards). The pattern is as follows: clause of earlier action + ránhòu + clause of later action, as in "Mínglěi gēn tā de nǔpéngyou zài fēijīchǎng liáo tiān. Ránhòu, tāmen yìqǐ shàng fēijī" (Mínglěi and his girlfriend were having a chat at the airport. Afterwards, they got on the airplane together).

The body parts are illustrated and named below.

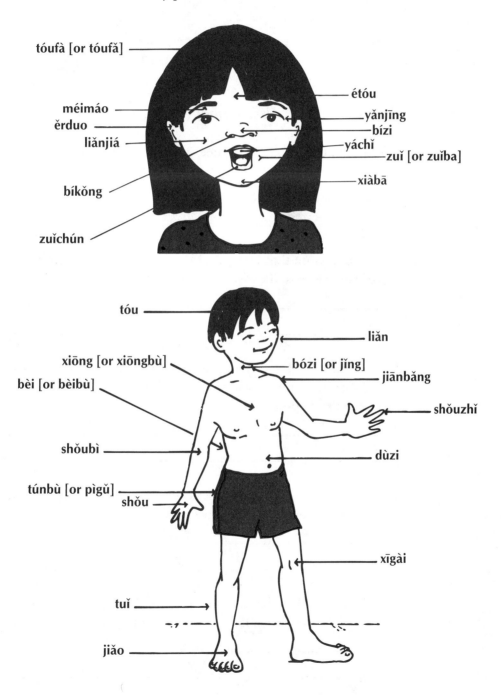

tóufà [or tóufǎ] (hair)	étóu (forehead)
yǎnjīng (eyes)	méimáo (eyebrows)
liǎnjiá (cheek)	xiàbā (chin)
bízi (nose)	bíkǒng (nostril)
ěrduo (ear)	yáchǐ (teeth)
zuǐ [or zuǐba] (mouth)	zuǐchún (lip)
tóu (head)	jiānbǎng (shoulder)
liǎn (face)	bózi [or jǐng] (neck)
xiōng [or xiōngbù] (chest)	bèi [or bèibù] (back)
dùzi (stomach)	shǒubì (arm)
shǒu (hand)	shǒuzhǐ (finger)
túnbù [or pìgǔ] (buttocks)	tuǐ (leg)
xīgài (knee)	jiǎo (foot)

Exercises for 17.2: Use "ránhòu" in the following situations.

1. Tell the doctor that your knee started to hurt last Saturday; afterwards, your feet also started to ache.

   _____

   _____

2. Tell your mom that Lìlián and her boyfriend first went to the park; afterwards, they went to a French restaurant.

   _____

   _____

3. Tell your friend that Xiǎo Wěi (Young Wěi), your little cousin, said that his stomach was hurting; afterwards, he said he wanted to drink soda pop.

   _____

   _____

4. Tell your dad that you started to run a fever last Wednesday; afterwards, you started to have a runny nose.

   _____

   _____

5. Tell your teacher that Mr. Zhāng started to have a sore throat last week; afterwards, he contracted bronchitis.

   _____

   _____

6. That old man contracted pneumonia (fèi yán) last month; afterwards, he died (sǐ le).

17.3 Completed-action "le" with Duration Continuing through to the Present

Subject	(Verb Object)	Verb	le	Duration	(le)
Tāmen (They walked for two hours.)		zǒu	le	liǎngge zhōngtóu.	
Wǒ zǔfù (My grandfather coughed for a month.)	ké sòu	ké	le	yíge yuè.	
Tā (She has been sick for three days so far.)		bìng	le	sāntiān	le.
Nǐ (How long have you been learning Chinese?)	xué Zhōngwén	xué	le	duōjiǔ	le?
Wǒ (I have been learning Chinese for a year.)	xué Zhōngwén	xué	le	yìnián	le.

As indicated in preceding chapters, the duration of an action goes after the verb, and the completed-action "le" is inserted directly after the verb if the action is completed. For instance, if you had completed the action of waiting for one week but were no longer waiting, you could say, "Wǒ děng le yíge xīngqī" (I waited for a week). This pattern can be schematized as SUBJ + VERB + le + duration.

On the other hand, if this action of waiting for a week was still going on up to and including the present moment, you would need to add a sentence-end "le": "Wǒ děng le yíge xīngqī le" (I've been waiting for a week so far). This pattern is SUBJ + VERB + le + duration + le.

If there is a direct object of the verb in this pattern, it cannot be sandwiched anywhere between the verb and the time duration expression, which is a unit that must be uninterrupted. Instead, the direct object is ordinarily placed before this uninterruptable unit, usually by repeating the verb once, as in "Wǒ děng Jiějie, děng le yíge xīngqī" (I waited for Elder Sister for a week), or SUBJ + VERB + OBJ + VERB + le + duration.

If the completed action continues up to the present moment, you simply add a sentence-end "le": "Wo děng Jiějie, děng le yíge xīngqī le" (I have been waiting for Elder Sister for a week so far), or SUBJ + VERB + OBJ + VERB + le + duration + le. Because "késòu" (to cough) is a VERB-OBJ combination, the doctor uses this pattern to ask Lìlián, "Nǐ késòu ké le duōjiǔ le?" (How long have you been coughing so far?)

Exercises for 17.3: Translate the following sentences using the patterns given.

1. That old man sat for an hour (zhōngtóu). (SUBJ + VERB + le + duration)

   _____

2. Your manager has been working for four weeks so far. (SUBJ + VERB + le + duration + le)

   _____

3. How long were you eating lunch (wǔfàn)? (SUBJ + VERB + OBJ + VERB + le + duration)

   _____

4. This young man has been learning Chinese for five months so far. (SUBJ + VERB + OBJ + VERB + le + duration + le)

   _____

5. How long have they been swimming? (SUBJ + VERB + OBJ + VERB + le + duration + le)

   _____

17.4 Indicating Who Grants or Denies Permission with "Ràng" (Allow)

Suppose you were to tell Mínglěi, "Nǐ bù kěyǐ hē píjiǔ" (You may not drink beer). From this statement alone, it would not be clear whether you yourself were denying him permission, or you were merely enforcing a rule laid down by somebody else. To indicate clearly who is granting or denying permission, use the verb "ràng," as in "Wǒ bú ràng nǐ hē píjiǔ" (I'm not letting you drink beer), and "Nǐ ràng wǒ kànkan nǐ de hùzhào" (Let me take a look at your passport).

Exercises for 17.4: Use "ràng" in the following sentences.

1. Those teachers let the students read this book.

   _____

2. My dad does not let my elder brother drive Dad's car.

   _____

3. Her mom lets her drink only water and juice (guǒzhī).

   _____

4. Does your friend let you borrow her dictionary?

   _____

5. My boyfriend doesn't like to let me see his photographs.

   _____

17.5 Expressing the "Type" or "Kind" of Thing with the Measure "Zhǒng"

yìzhǒng	(one kind)
liǎngzhǒng	(two kinds)
hěn duō zhǒng	(many kinds)
zhèizhǒng	(this kind)
nèizhǒng	(that kind)
něizhǒng	(which kind?)

The measure "zhǒng" (kind), like the pluralizing measure "xiē," can be used with practically any noun. Examples are "Zhèizhǒng yào duì hóulóng hěn hǎo" (This kind of medicine is good for the throat), "Yǒu liǎngzhǒng tán: yìzhǒng shì lǜ de, yìzhǒng shì bái de" (There are two kinds of phlegm: one kind is green, and one kind is clear), and "Nèizhǒng yīshēng fēicháng hǎo" (That kind of doctor is extremely good).

Exercises for 17.5: Use "zhǒng" in translating the following dialogue into Chinese.

1. A: Which kind of computers do you like?

_____

2. B: I like this kind of computer.

_____

3. A: What kind of beer is this?

_____

4. B: This is German (Déguó) beer.

_____

5. A: Is that kind of dish (cài) delicious?

_____

6. B: No, that kind of dish is not very (bútài) delicious.

_____

17.6 "Duì" as a Coverb in Phrases Such As "Duì nǐ shēntǐ hěn hǎo" (Good for Your Health)

Subject	duì	Noun	Adverb	Adjective
Yǒuxiē Zhōng yào (Some Chinese medicine is good for your health.)	duì	shēntǐ	hěn	hǎo.
Chī tài duō táng (Eating too much candy is bad for your teeth.)	duì	yáchǐ	bù	hǎo.

To express the idea that something is good or bad for you, the coverb "duì" (the same word as in "duìbùqǐ") functions a bit like the English preposition "for" in such a structure, which can be generalized as SUBJ + duì + NOUN (+ ADV) + ADJ (the subject is adjective for the noun). Examples are "Fēicháng là de cài duì dùzi bùhǎo" (Extremely spicy food isn't good for the stomach), and "Gāncǎo wán duì hóulóng hěn hǎo" (Licorice pills are good for the throat).

Exercises for 17.6: Translate the following, using "duì" as a coverb.

1. That mom is extremely nice to her child.

_____

2. I think swimming is good for your health.

_____

3. Is eating green vegetables good for old folks?

_____

4. When you have a sore throat (. . . de shíhòu), hot-and-sour soup is not very good for you.

_____

5. When you contract bronchitis, taking antibiotics is good for you.

_____

17.7 "Dūo VERB OBJ" as "Verb More of the Object"

Dūo/Shǎo	Verb	Object	
Dūo	xiūxi.		(Get more rest.)
Shǎo	gōngzuò.		(Work less.)
Dūo	yòng	Zhōngwén.	(Use more Chinese.)

Many adjectives such as "dūo" (much, many) can function as adverbs under certain circumstances, as when they are placed before the verb. Especially in the imperative form, the meaning of "dūo" shifts somewhat to "more," or "verb more of the object" (dūo VERB OBJ), while "shǎo" (few) means "less" or "fewer" when used in similar fashion (shǎo VERB OBJ).

Thus, if you have high blood pressure or a weight problem, a concerned relative or friend may suggest, "Dūo chī qīngcài, shǎo chī ròu" (Eat more green vegetables, and eat less meat). As another example, your teacher might say, "Dūo shuō Zhōngguóhuà, shǎo shuō Yīngwén" (Speak more Chinese, and speak less English).

Exercises for 17.7: Use either "duō" or "shǎo" in the following situations.

1. When you and your boyfriend are invited to a banquet, the host tells you, "Please eat a little more food (cài)."

   _____

   _____

2. Your doctor tells you, "When you have a fever, drinking more water is good for you."

   _____

   _____

3. You wonder why your friend can read Chinese so well. She tells you her secret: "I read more Chinese books and fewer English books."

   _____

   _____

4. Mrs. Lǐ tells her children, "Watching more movies (diànyǐng) and television (diànshì) is not good for you."

   _____

   _____

5. On New Year's Eve, you made the following decision: Next year I'm going to start writing letters more and making phone calls less.

   _____

   _____

CULTURE NOTES

Many doctors in China are educated in both modern Western medicine and traditional Chinese medical practices. These physicians often combine the strengths of both systems of healing, as when Lìlián's doctor prescribes an antibiotic to counter her bronchial infection, along with an anti-inflammatory herbal remedy, licorice root pills, for her sore throat.

SUMMARY

If the duration of an action has not continued to the present, use only the completed-action "le," not the sentence-end "le": "Shàngge yuè, wǒ dùzi tòng le yíge xīngqī" (Last month, my stomach hurt for a week). On the other hand, if the duration of the action continues to the present, use both the completed-action "le" and the sentence-end "le": "Wǒde tóu tòng le yíge xīngqī le" (My head has been aching for a week so far).

To express the idea that the subject of the sentence is good for some noun, use the coverb "duì" before the noun and conclude with "hěn hǎo." An example is "Gāncǎo wán duì hóulóng hěn hǎo" (Licorice pills are good for the throat).

Like the plural measure "xiē," the measure "zhǒng" (type) goes with practically all nouns. For instance, "Wǒde yīshēng yóuqí xǐhuān zhèizhǒng yào" (My doctor especially likes this kind of medicine).

To urge the listener to verb more of the object, use "duō" in an adverbial position right before the verb: "Duō hē shuǐ, duō xiūxi" (Drink more water and get more rest). To urge the listener to verb less, use "shǎo" in the same way: "Shǎo hē jiǔ, shǎo chī táng" (Drink less liquor, and eat less candy).

Traditional Chinese culture has typically represented the flow of time in spatial terms as a downward movement, causing the past to be higher than the present, which in turn is higher than the future. Last week is thus "shàng(ge) xīngqī," next week is "xià(ge) xīngqī," and last month and next month are "shàngge yuè" and "xiàge yuè," respectively.

The wandering souls of the dead within the watery realm are guided by floating lanterns during the Ghost Festival in late summer.

CHAPTER 18

NǏ KÀNGUÒ JĪNGJÙ MÉIYǑU?

(Have you ever watched Běijīng Opera?)

CHAPTER OVERVIEW

1. Having Had the Experience of Verbing: VERB-guò

2. "Every Noun" with Měi + MEAS + NOUN

3. Manner-of-verbing Complements Such As "Biǎoyǎn de hěn hǎo" (Performed Well)

4. The Adversative Expression "ADJ-sǐ le" as "Terribly Adjective"

5. Adverbs of Frequency: "Yǒu shíhòu" (Sometimes) and "Chángcháng" (Often)

6. The Comparative "ADJ Yìdiǎnr" versus the Noncomparative "Yǒu Yìdiǎnr ADJ"

7. VERB-bùqǐ as "Can't Afford to Verb," and Some Variations

NEW VOCABULARY

1.	kànguò	have watched before	VERB-COMP
2.	SUBJ-VERB-guò-OBJ-méiyǒu?	Have SUBJ ever verbed OBJ before?	experiential question pattern
3.	Jīngjù	Běijīng Opera	NOUN
4.	méi kànguò	have never watched	ADV-VERB-COMP
5.	juéde	to feel	VERB
6.	zěnmeyàng	How was it?/ How are things?	QW
7.	yǒu yìsi	be interesting, be fun	ADJ
8.	měi-MEAS-NOUN	every noun, each noun	SPEC-MEAS-NOUN
9.	yǎnyuán	actor	NOUN
10.	biǎoyǎn	to perform, to act	VERB
11.	VERB-de-ADJ	verb adjective-ly	manner-of-verbing complement
12.	dànshì	but, however	CONJ
13.	kàndào yíbàn	watched it halfway through ("to the point of half")	VERB-COMP-OBJ
14.	yíbàn	half, halfway	NOUN
15.	tūrán	suddenly	MADV
16.	dà jiào	to shout loudly, to bellow	ADV-VERB
17.	xiàsǐ le	be scared to death	ADJ-COMP-PART
18.	ADJ-sǐ le	be terribly adjective (adversative adjectives only)	
19.	jiǎng	to recount, to talk, to explain	VERB
20.	hǎoxiào	be funny, be laughable	ADJ
21.	háiyǒu	what's more, moreover	ADV
22.	zuòde tài yuǎn	was sitting too far away	VERB-PART-ADV-ADJ
23.	yǒu (de) shíhòu	sometimes	MADV

24. kànbújiàn	couldn't see, can't see	VERB-bù-COMP
25. tīngbùqīngchǔ	couldn't hear clearly, can't hear clearly	VERB-bù-COMP
26. qīngchǔ	be clear	ADJ
27. zuò de jìn yìdiǎnr	sit a bit closer	manner-of-verbing complement
28. zuòwèi	seat, place to sit	NOUN
29. mǎibùqǐ	can't afford to buy	VERB-bù-COMP
30. VERB-bùqǐ	can't afford to verb	VERB-bù-COMP

DIALOGUE

TRACK
38

Lǐ Lǎoshī: Nǐmen kànguò Jīngjù méiyǒu?

Ānnà: Wǒ méi kànguò.

Mínglěi: Wǒ kànguò yícì.

Lǐ Lǎoshī (to Mínglěi): Nǐ juéde zěnmeyàng?

Mínglěi: Wǒ juéde hěn yǒu yìsi. Měige yǎnyuán dōu biǎoyǎn de hěn hǎo. Dànshì, wǒ kàndào yíbàn, tūrán yǒu ge yǎnyuán dà jiào. Wǒ xiàsǐ le!

Lǐ Lǎoshī: Nǐ jiǎngde nàme hǎoxiào!

Mínglěi: Háiyǒu, wǒ zuòde tài yuǎn, yǒu shíhòu kànbújiàn, yě tīngbùqīngchǔ.

Lǐ Lǎoshī: Nǐ zěnme méi zuò de jìn yìdiǎnr?

Mínglěi: Jìnde zuòwèi tài guì le. Wǒ mǎibùqǐ.

DIALOGUE TRANSLATION

Teacher Lǐ: Have you ever watched Běijīng Opera?

Ānnà: I've never watched it.

Mínglěi: I've watched it once.

Teacher Lǐ (to Mínglěi): How did you feel about it?

Mínglěi: I felt it was interesting. Every actor performed well. But once I had watched it halfway through, there was an actor who suddenly bellowed loudly. I was scared to death!

Teacher Lǐ: You recounted it in such a funny way!

Mínglěi: What's more, I was sitting too far away, and sometimes couldn't see the goings-on and couldn't clearly hear them, either.

Teacher Lǐ: How come you didn't sit a bit closer?

Mínglěi: Tickets for the seats up front were too expensive. I couldn't afford to buy them.

Though Chinese opera is a relatively youthful art form by Chinese standards, it enjoys a rich variety of popular regional variants such as Běijīng Opera.

18.1 Having Had the Experience of Verbing: VERB-guò

Subject	(méiyǒu)	Verb	le	Object	(méiyǒu)
Nǐ (Have you eaten the crabs?)		chī	le	pángxiè	méiyǒu?
Wǒ (I have eaten the crabs.)		chī	le	pángxiè.	
Wǒ (I haven't eaten the crabs.)	méi(yǒu)	chī		pángxiè.	

Subject	(méiyǒu)	Verb	guò	Object	(méiyǒu)
Nǐ (Have you ever eaten crabs?)		chī	guò	pángxiè	méiyǒu?
Wǒ (I have eaten crabs.)		chī	guò	pángxiè.	
Wǒ (I have never eaten lobsters.)	méi(yǒu)	chī	guò	lóngxiā.	

In a sentence such as "Lǎo Wáng chī le èrshíge yángròu jiǎozi" (Ol' Wáng ate 20 mutton dumplings), the "le" appended to the verb indicates the completion of the subject's verbing, in this case eating. If, however, Ol' Wáng is a southeasterner on vacation in the North who may have never eaten mutton dumplings, a specialty of northern and northwestern China, you may be more interested in whether he has ever had the experience of eating them than in how many he completed eating on some particular occasion.

Assuming that you were not present at the time he ate those 20 dumplings, you might ask, "Nǐ chīguò yángròu jiǎozi méiyǒu?" (Have you ever eaten mutton dumplings?), in line with the pattern SUBJ + VERB + guò + OBJ + méiyǒu (Has the subject ever verbed the object?). Remembering the dumplings he had eaten, Ol' Wáng would reply, "Duì, wǒ chīguò yángròu jiǎozi" (That's right, I've eaten mutton dumplings before), according to the pattern, SUBJ + VERB + guò + OBJ. Notice that the basic structures in the question form and the affirmative declarative sentence form are the same for the completed-action "le" and the experiential aspect "guò": SUBJ + VERB + le + OBJ + méiyǒu versus SUBJ + VERB + guò + OBJ + méiyǒu, and SUBJ + VERB + le + OBJ versus SUBJ + VERB + guò + OBJ.

The major structural difference between the completed-action "le" pattern and the experiential "guò" pattern occurs in negative declarative sentences, where "le" drops out in the completed-action pattern while "guò" is retained in the experiential pattern. Compare SUBJ + méiyǒu + VERB + OBJ (negative completed action) with SUBJ + méiyǒu + VERB + guò + OBJ (negative experiential action).

In other words, if Ol' Wáng hadn't completed the action of eating those 20 dumplings, "le" would have to drop out: "Wǒ méiyǒu chī èrshíge yángròu jiǎozi" (I haven't eaten 20 mutton dumplings). In contrast, if he had never had the experience of eating the dumplings before, "guò" would stay in: "Wǒ méiyǒu chīguò yángròu jiǎozi" (I've never eaten mutton dumplings). Note that "méiyǒu" can be contracted to "méi."

Exercises for 18.1: Complete the following dialogues using either the completed-action "le" pattern or the experiential "guò" pattern.

1. A: _____ ma? (Did you [plural] eat four *jīn* of pork altogether?)
   B: Bù, wǒmen méi chī sì jīn zhūròu.

2. A: _____ méiyǒu? (Have you ever caught [zhuā] cockroaches?)
   B: _____ (I've caught one at home.)

3. A: _____? (Has your mom ever drunk French
liquor?)
   B: _____. (She has never drunk French
liquor.)

4. A: Nǐ qùguò Rìběn méiyǒu?
   B: _____. (I've been to [Japan] once.)

5. A: _____?
   B: Wǒ méi kànguò zhèiběn shū.

18.2 "Every Noun" with Měi + MEAS + NOUN

měi	Measure	Noun	
měi	ge	rén	(everyone)
měi	zhī	lǎoshǔ	(every mouse)
měi	bēi	shuǐ	(every glass of water)
měi	fēn	zhōng	(every minute)
měi	ge	zhōngtóu	(every hour)
měi	tiān		(every day)
měi	ge	xīngqī	(every week)
měi	ge	yuè	(every month)
měi	nián		(every year)

(Subject)	měi	Measure	Noun	dōu		Verb	(Object)
	Měi	ge	nǚháizi	dōu	hěn	piàoliàng.	
(Every girl is pretty.)							
Tā	měi	ge	xīngqī	dōu		qù mǎi	cài.
(He goes to buy groceries every week.)							

Like "zhèi," "nèi," and "něi," "měi" (every) must be followed by a
measure word according to the pattern měi + MEAS + NOUN, as in
"měige xuéshēng" (every student) and "měizhāng zhuōzi" (every
table). More often than not, the adverb "dōu" is included before the
verb in sentences with a subject modified by "měi," even though
English would not call for "both" or "all" in such a sentence: "Měige
jīnglǐ dōu mángsǐ le" (Every manager is terribly busy), and
"Měizhāng chuáng dōu yǒu yìdiǎn zāng" (Every bed is a bit dirty).

A small number of special nouns such as "tiān" and "nián" are
quasi measures, and thus directly follow "měi." Examples are

"Lìlián měitiān dōu zuò chē" (Lìlián rides the bus every day), and "Bǐdé měinián dōu qù kàn tā bàba māma" (Peter goes to see his dad and mom every year).

Exercises for 18.2: Use "měi" in each of the following sentences.

1. Every book is cheap here.

_____

2. Everyone is happy in the park.

_____

3. Has each child raised a mouse before (VERB + guò)?

_____

4. She is accustomed to going to bed (shàng chuáng) at nine every night.

_____

5. Mrs. Chén and her husband go to eat at that restaurant every month.

_____

18.3 Manner-of-verbing Complements Such As "Biǎoyǎn de hěn hǎo" (Performed Well)

Subject	Verb	de	Adverb	Adjective
Wǒmen (We ate it happily.)	chī	de	hěn	gāoxìng.
Tā (He doesn't sing well.)	chàng	de	bù	hǎo.

In English, an adjective such as "happy" modifies a noun, but the adjective can be changed into an adverb that modifies a verb simply by adding "-ly" as a suffix ("happily"), as in "The children are playing happily." A similar process occurs in many Chinese declarative sentences, where the particle "de" must be included after the verb in the "manner-of-verbing" complement of de + ADV + ADJ.

The structure of the pattern is as follows: SUBJ + VERB + de + ADV + ADJ, and the Chinese version of the above English sentence is "Háizi wán de hěn gāoxìng." Some other examples are "Tāmen xiě de nàme piàoliàng!" (They wrote it so prettily!), "Nèiwèi yīshēng shuō de hěn kèqì" (That doctor said it politely), and "Nǐ de háizi jiǎng de zhēn hǎo" (Your child recounted it really well).

Exercises for 18.3: Rearrange the words in each entry to make a correct sentence according to the English meaning given.

1. hěn de lǎorén kuài nèige zǒu (That old man walks very fast.)

   _____

2. chī bù duō wǒ nǐmen de nàme zhīdào (I didn't know that you eat so much.)

   _____

3. dōu měizhī gāoxìng wán gǒu de hěn (Every dog is playing happily.)

   _____

4. nàme méi hǎo de gēge xiǎngdào kāi bàba (Dad didn't realize that Elder Brother drives so well.)

   _____

5. fēicháng zǔfù zhèr kàn tāde de qīngchǔ kěyǐ cóng (His grandfather can see extremely clearly from here.)

   _____

18.4 The Adversative Expression "ADJ-sǐ le" as "Terribly Adjective"

Subject	Adjective	sǐ	le	
Wǒ	è	sǐ	le.	(I'm terribly hungry.)
Zǔfù	qì	sǐ	le.	(Grandfather is terribly angry.)

The modifier of an adjective is usually an adverb that precedes the adjective, such as "tài" in "tài xiǎo" (too small), and "búgòu" in "búgòu gānjìng" (not clean enough). However, Chinese has another type of structure, parallel to English's "adjective to the point of X (or to the extent of X)," as in "hungry to the point of dying (from starvation)."

In this structure, the modifier comes directly after the adjective, as in the pattern SUBJ + adjective + sǐ le, "Subject is terribly adjective," which is used to describe an adverse or unfavorable situation and hence is called the adversative pattern. A sentence in this pattern literally means that the subject is adjective to death or to the point of dying, as in "xiàsǐ le" (scared to death) and "èsǐ le" (hungry to the point of dying), but is often more accurately understood as "terribly adjective," as in "terribly hungry" (èsǐ le) and "terribly tired" (lèisǐ le). Note that the only type of adjective you can use in the ADJ-sǐ le pattern is one that denotes a state of adversity or discomfort on the part of the subject, such as "lèi" (tired), "è" (hungry), "qì" (angry), and "kě" (thirsty).

Subject	Adjective	jí	le.	
Tā	piàoliàng	jí	le.	(She is extremely pretty.)
Zhèige cài	hǎochī	jí	le.	(This dish is extremely tasty.)

A similar but more versatile structure that means "extremely adjective" and yet is neutral with regard to the adjective being adversative or nonadversative is ADJ + jí le. Examples include "hǎojí le" (wonderful, extremely good), "huàijí le" (terrible, extremely bad), and "piàoliàngjí le" (extremely pretty).

Exercises for 18.4: Use the patterns ADJ + sǐ le and ADJ + jí le in the following sentences.

1. This dog is terribly thirsty.

_____

2. Look; that child is terribly hungry.

_____

3. Those actors' performance is extremely good.

_____

4. His grandfather is terribly angry (qì).

_____

5. These crabs are extremely tasty.

_____

18.5 Adverbs of Frequency: "Yǒu shíhòu" (Sometimes) and "Chángcháng" (Often)

"Yǒu shíhòu"

Subject	yǒu shíhòu	Verb	Object	
Tā lǎoshī (Her teacher sometimes teaches her Chinese.)	yǒu shíhòu	jiāo	tā	Zhōngwén.

Yǒu shíhòu	Subject	Verb		Object
Yǒu shíhòu (Sometimes my uncle likes to crack jokes.)	wǒ shúshu	xǐhuān	kāi	wánxiào.

As a moveable adverb, "yǒu shíhòu" (sometimes) may either precede or follow the subject, but it must go somewhere before the verb. Examples are "Yǒu shíhòu, Lǐ Lǎoshī qù kàn Jīngjù" (Sometimes Teacher Lǐ goes to watch Běijīng Opera), and "Lín Tàitai yǒu shíhòu yòng dāochā chī fàn" (Mrs. Lín sometimes eats with a knife and fork).

"Chángcháng"

Subject	(bù)	chángcháng	Verb	Object
Wǒmen (We often eat American food.)		chángcháng	chī	Měiguó cài.
Tā (He doesn't drink red wine often.)	bù	cháng(cháng)	hē	hóng jiǔ.

"Chángcháng" (often) is a standard adverb, and thus must go somewhere before the verb and after the subject, as in "Lìlián chángcháng qù yóuyǒng" (Lìlián often goes swimming).

Exercises for 18.5: Use the appropriate adverbs of frequency in the following dialogues.

1. A: _____ ma? (Do you often go to watch Běijīng Opera?)

_____

2. B: Bù, wǒ _____. (No, I don't often go.)

_____

3. A: Nǐ měige xīngqītiān dōu gēn nǐ māma qù mǎi cài ma? (Do you go with your mom to buy groceries every Sunday?)

B: Bù, _____. (I don't go every Sunday.)
Kěshì, _____. (I sometimes go with her.)

4. A: Nǐmen qù Zhōngguó fànguǎn chī fàn de shíhòu, diǎn xiē shénme cài? (What dishes do you order when you go to a Chinese restaurant?)
B: _____. (We sometimes order sweet-and-sour fish, and sometimes order sautéed green vegetables and soup.)

5. A: _____? (Do you often listen to classical music [gǔdiǎn yīnyuè]?) [Use a "ma" question.]
B: _____. (Yes. Because I like classical music very much, I often listen to it.)

18.6 The Comparative "ADJ Yìdiǎnr" versus the Noncomparative "Yǒu Yìdiǎnr ADJ"

Subject	(Verb de)	Adjective	yìdiǎnr	
Tā	zuò de	yuǎn	yìdiǎnr.	(He sat a bit farther away.)
Nǐ	zhàn de	jìn	yìdiǎnr.	(You stood a bit closer.)
Zhèige cèsuǒ		dà	yìdiǎnr.	(This toilet is a bit bigger.)

Teacher Lǐ is speaking in comparative terms when she asks why Mínglěi didn't "zuòde jìn yìdiǎnr" (sit a bit closer) to the stage. Any time "yìdiǎnr" follows an adjective, the phrase means "a bit more adjective" or "a bit adjective-er," as in "Zhèige fángjiān gānjìng yìdiǎnr, yě guì yìdiǎnr" (This room is a bit cleaner, and also a bit more expensive). In the latter sentence the speaker is implicitly comparing this room with another one that is neither as clean nor as expensive.

Subject	yǒu yìdiǎnr (= yǒudiǎn)	Adjective	
Nèige cài	yǒu yìdiǎnr	là.	(That dish is a bit spicy.)
Zhèige fángzi	yǒu yìdiǎnr	guì.	(This house is a bit expensive.)

Subject	Verb		yìdiǎnr	Noun		
Nǐ	yào	hē	yìdiǎnr	píjiǔ	ma?	(Do you want to drink a little beer?)
Wǒ	xiǎng	kàn	yìdiǎnr	diànshì.		(I'd like to watch a little TV.)

If you do not want to suggest a comparison and yet wish to say "a bit adjective," use the longer phrase "yǒu yìdiǎnr," and place it before the adjective instead of after it, as in "Nèige fángjiān yǒu yìdiǎnr zāng" (That room is a bit dirty) and "Zhèiběn shū yǒu yìdiǎnr guì" (This book is a bit expensive). Note that "yǒu yìdiǎnr" is an adverbial phrase, whereas "yìdiǎnr" can function as an adjective when it is placed before a noun, as in "Tā xiǎng hē yìdiǎnr shuǐ" (He would like to drink a little water).

Exercises for 18.6: Use either "ADJ yìdiǎnr" or "yǒu yìdiǎnr ADJ" in each of the following sentences.

1. That bank is far away; this bank is a bit closer.

_____

2. His manager's airplane ticket is a bit expensive.

_____

3. That hot-and-sour soup is not sour; this soup is a bit sour.

_____

4. Their clothes are all a bit dirty.

_____

5. This room is a bit smaller, and also a bit cheaper.

_____

18.7 VERB-bùqǐ as "Can't Afford to Verb," and Some Variations

Subject	Verb –bùqǐ	Object	
Tā	duìbùqǐ	tāde lǎoshī.	(He's let down his teacher.)
Tāmen	kànbùqǐ	xiǎo háizi.	(They look down upon children.)

"VERB-bùqǐ" usually means "can't afford to verb." Examples are "Wáng Xiānsheng chībùqǐ lóngxiā" (Mr. Wáng can't afford to eat lobster), and "Wǒ zuòbùqǐ fēijī" (I can't afford to take an airplane).

Less frequently, "VERB-bùqǐ" means that the subject can't verb due to feelings of disgust or regret, especially when the verb means "to look at" or "to face" someone, respectively. An example of the subject's inability to look at some particular person(s) as respectable is "Nèige rén kànbùqǐ yǎnyuán" (That person looks down upon actors). An example of the subject's inability to raise his or her head and look someone else in the eye because of regret or shame is "Wǒ duìbùqǐ nǐ" (I can't face you), which has been abbreviated to the conventional "Duìbùqǐ," meaning "Sorry" or "Excuse me."

Exercises for 18.7: Use the VERB-bùqǐ pattern in the following sentences.

1. I'm truly sorry (I truly can't face you).

_____

2. You shouldn't look down upon that person.

_____

3. He thought you could not afford to buy a computer [when in fact you can].

_____

4. Because she and her husband have no jobs, they cannot afford to raise children.

_____

5. Because they can't afford to take an airplane, they must drive to New York.

_____

Elaborately carved and costumed puppets bustle about on a miniature version of a Chinese opera stage.

CULTURE NOTES

Before the strong currents of Western cultural influences swept over China in the twentieth century, all Chinese drama was operatic. Aside from memorizing lines from the script and mastering the art of acting, actors had to develop proficiency in singing, pantomime, and circular, dancelike movements on the stage. Even now, at the dawn of a new century, traditional operatic Chinese drama still draws sizable audiences in China, in spite of strong competition from television, movies, Western-style "spoken drama," computer games, and other forms of mass entertainment.

Operatic performances are especially numerous during the traditional festivals in a given year when people take time off from work to enjoy various forms of entertainment and cultural pursuits. The generic term for "holiday" is "jiérì," and Chinese people often speak of "guò jié" (celebrating the holiday), as distinct from the more neutral and universal concept of "fàng jià" (going on vacation).

Traditional holidays often follow the old lunar or "agriculture calendar" (nónglì) instead of the solar or "new calendar" (xīnlì). For this reason the exact dates of a given holiday vary from year to year according to the new calendar, which is the basis for work and school schedules.

The longest and most important holiday is "chūnjié" (Spring Festival), which is the old lunar calendar's New Year (xīnnián), and fills a time block of a couple of weeks in February, sometimes beginning as early as late January. Family and friends often gather for special feasts at that time, and many people shoot off fireworks and indulge in such pastimes as opera-going and folk performing arts.

The major holiday for paying one's respects to deceased ancestors, relatives, and other respected souls is "Qīngmíngjié" (Grave-sweeping Festival), usually in April, when the living tidy up the graves of the dead along with bowing repeatedly in remembrance. (The "kētóu" or kowtow prostration may on rare occasion still be observed in some remote parts of China, but it is mostly a relic of bygone days, especially in urban areas.)

The most important fall holiday is "Zhōngqiūjié" (Midautumn Festival), typically in September. Family members and friends traditionally gather to celebrate harvest time by feasting on delicacies such as a rich, sweet pastry known as a "yuèbǐng" (moon cake).

SUMMARY

To discuss having had the experience of verbing, use the VERB-guò pattern: "Lìlián fúguò Zhōng yào" (Lìlián has taken traditional Chinese medicine before). In the negative version, "guò" remains, in contrast to the completed-action "le," which drops out in the negative: "Nèige niánqīngrén méi kànguò Jīngjù" (That youth has never watched Běijīng Opera before).

When referring to "every noun," use the pattern měi + MEAS + NOUN, and insert the adverb "dōu" right before the verb; for example, "Měige nǚháizi dōu hěn piàoliàng" (Every girl is pretty). Because a handful of nouns such as "nián" (year) and "tiān" (day) are quasi measures, they do not require a measure word in this construction: "měinián" (every year), "měitiān" (every day).

An English adjective such as "happy" can be converted into an adverb that modifies a verb simply by adding "-ly" as a suffix ("happily"). A similar process occurs in many Chinese declarative sentences, where the particle "de" must be appended right after the verb in the "manner-of-verbing" construction SUBJ + VERB + de + ADV + ADJ, as in "Háizi wán de hěn gāoxìng" (The children are playing happily).

Use the adversative expression "sǐ le" (lit., "to have died") right after an adjective to mean "terribly adjective" or "adjective to death," as in "Wǒ èsǐ le" (I'm terribly hungry), and "Mínglěi xiàsǐ le" (Mínglěi was scared to death).

If you wish to speak in comparative terms about something, it is possible to say that the subject is "ADJ yìdiǎnr," as in "Zhèige fángjiān dà yìdiǎnr" (This room is a bit larger). To avoid any such comparisons, use "yǒu yìdiǎn ADJ": "Wǒ yǒu yìdiǎnr kě" (I'm a bit thirsty).

CHAPTER 19

NǏ ZĚNME BǏ WǑ SHÒU?
(How come you're slimmer than I am?)

CHAPTER OVERVIEW

1. Superlatives ("Zuì ADJ") and "Not Even a Little Bit ADJ" ("Yìdiǎnr yě bù ADJ")

2. Placing Direct Objects Before Manner-of-verbing Complements

3. Comparing Things with the Coverb "Bǐ" and an Adjective

4. Comparing Actions with the Coverb "Bǐ" and Manner-of-verbing Complements

5. Being the Same ("Yíyàng") and Different ("Bù Yíyàng")

6. Prestating Objects to Which "Dōu" Refers: OBJ1, OBJ2, SUBJ dōu VERB

7. "Lǎoshì VERB" (Always Verb) and "Chángcháng VERB" (Often Verb)

NEW VOCABULARY

TRACK 39

1.	chuān	to wear (clothing that body parts "pierce"—go into—such as pants, shirt, shoes, socks)	VERB
2.	jiàn	(measure for "shì"—things to do—and many garments)	MEAS
3.	chènshān	shirt	NOUN
4.	búcuò	be pretty good, be not bad	IDIO
5.	cuò	be wrong	ADJ
6.	bǎihuò gōngsī	department store (lit., "hundred-wares company")	PW/NOUN
7.	dōngxi	thing	NOUN
8.	zuì + ADJ	the most adjective, the adjective-est	ADV
9.	lěng	be cold	ADJ
10.	máoyī	sweater	NOUN
11.	zuìjìn	recently	TW
12.	lèi	be tired	ADJ
13.	gēn nǐ bù yíyàng	be different from you, be not the same as you	
14.	bù yíyàng	be different	ADV-ADJ
15.	yíyàng	be the same	ADJ
16.	yìdiǎnr yě bù ADJ	not even a little bit adjective	
17.	shēntǐ	body, physique	NOUN
18.	bǐ	compared to	COV
19.	qùnián	last year	TW
20.	jiànkāng	be healthy	ADJ
21.	SUBJ dōu méi VERB	SUBJ didn't verb at all	ADV1-ADV2
22.	měitiān zǎoshàng	every morning	TW
23.	yùndòng	exercise; to exercise	NOUN/VERB
24.	zuò yùndòng	to do exercises, to get exercise	VERB-OBJ
25.	shénmeyàng de NOUN	what kind of NOUN?	QW
26.	chángcháng	often	ADV

27. mànpǎo	to jog	VERB
28. màn	be slow	ADJ
29. pǎo	to run	VERB
30. liàn qìgōng	to practice "qìgōng"	VERB-OBJ
31. qìgōng	deep-breathing exercises	NOUN
32. qì	breath, air	NOUN
33. gāo	be tall	ADJ
34. A bǐ B ADJ	A is more adjective than B.	comparative pattern
35. yěxǔ	perhaps, maybe	MADV
36. kuài	be fast	ADJ
37. shòu	be thin, be slim	ADJ
38. kuàngquán shuǐ	spring water (usually the bottled fizzy type)	NOUN
39. guàibùdé	no wonder . . .	IDIO
40. guài	be strange	ADJ
41. lǎoshì VERB	always VERB	ADV
42. dǎgé	to burp	VERB-OBJ

DIALOGUE

TRACK
40

Bǐdé: Mínglěi, nǐ chuān de nèijiàn chènshān hěn búcuò. Zài nǎr mǎi de?

Mínglěi: Zài Běijīng yìjiā bǎihuò gōngsī mǎi de. Tāmen de dōngxi zuì piányi. Bǐdé, jīntiān bù lěng. Nǐ wèishénme chuān máoyī?

Bǐdé: Wǒ juéde yǒudiǎn lěng. (He yawns.) Wǒ zuìjìn yě hěn lèi.

Mínglěi: Nà wǒ jiù gēn nǐ bù yíyàng le. Wǒ yìdiǎnr yě bú lèi. Wǒde shēntǐ jīnnián bǐ qùnián jiànkāng. Wǒ dōu méi shēngbìng, yīnwèi wǒ měitiān zǎoshàng dōu yùndòng.

Bǐdé: Nǐ zuò shénmeyàng de yùndòng?

Mínglěi: Wǒ chángcháng mànpǎo. Yǒu shíhòu gēn wǒ sānjiě qù yóuyǒng, yǒu shíhòu liàn qìgōng.

Bǐdé: Nǐ bǐ Lìlián gāo, yěxǔ pǎode bǐ tā kuài.

Mínglěi: Duì. Kěshì wǒ yóuyǒng yóude bǐ tā màn. Bǐdé, nǐ bú zuò yùndòng, zěnme bǐ wǒ shòu?

Bǐdé: Yīnwèi wǒ qìshuǐ, jiǔ dōu bù hē. Wǒ zhǐ hē kuàngquán shuǐ.

Mínglěi: Guàibùdé nǐ lǎoshì dǎgé!

DIALOGUE TRANSLATION

Peter: Mínglěi, that shirt you're wearing is pretty good. Where did you buy it?

Mínglěi: I bought it at a department store in Běijīng. Their things are the cheapest. Peter, it's not cold today. Why are you wearing a sweater?

Peter: I feel a bit cold. (He yawns.) I've also been tired lately.

Mínglěi: Well, then, I'm different from you. I'm not even a little bit tired. My body's healthier this year than last year. I haven't gotten sick at all because I exercise every morning.

Peter: What sort of exercise do you do?

Mínglěi: I often jog. Sometimes I swim with my third elder sister, and sometimes I practice deep-breathing exercises [qìgōng].

Peter: You're taller than Lìlián; perhaps you run faster than she does.

Mínglěi: That's right, but I swim more slowly than Lìlián. Peter, you don't exercise. How come you're slimmer than I am?

Peter: Because I don't drink either soda pop or liquor. I drink only spring water.

Mínglěi: No wonder you're always burping!

19.1 Superlatives ("Zuì ADJ") and "Not Even a Little Bit ADJ" ("Yìdiǎnr yě bù ADJ")

Superlatives

Subject	zuì	Adjective/Verb		(Object)	
Nèijiàn máoyī	zuì	hǎokàn.			(That sweater is prettiest.)
Tā	zuì		ài	hē Yīngguó chá.	(He loves to drink English tea the most.)
Nàr de dōngxi	zuì	piányi.			(The things there are cheapest.)

To make a plain adjective into a superlative ("the most adjective," "adjective-est"), simply place the adverb "zuì" before the adjective. Examples are "Zhōngguó cài zuì hǎochī" (Chinese food is the tastiest), "Nèijiàn chènshān zuì zāng" (That shirt is dirtiest), and "Něiwèi xiǎojiě shì zuì piàoliàng de?" (Which young lady is the prettiest one?).

"Not Even a Little Bit ADJ"

Subject	yìdiǎnr yě bù	Adjective
Nǐ gēge (Your older brother is not short at all.)	yìdiǎnr yě bù	ǎi.
Zhèijiàn chènshān (This shirt is not short at all.)	yìdiǎnr yě bù	duǎn.

Subject	yìdiǎnr yě bù	Verb		(Object)
Tā mèimei (His younger sister doesn't like to cook at all.)	yìdiǎnr yě bù	xǐhuān	zuò	fàn.
Nèige háizi (That child would not like to go to school at all.)	yìdiǎnr yě bù	xiǎng	shàng	xué.

At the other end of the spectrum, use "yìdiǎnr yě bù ADJ" or "yìdiǎnr dōu bù ADJ" after the subject to express the idea of "not even a little bit adjective" or "not at all" adjective. Examples include "Shí'èrhào fángjiān yìdiǎnr yě bù zāng" (Room 12 isn't even a little bit dirty), "Zhèixiē dōngxi yìdiǎnr yě bù piányi" (These things aren't even a little bit cheap), "Háizi jīntiān yìdiǎnr dōu bú è" (The children aren't even a little bit hungry today).

You may plug in a verb for an adjective in this pattern, and a direct object can often be brought around before the verb to a position either before or after the subject: "Zhèige rén shì chī sù de, ròu yìdiǎnr yě bù chī" (This person is a vegetarian, and doesn't eat even a little bit of meat), "Zhāngláng, wǒmen yìdiǎnr dōu bù xǐhuān" (We don't like cockroaches even a little bit), and "Lǎoshī shuō de huà, Mínglěi yìdiǎnr yě bù dǒng" (Mínglěi doesn't understand even a little bit of what the teacher said).

Exercises for 19.1: Use "zuì" or "yìdiǎnr yě bù" when you translate the following into Chinese.

1. That hotel is the most expensive; their service (fúwù) is also the best.

   _____

   _____

2. In my family (wǒ jiālǐ) my mom is the busiest, but she is not even a little bit tired.

   _____

   _____

3. She loves to eat sautéed vegetables the most.

_____

_____

4. We don't like mice even a little bit.

_____

_____

5. In the restaurant, my younger brother eats only dumplings. He doesn't eat the other dishes at all.

_____

_____

19.2 Placing Direct Objects Before Manner-of-verbing Complements

Subject	(Verb	Object)	Verb	de	Adverb	Adjective
Nǐ dìdi	zuò	shì	zuò	de	fēicháng	hǎo.
(Your younger brother handles matters extremely well.)						
Tā	yóu	yǒng	yóu	de	bú	màn.
(She doesn't swim slowly.)						
Nǐ	xiě	zì	xiě	de	yóuqí	piàoliàng.
(You write especially prettily.)						

The preceding chapter introduced manner-of-verbing complements in sentences without direct objects, using the pattern SUBJ + VERB + de + ADV + ADJ, as in "Mínglěi zǒude nàme kuài" (Mínglěi walks so quickly). If you wanted to add a direct object such as "lù" (road), you could not insert it in its ordinary slot after the verb, because the manner-of-verbing unit VERB + de + ADV + ADJ is an integral whole that should not be split up through the insertion of an object.

The most common way of avoiding "traffic congestion" after the verb in such a sentence is to say the verb twice, first followed by the direct object and then followed by the manner-of-verbing complement: SUBJ + VERB + OBJ + VERB + de + ADV + ADJ, as in "Mínglěi zǒu lù zǒude nàme kuài" (same translation as above), "Lǐ Lǎoshī shuō huà shuōde hěn màn" (Teacher Lǐ speaks slowly), and "Zhèige Měiguórén ná kuàizi náde fēicháng hǎo" (This American holds chopsticks extremely well). Although the verb is repeated once in each of these examples, the sentences do not sound repetitious or excessively wordy in Chinese.

Exercises for 19.2: Use the SUBJ + (VERB + OBJ) + VERB + de + ADV + ADJ pattern in the following sentences.

1. Her mom runs extremely fast.

   _____

2. That American speaks Chinese very slowly.

   _____

3. These children hold knives and forks especially well.

   _____

4. His younger sister writes (xiě zì) extremely prettily (. . . jí le).

   _____

5. Does your boyfriend cook well?

   _____

19.3 Comparing Things with the Coverb "Bǐ" and an Adjective

Noun 1	bǐ	Noun 2	Adjective	
Nǐ	bǐ	wǒ	gāo.	(You are taller than I.)
Wǒ	bǐ	nǐ	ǎi.	(I am shorter than you.)
Tā	bǐ	nǐ	dà.	(He's bigger/older than you.)
Nǐ	bǐ	tā	xiǎo.	(You're smaller/ younger than he.)

To express the idea that NOUN1 is more adjective than NOUN2, use the coverb "bǐ" (lit., "compared to") in the comparative pattern, NOUN1 + bǐ + NOUN2 + ADJ: "Jīnnián bǐ qùnián lěng" (This year is colder than last year), "Shū bǐ bàozhǐ yǒu yìsi" (Books are more interesting than newspapers), and "Háizi bǐ dàrén kě'ài" (Children are cuter than adults ["big people"]).

Note that even in the absence of the coverb "bǐ," an adjective without any adverbial modifier such as "hěn" or "bù" has a comparative connotation: "Mínglěi gāo" implies that the speaker is comparing Mínglěi with someone shorter, and thus means "Mínglěi is taller." To avoid the comparative connotation of a predicate adjective when you don't particularly want to use "bù" or some other adverb, use the dummy adverb, an unstressed "hěn," as in "Mínglěi hěn gāo" (Mínglěi is tall).

Noun 1	bǐ	Noun 2	Adjective	de duō/ duō le	
Nǐ	bǐ	wǒ	shòu	de duō.	(You are much slimmer than I.)
Wǒ	bǐ	nǐ	pàng	duō le.	(I am much fatter than you.)
Lóngxiā	bǐ	zhūròu	guì	de duō.	(Lobster is much more expensive than pork.)

If you want to say that NOUN1 is *much* more adjective than NOUN2, never use the comparison-defeating "hěn"; instead add the two syllables "de duō" or "duō le" directly after the adjective: NOUN1 + bǐ + NOUN2 + ADJ + de duō (or duō le). Examples are "Tángcù yú bǐ chǎo fàn guì duō le" (Sweet-and-sour fish is much more expensive than fried rice), "Zhōngguó bǐ Yīngguó dàde duō" (China is much larger than England), and "Nǚrén de yīfu bǐ nánrén de hǎokàn duō le" (Women's clothing is much nicer looking than men's).

Noun 1	bǐ	Noun 2	Adjective	yìdiǎnr	
Pángxiè	bǐ	xiā(zi)	piányi	yìdiǎnr.	(Crabs are a bit cheaper than shrimps.)
Nǐ	bǐ	tā	cōngmíng	yìdiǎnr.	(You are a bit more clever than he.)

When NOUN1 is *a bit* more adjective than NOUN2, add "yìdiǎnr" instead of "de duō" or "duō le" directly after the adjective: NOUN1 + bǐ + NOUN2 + ADJ + yìdiǎnr. Three examples are "Zhèijiàn chènshān bǐ nèijiàn piányi yìdiǎnr" (This shirt is a bit cheaper than that one), "Lìlián bǐ Ānnà lèi yìdiǎnr" (Lìlián is a bit more tired than Ānnà), and "Lǎoshǔ bǐ zhāngláng zāng yìdiǎnr" (Mice are a bit dirtier than cockroaches).

Exercises for 19.3: Rearrange the words in each entry to make a correct sentence according to the English meaning given.

1. nèiběn shū bǐ guì shū zhèiběn (This book is more expensive than that book.)

   _____

2. suān tángcù suānlà duō tāng yú de bǐ (Hot-and-sour soup is much more sour than sweet-and-sour fish.)

   _____

3. piào le piào bǐ duō huǒchē guì fēijī (Airplane tickets are much more expensive than train tickets.)

   _____

4. yìdiǎnr Měiguó bǐ xiǎng Zhōngguó dà wǒ (I think China is a bit bigger than the United States.)

   _____

5. nǚrén yǐwéi de chènshān piàoliàng duō de tā nánrén bǐ de (He mistakenly thought that men's shirts were much prettier than women's.)

   _____

19.4 Comparing Actions with the Coverb "Bǐ" and Manner-of-verbing Complements

Subject	(Verb Object)		Verb	de	bǐ	Noun	Adjective
Nǐ	kàn	shū	kàn	de	bǐ	tā	kuài.
(You read books faster than he.)							
Nèige rén	yóu	yǒng	yóu	de	bǐ	nǐ	màn.
(That person swims more slowly than you.)							
Měiguórén	chī	shēngcài	chī	de	bǐ	Zhōngguórén	duō.
(Americans eat more lettuce than the Chinese.)							
Nǐ	xiě	Zhōngguózì	xiě	de	bǐ	wǒ	hǎokàn.
(You write Chinese characters more prettily than I.)							

In order to say that Mínglěi swims more slowly than Lìlián, we can combine the basic patterns of Sections 19.2 and 19.3 into SUBJ + VERB + OBJ + VERB + de + bǐ + NOUN + ADJ, which states that the subject verbs the object more adjectively than the noun: "Mínglěi yóuyǒng yóude bǐ Lìlián màn." Other examples are "Ānnà mǎi dōngxi mǎide bǐ Lìlián shǎo" (Ānnà buys fewer things than Lìlián), "Mínglěi chī fàn chīde bǐ Bǐdé kuài" (Mínglěi eats more quickly than Peter), and "Dàrén yòng kuàizi yòngde bǐ xiǎo haízi hǎo" (Adults are better at using chopsticks than young children are). In a less common but acceptable variation on this pattern, the coverbial phrase (bǐ + NOUN) is moved up between the subject and the verb. When this variant, SUBJ + bǐ + NOUN + VERB + OBJ + VERB + de + ADJ, is used, the last sentence above is "Dàrén bǐ xiǎo háizi yòng kuàizi yòngde hǎo." There is no change in meaning.

Exercises for 19.4: Use the SUBJ + (VERB + OBJ) + VERB + de + bǐ + NOUN + ADJ pattern to answer the following questions.

1. A: Nǐ zǔmǔ mǎi dōngxi mǎide duō bùduō?
   B: _____. (My grandmother buys more things than I.)

   _____

2. A: Nǐde Měiguó péngyou shuō Zhōngguóhuà shuōde zěnmeyàng?
   B: _____. (She speaks Chinese faster than my Japanese friend.)

   _____

3. A: Nǐ gēn nǐ péngyou dōu zhùde lí huǒchēzhàn hěn jìn ma? (Do both you and your friend live close to the train station?)
   B: Bù, _____. (No, he lives closer than I.)

   _____

4. A: Lín Tàitai de jiějie bāo jiǎozi bāode zěnmeyàng?
   B: _____. (Her elder sister wraps dumplings more slowly than she, but better than she.)

   _____

5. A: Nǐ kàn Zhōngwén bào kànde bǐ nǐ māma kuài ma?
   B: _____. (No. My mom reads Chinese newspapers faster than I do.)

   _____

19.5 Being the Same ("Yíyàng") and Different ("Bù Yíyàng")

Noun 1	gēn/hé	Noun 2	(bù)	yíyàng	(Adjective)
Zhèige zì (This character is the same as that one.)	gēn	nèige zì		yíyàng.	
Nǐ jiā (Your home is different from mine.)	gēn	wǒ jiā	bù	yíyàng.	
Nǐ jiějie (Your older sister is as clever as you.)	gēn	nǐ		yíyàng	cōngmíng.

To express the idea that two nouns are the same or different, use "gēn" instead of "bǐ" as the coverb: first, NOUN1 + gēn + NOUN2 + yíyàng (NOUN1 is the same as NOUN2); second, NOUN1 + gēn + NOUN2 + bù yíyàng (NOUN1 is different from NOUN2). You would say, for example, "Nǐde máoyī gēn wǒde yíyàng" (Your sweater is the same as mine), and "Zhèijiā bǎihuò gōngsī gēn nèijiā bù yíyàng" (This department store is different from that one).

By simply adding an adjective at the end of the pattern of sameness above (NOUN1 + gēn + NOUN2 + yíyàng + ADJ), you can indicate that NOUN1 is as adjective as NOUN2. Examples are "Hǎixiān tāng gēn tángcù yú yíyàng guì" (Seafood soup is as expensive as sweet-and-sour fish), and "Xiě xìn gēn dǎ diànhuà yíyàng fāngbiàn" (Writing letters is as convenient as making phone calls).

Exercises for 19.5: Use "gēn" and "yíyàng" to say each of the following in Chinese.

1. This airport is different from that one.

_____

2. Is that bank as convenient as this one?

_____

3. I think this deer is as cute as that one.

_____

4. Mr. Lǐ is as tired as Mr. Hán.

_____

5. Is writing with the hand as nice-looking as writing done with the computer?

19.6 Prestating Objects to Which "Dōu" Refers: OBJ1, OBJ2, SUBJ dōu VERB

Object 1,	Object 2,	Subject	dūo	Verb	
Yīngguó chá, (She drinks both English tea and Chinese tea.)	Zhōngguó chá,	tā	dōu	hē.	
Lóngxiā, (We love to eat both lobster and crabs.)	pángxiè,	wǒmen	dōu	ài	chī.

When "dōu" refers to the subjects in a sentence, there is no reason to alter the basic Chinese word order of subject-verb-object, as in "Lìlián gēn Mínglěi dōu xǐhuān qù yóuyǒng" (Both Lìlián and Mínglěi like to go swimming). However, "dōu" cannot ordinarily go before any word to which it refers, so any direct objects to which "dōu" refers must be pulled back in front of the verb and prestated before or after the subject.

Moreover, when these direct objects are prestated, usually no conjunction such as "gēn" or "hé" connects them; there is merely a pause marked by a comma: "Lǜchá, píjiǔ, bàba dōu xǐhuān hē" (Dad likes to drink both green tea and beer), "Wǒ yángròu, gǒuròu dōu bù chī" (I eat neither mutton nor dogmeat), "Yīfu, chīde dōngxi, Māma dōu xiǎng mǎi" (Mom would like to buy both clothing and things to eat).

Exercises for 19.6: Use the OBJ1, OBJ2, SUBJ dōu VERB pattern in the following sentences.

1. My manager likes neither swimming nor jogging.

---

2. Miss Wáng would like to eat both Chinese and American food (cài).

---

3. My uncle is not allowed to drink either beer, soda pop, or liquor.

_____

4. That young man should not buy either expensive or useless (méiyòng de) things.

_____

5. This clerk knows how to write both Chinese and English letters.

_____

19.7 "Lǎoshì VERB" (Always Verb) and "Chángcháng VERB" (Often Verb)

Chinese adverbs that describe the frequency of verbing typically contain two syllables and fit into the standard adverbial slot between the subject and the verb. Examples include "Mínglěi chángcháng yùndòng" (Mínglěi often exercises), and "Bǐdé lǎoshì hē kuàngquán shuǐ" (Peter always drinks bottled spring water).

Exercises for 19.7: Make up conversations using the situations given.

You go to China to visit a friend. She looks even younger and prettier than before. You ask her, "How come you're so pretty recently?" She says, "Because I often practice deep-breathing exercise, my body's healthier this year than last year."

You go mountain climbing with her. You say you're extremely tired (-jí le). She says, "I don't feel even a little bit tired."

You ask her what kinds of things she eats. She says, "I like to eat vegetables the most." You ask, "Do you always eat vegetables?" She replies, "No, I eat both vegetables and meat. These two kinds of things are both good for your health."

You ask her what kinds of exercises she thinks you should do. She suggests, "Perhaps you can jog often, and sometimes you can also go swimming. Moreover, I will teach (jiāo) you deep-breathing exercises."

CULTURE NOTES

Speakers of English can "wear" or "don" just about any garment or type of jewelry. However, the Chinese language uses a few different verbs, depending on the way in which the garment is worn or the nature of the garment itself.

The most important Chinese verb in matters of clothing is "chuān," which still carries its original meaning of "pierce" in that its direct objects are garments that are "pierced" by various body parts. You "chuān" (wear) most kinds of clothing from the neck down, including "dàyī" (overcoats), "yǔyī" (raincoats), "xīfú" (suits), "yīshang" (dresses), "wàitào" (jackets), "bèixīn" (vests), "chènshān" (shirts and blouses), "kùzi" (pants), "qúnzi" (skirts), "nèiyī" (underwear), "duǎnkù" (shorts), "wàzi" (socks), "xiézi" (shoes), "liángxié" (sandals), and "tuōxié" (slippers).

The next most important verb for wearing is "dài," which is used for wearing such things as "zhūbǎo" (jewelry), "màozi" (hats), "shǒubiǎo" (wristwatches), "shǒutào" (gloves), "yǎnjìng" (eyeglasses), and "lǐngdài" (neckties). Less important, the "bāo" of "wrapping" dumplings is also used for babies or toddlers wearing "niàobù" (diapers), and "wéi" (encircling) is the correct choice for wearing a "wéijīn" (muffler).

SUMMARY

To make an adjective into a superlative ("the most ADJ, the ADJ-est"), simply insert the adverb "zuì" before the adjective: "Zhōngguó chá zuì hǎohē" (Chinese tea is the tastiest).

If instead you wish to compare two things by saying that one thing is "more ADJ" or "ADJ-er" than the other, use the pattern NOUN1 + bǐ + NOUN2 + ADJ, as in "Háizi bǐ dàrén kě'ài" (Children are cuter than adults). To express the idea "a bit more ADJ," simply append "yìdiǎnr" to the adjective, as in "Jīnnián bǐ qùnián rè yìdiǎnr" (This year is a bit hotter than last year). If the first noun is "much more ADJ," affix "de duō" or "duō le" to the adjective instead: "Kuàngquán shuǐ bǐ qìshuǐ hǎo duō le," or "Kuàngquán shuǐ bǐ qìshuǐ hǎo de duō" (Spring water is much better than soda pop).

When saying that two things are the same (or different), use the coverb "gēn" and the adjective "yíyàng" (or "bù yíyàng" for "different"). Examples are "Nǐde máoyī gēn wǒde yíyàng" (Your sweater is the same as mine), and "Zhōngguó cài gēn Rìběn cài

Eye-catching ornamentation of the roof and eaves is a hallmark of traditional Chinese architecture, as in this four-story pavilion in Sìchuān province.

bù yíyàng" (Chinese cuisine is different from Japanese cuisine). By simply adding an adjective at the end of the first sample sentence in this paragraph, you can indicate that NOUN1 is as ADJ as NOUN2: "Nǐde máoyī gēn wǒde yíyàng guì" (Your sweater is as expensive as mine).

When the adverb "dōu" (both/all) refers to two or more direct objects, they must be pulled back before the verb to a position either preceding or following the subject: "Chènshān, máoyī, wǒ dōu xiǎng mǎi" (I would like to buy both shirts and sweaters), and "Tā píjiǔ, qìshuǐ, dōu bù hē" (She drinks neither beer nor soda pop).

CHAPTER 20

ZHŌNGGUÓ ZÌ, ZĚNME XUÉ?

(How do you study Chinese characters?)

CHAPTER OVERVIEW

1. Speaking and Understanding Chinese versus Reading and Writing Chinese

2. Clearing Up Common Misconceptions About the Chinese Writing System

3. Traditional or Long-form Characters versus Simplified Characters

4. Character-practice Paper and Stroke Order in Writing Characters

---

20.1 Speaking and Understanding Chinese versus Reading and Writing Chinese

Conservative estimates indicate that well over 100 million teenage and adult Chinese who can speak and understand their language cannot read or write it. This army of illiterates naturally tends to encounter more inconveniences in life than their educated fellow citizens, but the fact that they can function in their daily lives is worth noting for the beginning Chinese student with limited time for language study.

If you have the time and staying power to study Chinese intensively over an extended period, you should by all means work toward a proficiency in reading and writing, along with improving your skills in listening comprehension and speaking; experience shows that each of the four skills helps reinforce the others. If, however, you are working under severe time constraints or simply lack the means to study Chinese over the long term in a comprehensive way, you will achieve more practical results by focusing on speaking and listening comprehension than by spreading yourself too thin in four different directions.

20.2 Clearing Up Common Misconceptions About the Chinese Writing System

It is widely known that the Chinese character writing system differs greatly from the alphabetic systems in common use throughout most of the world. The problem is that in describing *how* written Chinese differs from alphabetic writing systems, much baseless speculation and wishful thinking on the subject have been repeated so often that the sober interpretations of *bona fide* linguists and other qualified scholars are frequently overlooked.

The Misconception That Chinese Characters Are Pictographic

One popular notion that has survived a mountain of evidence to the contrary is that Chinese characters are pictographic or like little pictures, and that you have to learn many thousands of these totally unique little pictures before you can hope to read the front page of a Chinese newspaper. Admittedly, a very small number (less than one percent) of Chinese characters such as the "rì" of "Xīngqīrì" (Sunday) and the "yuè" of "yuèliàng" (moon) originally developed from pictographs.

What is more important, however, is that these pictographic elements have been assimilated into a real-world writing system in which they most commonly appear as merely one component within more complex characters that contain components related to both sound and meaning. There is a large but finite number of these components, and the task of learning new characters eventually becomes one of reassembling these familiar if sometimes cumbersome components into new configurations, and mastering the relevant pronunciations and meanings.

Moreover, the vast majority of characters combine with other characters to form a multitudinous variety of compounds, most commonly of two characters and the same number of syllables; truly advanced students of Chinese typically spend more time learning new combinations of familiar characters than on mastering new characters from scratch. Even very well-educated native speakers typically learn no more than a few thousand characters altogether, and a well-rounded student with a solid foundation in the language who has mastered from 1,200 to 1,500 characters can tackle a contemporary newspaper with the aid of a good dictionary.

(1) Oracle bone graphs	(2) Seal script characters	(3) Brush-written characters	(4) Standard form characters	Pīnyīn	English meaning
		月	月	yuè	moon; month
		水	水	shuǐ	water
		雨	雨	yǔ	rain
		人	人	rén	person
		女	女	nǔ	woman
		母	母	mǔ	mother

Most characters in common use today evolved from less abstract prototypes that date back to ancient times. The pictographs above amount to only 1% of all characters when occurring as independent graphs. More commonly, such pictographs appear as simply one component within a more complex character consisting of two or more components, one of which hints at the character's pronunciation, while another hints at the character's meaning. A sense of the evolution of characters may be perceived in the above chart, starting from the left: (1) Oracle bone graphs are the earliest known version of Chinese characters. Over three millennia ago, during the Shāng dynasty, oracle bone graphs were carved on bony surfaces, either the relatively flat underside of large tortoise shells, or else on an ox's shoulder blade. (2) Seal script characters were a subsequent development, having been the dominant form of writing during the Qín dynasty over 22 centuries ago. Since then, they were significantly but less frequently used in the carved seals or chops that were stamped on documents or pictorial art. (3) Over most of the past 2000 years, characters have usually been written with a brush such as that used by a painter to sketch portraits, allowing lines of varying thickness to be drawn. (4) This is the modern standard form of the character, less cursive in style than in the row to its immediate left.

The Misconception That Chinese Is Essentially "Ideographic"

Another widespread misconception about the Chinese writing system that many intellectuals with no real expertise in linguistics still espouse is that Chinese is essentially "ideographic," and that all characters are "ideographs." To be sure, a very small number of characters out of the total are ideographs that graphically represent an idea without providing any phonetic clues as to the pronunciation, such as "shàng" (above/on), "zhōng" (middle), and "xià" (below).

However, these true ideographs amount to only one to two percent of the total number of characters, and a given ideograph often appears less commonly standing alone than as one component within a more complex character, where it may serve a phonetic function. For instance, the right-hand side of the first character in Confucius's given name, Zhòngní, is the above-mentioned ideographic component "zhōng," which is used phonetically in this famous case. In other words, a character that originated as an ideograph soon began functioning as a phonetic component in more complex characters, thus pointing to the sound rather than the meaning of the more complex characters.

The Phonetic and "Signific" Elements in Chinese Characters

The vast majority of Chinese characters—over 90 percent of the total—are complex characters that contain both a phonetic element that hints at the pronunciation and a "signific" element that provides a rough clue to the meaning. The reasons that the phonetic and signific elements of a character provide no more than hints of a given character's pronunciation and meaning are complex, and include the very limited number of significs (214 is the most widely accepted number) and the myriad changes in pronunciation and usage since the ancient origins of written Chinese during the Shāng dynasty, some three and a half millennia in the past. What this means in practical terms is that while characters become easier to learn over time as the student masters more and more of the hundreds of basic building blocks or components, much memorization is required to yoke a pronunciation to each new character the student learns.

The Special Problem of Pronunciation

Chinese characters are thus very far from being self-pronouncing, especially if compared with the clear, systematic spelling of orthographically tidy languages like Spanish and Italian. Still, recent linguistic studies of how the brain processes written Chinese suggest that once a student has mastered a typical character's graphical form and pronunciation, he depends largely on the phonetic cue in the character when identifying and processing it during reading. The problem is that sustained study and repeated practice of characters and their pronunciation are required before these phonetic cues can be processed efficiently in reading. Nevertheless, tens of millions of Chinese schoolchildren achieve this feat every year, though at a cost in classroom hours and after-school homework assignments that far exceeds the amount of time schoolchildren elsewhere must typically spend to gain a solid foundation in their own alphabetic written languages.

Arguments Against Replacing Characters with Romanization

One might wonder why the Chinese do not simply convert from a character-based writing system to an alphabetic system such as that of the pīnyīn romanization used in this book. Several practical problems militate against such a change. Chinese is not actually a single language, but rather an assemblage of half a dozen related Sinitic languages that share a single writing system. If standard Mandarin ("pǔtōnghuà") were romanized to the exclusion of other important Sinitic languages such as Cantonese in southeast China, China's linguistic and even political unity might unravel, for well over 100 million people in one of China's most dynamic and prosperous regions would probably feel disenfranchised.

Many well-educated Chinese particularly fear the prospect that romanization would cut off future generations from China's singularly massive and unbroken cultural legacy of over 3,500 years, since the very thought of converting mountains of old Chinese books to romanized form boggles the mind. Even if someone were to wave a magic computerized wand and thereby convert all these books to romanized form, the books written in classical Chinese would often be barely intelligible in romanization. The Chinese language teems with homonyms and near sound-alike terms that are more easily distinguished from one another via characters than through romanization; this problem is more severe with terse classical Chinese writings than with the more expansive idiom characteristic of modern-day vernacular Chinese. For these reasons, at least over the foreseeable future, the character-based writing system appears to be well entrenched.

20.3 Traditional or Long-form Characters versus Simplified Characters

If Chinese characters cannot be replaced with an alphabetic system because of practical difficulties, at least they can be simplified somewhat to a smaller number of strokes per character. This has happened to some extent on both sides of the Taiwan Straits on an informal level, for people have typically preferred the simpler of two competing forms of the same character, especially when writing longhand.

Simplification in the PRC

The process of simplifying characters accelerated quite a bit during the early 1950s in the PRC, where standard lists of simplified characters came out in batches and were systematically incorporated into new textbooks and even most scholarly books. However, this government-enforced simplification of the language tended not to be observed in many Chinese-speaking areas outside of the PRC, so the practical effect on foreign learners interested in Chinese writings from all over the map has been the need to develop familiarity with both the traditional and simplified versions of characters. Needless to say, character simplification has not necessarily led to a simplification of the process of learning written Chinese!

Moreover, as in many other areas of life, it is easy to get too much of a good thing: one of the PRC's later batches of official simplified characters took simplification too far, creating so many unnecessary new ambiguities and easily mistaken look-alike characters that the batch had to be withdrawn.

The Best Way to Learn Characters

Experience has shown that it is easier for students to begin with the traditional long-form characters and then progress to the simplified versions than the other way around. For this reason the character glossary in Appendix 4 of this book places traditional characters before their simplified equivalents, which are in parentheses. The provision of traditional characters in Appendix 4 should not be interpreted, however, as slighting the importance of simplified characters, for relatively advanced learners need to be able to read materials written in both simplified and traditional characters. The dialogues and vocabulary lists in Appendix 5 are thus in simplified characters.

20.4 Character-practice Paper and Stroke Order in Writing Characters

Preparing Character-practice Paper

Because a character should fit neatly into a square, beginners and seasoned writers alike have often used writing paper with preprinted squares. If you have no such paper, you can make your practice master on an ordinary 8½-by-11-inch sheet of paper. After leaving almost an inch margin on all four edges of the sheet, you should have enough room left for 15 squares going across in rows and 20 squares going down in columns, or 300 squares in all per sheet. Make your 300 squares with a ruler, and check the consistency of the squares' size. Then photocopy the character-practice-sheet master and file it away for future use.

Mastering Stroke Order

You are now ready to search for an appropriate character workbook, which should have clear and fairly large model characters, some sort of indication of proper stroke order, accurate pronunciation and meaning entries, and exercises that encourage you to place newly studied characters in phrases and sentences. Characters seldom look properly proportioned if the stroke order is wrong, so it is important to learn the standard stroke order for each character and stick with it. You will also master a character more quickly if you use the same stroke order every time you write it. Also, by intoning the pronunciation of a new character out loud a few times while writing it, you can hasten the time when you have forged a strong link in your memory between the pronunciation of a character and its graphical appearance.

Five Common Characters

This chapter concludes with five common characters of large size and with stroke-order numbers denoting the place where a given stroke should begin. The five characters form the sentence "Tā shì Zhōngguó rén" (She is Chinese). Note that these characters usually consist of components that spread horizontally across the square from left to right, as with "tā," or vertically down the square from top to bottom, as in "shì." An individual given stroke also follows the pattern of left before right and top before bottom: vertical

strokes begin at the top and conclude at the bottom, while horizontal strokes begin at the left and conclude at the right. A stroke may change direction once or even twice over the course of the stroke, so it is important to begin the stroke at the point indicated by the stroke order number and to proceed downward with vertical portions of the stroke and to the right with horizontal portions. Diagonal strokes may go either from left to right or from right to left, so it is doubly important to pay attention to where the stroke begins when writing diagonals.

Any strokes located near the upper left-hand corner of the character square tend to be written first, as with "tā," while strokes that end in the bottom right-hand corner usually come at or near the very end of the stroke order, as is the case with each of the characters except "zhōng." For characters such as "guó" that are divisible into an outer enclosure and inner contents, it is standard practice to complete any top and left-hand portions of the enclosure before filling in the inner contents and concluding with the bottom of the enclosure.

Practice in writing characters for half an hour now and then can serve as a pleasant change of pace from the more fundamental tasks of learning Chinese at the beginning level: improving speaking and listening comprehension. Students who have been working with the materials in this textbook may further enhance their study of Chinese by occasionally turning to such supplements as beginning-level audio CDs, introductory language videotapes or DVDs, and a character workbook.

CULTURE NOTES

Since the 1950s, Chinese books published in the PRC have looked very similar to Western books in terms of format in that typeset sentences run horizontally from left to right on the page, and the spine of the book is on the left side as the reader opens to the first page. After all, our eyes are arranged in a horizontal line on the face, which makes horizontal type less of a strain for the eyes to follow as compared with a vertical array of words. Moreover, interspersed Western-language words and names fit more conveniently into a horizontal alignment than into the vertical alignment of a Chinese printed page. Most important, after coming to power in 1949, the present Chinese government was at loggerheads with what it derided as "feudal" Chinese cultural traditions—including the writing system—and thus felt free to intervene quite aggressively in traditional cultural practices.

On the other hand, Chinese books from Táiwān and Hong Kong and virtually all books printed in mainland China before the 1950s are printed in the traditional manner, as are practically all overseas Chinese-language publications, including newspapers. They are printed vertically, starting at the upper right-hand side of the page. Also, the spine of the book is on the right side as the reader opens

Mist-shrouded limestone cliffs rise from both banks of the mighty Cháng jiāng, or Yángzǐ River, in the Three Gorges region in eastern Sìchuān and western Húběi.

to the first page, which makes the table of contents of a traditional book appear exactly where you would expect to find the index or bibliography of a modern PRC book, and vice versa.

Vertical writing that begins at the upper-right corner is a cultural habit that extends all the way back in time to Shāng dynasty oracle-bone and bronze inscriptions of the second millenium B.C.—the millenium in which written Chinese first emerged as a sophisticated writing system. Most Chinese scribes were and still are right-handed, and it is easier for the right hand to begin writing things down on the right side of a writing medium than on the left side. The long wooden or bamboo slats of which the first Chinese books were made also seemed to lend themselves better to vertical writing than to its horizontal counterpart.

At any rate, most readers of Chinese nowadays encounter few difficulties when moving back and forth between the traditional vertical page layout and the modern horizontal array of sentences on the page.

SUMMARY

If you have the time and staying power to study Chinese intensively over an extended period, you should by all means work toward a proficiency in reading and writing characters, along with improving your skills in listening comprehension and speaking. If, however, you are working under severe time constraints or simply lack the means to study Chinese over the long term in a comprehensive way, you will achieve more practical results by focusing on speaking and listening comprehension than by spreading yourself too thin in four different directions.

Though some dictionaries include tens of thousands of characters, only a few thousand characters are commonly used, and even very well-educated Chinese usually know no more than 3,000 to 5,000 characters. If learners have a solid foundation in the language and know over 1,200 of the highest-frequency characters, they can usually read a newspaper with the aid of a good Chinese dictionary.

Contrary to popular belief, only a tiny percentage of Chinese characters are "ideographs" that convey no hints about pronunciation. Over 90 percent of Chinese characters are complex graphs that contain both a phonetic element that hints at the pronunciation and a "signific" element that provides rough clues to the meaning.

A character should be written according to the prescribed stroke order, and must fit neatly within a square. Character components spread horizontally across the square from left to right, vertically down the square from top to bottom, or a combination thereof. An individual stroke also typically follows the pattern of moving from left to right and from top to bottom. However, diagonal strokes may go either from right to left or from left to right, so beginners must always note where a stroke begins.

APPENDIX 1: ANSWERS TO EXERCISES IN CHAPTERS 3–19

CHAPTER 3

Exercises for 3.1
1. Nǐhǎo!
2. Nǐ bàba hǎo ma?
3. Tā hěn hǎo.
4. Nǐ māma ne?
5. Nínhǎo!
6. Wáng Lǎoshī hǎo!
7. Mínglěi, zàijiàn.

Exercises for 3.2
1. Mínglěi, wǒ búshì nǐ māma.
2. Mínglěi, nǐ búshì lǎoshī.
3. Lǎoshī, nǐ bù máng.
4. Wǒ shì māmī, búshì māomī.
5. Wǒ shì Mǐ Lǎoshī, búshì Mǐ Lǎoshǔ.

Exercises for 3.3
1. Lǎoshī, nǐ máng ma? (OR Lǎoshī, nín máng ma?)
2. Wǒ hěn máng.
3. Nǐ ne?
4. Wǒ yě hěn máng.
5. Wǒ búshì lǎoshī.
6. Wǒ bàba yě búshì lǎoshī.

Exercises for 3.4
1. Nǐ shì tā māma. Nǐ shì tā māma ma?
2. Tā búshì nǐ bàba. Tā shì nǐ bàba ma?
3. Lǐ Lǎoshī búshì lǎoshǔ. Lǐ Lǎoshī shì lǎoshǔ ma?
4. Wǒ māma bù máng. Wǒ māma máng ma?
5. Tā bàba búshì lǎoshī. Tā bàba shì lǎoshī ma?

CHAPTER 4

Exercises for 4.1
1. Qǐngwèn, guìxìng, shénme
2. Wǒ jiào, nǐ jiào shénme míngzi?
3. xìng, Xiǎojiě, gāoxìng rènshì nǐ

4. nǐ jiào shénme míngzi?

Wǒ jiào Hán Lìlián.

5. Tā jiào shénme míngzi?

Tā jiào Chén Dàwèi.

Exercises for 4.2

1. Tā shì wǒde xuéshēng.

2. Tā shì nǐ jiějie ma?

3. Tāde míngzi búshì Hán Lìlián.

4. Wǒ shì tā(de) gōngsī de jīnglǐ.

5. Hán Lǎoshī shì wǒ péngyou de māma.

6. Tā búshì nǐ péngyou de yóuyǒng jiàoliàn ma?

Exercises for 4.3

1. Tā shì nǐde nǚpéngyou. Tā shì búshì nǐde nǚpéngyou?

2. Wǒ shì Wáng Lǎoshī de xuéshēng. Wǒ shì búshì Wáng Lǎoshī de xuéshēng?

3. Tā shì Lǐ Jiàoliàn de péngyou. Tā shì búshì Lǐ Jiàoliàn de péngyou?

4. Nǐ shì Mínglěi de bàba. Nǐ shì búshì Mínglěi de bàba?

5. Tā shì Hán Jīnglǐ de Sānjiě. Tā shì búshì Hán Jīnglǐ de Sānjiě?

Exercises for 4.4

1. A: Tā shì shéi?

2. B: Tā shì wǒ(de) gōngsī de jīnglǐ.

3. A: Tā jiào shénme míngzi?

4. B: Tā jiào Lǐ Míng.

5. A: Tā shì shéi?

6. B: Tā shì wǒ jiějie.

7. A: Tā shì xuéshēng ma?

8. B: Bù (OR Búshì), tā búshì xuéshēng.

9. A: Tā shì lǎoshī ma?

10. B: Shì (OR Duì), Tā shì lǎoshī.

Exercises for 4.5

1. nǚ, nán

2. nán lǎoshī, nǚ lǎoshī

3. nǚxuéshēng, nǚpéngyou

4. nán

5. nǚ

CHAPTER 5

Exercises for 5.1

1. yǒu

2. háiyǒu

3. yǒu méiyǒu
4. yígòng yǒu
5. méiyǒu
6. yě yǒu

Exercises for 5.2
1. qīge
2. yìtiáo
3. sìge
4. liùzhī
5. jiǔzhāng
6. bātiáo
7. wǔge
8. sānzhī
9. shízhāng
10. liǎngzhī

Exercises for 5.3
1. Zhè shì wǒ bàba.
2. Nèige rén shì shéi?
3. Nèige rén shì tāde Zhōngwén lǎoshī.
4. Zhè shì shénme?
5. Zhè shì wǒ dìdi de gǒu.
6. Nèige gōngsī de jīnglǐ hěn máng.
7. Zhèizhāng zhàopiàn búshì wǒ mèimei de.

Exercises for 5.4
1. zěnme shuō
2. yǒu jǐge
3. yǒu jǐzhī
4. Zhōngwén zěnme shuō.
5. Nǐ yǒu jǐge xiōngdì jiěmèi?
   Yígòng (yǒu) sānge rén.

CHAPTER 6

Exercises for 6.1
I. shíjiǔ, èrshísì, sānshíwǔ, sìshíqī, wǔshíliù, liùshísān, qīshíyī, bāshíèr, jiǔshíjiǔ
II. 1. Jǐdiǎn, shíèr, sìshíbā
   2. zǎoshàng jiǔ, bàn
   3. wǎnshàng bā, èrshíqī
   4. xiàwǔ sān, sānshíliù
   5. jǐdiǎn, shídiǎn wǔshíwǔ (fēn)
   6. shíyīdiǎn èrshíwǔ (fēn)

Exercises for 6.2
1. Wǒmen yào qù fēijīchǎng.
2. Tāmen liǎngdiǎn shíèrfēn yǒu shì.
3. Wǒmen gōngsī yǒu liǎngge jīnglǐ.
4. Tāmen liǎngdiǎn èrshí yào hē chá.
5. Wǒmen lǎoshī jiā yǒu liǎngzhī māo.

Exercises for 6.3
1. Wǒmen hē chá ba.
2. Bié jiào chūzū qìchē.
3. Nǐmen qù fēijīchǎng ba.
4. Qǐng bié jiào wǒ lǎoshī.
5. Qǐng bié kàn wǒde zhàopiàn.

Exercises for 6.4
1. yào yìzhāng zhàopiàn.
2. yào hē chá.
3. Tā sìdiǎn sānshíwǔ yào jiào chūzū qìchē.
4. Wǒmen yào qù tāde gōngsī.
5. qù Hán Jiàoliàn jiā yóuyǒng.

Exercises for 6.6
1. Yǐjīng sāndiǎn le.
2. Lǐ Xiānsheng búshì jīnglǐ le.
3. Wǒmen bú qù fēijīchǎng le.
4. Tāde lǎoshī bú jiào chūzū qìchē le.
5. Wǒ dìdi búyào kàn nǐde chǒngwù le.

CHAPTER 7

Exercises for 7.1
1. Wǒmen yǒu dìtú.
2. Nǐmen yǒu méiyǒu Yīngwén cídiǎn?
3. Zhōngguó dìtú yìzhāng shísānkuài wǔmáo.
4. Cídiǎn yìběn duōshǎo qián?
5. Shū yìběn jǐkuài qián?

Exercises for 7.2
1. Yīngwén
2. Zhōngguó
3. Měiguó
4. Zhōngwén
5. Yīngguó
6. Fǎwén

Exercises for 7.3
1. A: Nǐmen mài Zhōngwén shū ma?
2. B: Duì, wǒmen mài (Zhōngwén shū).
3. A: Yìběn duōshǎo qián?
4. B: Yìběn jiǔkuài liǎngmáo.
5. A: Wǒ mǎi sìběn, gěi nǐ wǔshíkuài.
6. B: Zhǎo nǐ shísānkuài liǎngmáo.

Exercises for 7.4
1. Nǐ yào mǎi bàozhǐ ma?
2. Nǐmen mài Yīngwén bào(zhǐ) ma?
3. Nàme, nǐmen mài búmài Zhōngwén bào(zhǐ)?
4. Yífèn bào(zhǐ) duōshǎo qián?
5. Nǐmen yě mài Zhōngguó dìtú ma?

Exercises for 7.5
1. Tāmen zhǐ mài Yīngwén zázhì.
2. Wǒ bàba yě bú kàn Zhōngwén bàozhǐ.
3. Wǒ zài gěi nǐ yìběn Hànyǔ cídiǎn.
4. Tā māma yě méiyǒu Měiguó péngyou.
5. Nèige háizi yào zài mǎi yìzhī chǒngwù.

Exercises for 7.6
2. B: Yìběn shíqīkuài wǔmáo.
3. A: Wǒ mǎi sānběn. Gěi nǐ liùshíkuài.
5. A: Búshì yígòng wǔshíèrkuài wǔmáo ma?
7. A: Wǒ hái yào mǎi yìběn Yīng-Hàn cídiǎn.
9. A: Nèiběn búshì Yīng-Hàn cídiǎn ma?

CHAPTER 8

Exercises for 8.1
1. Wǒmen wǔge rén.
2. Nǐmen Měiguórén
   Wǒmen Měiguórén
3. tāde Měiguó péngyou Hán Mínglěi
4. Nèiwèi lǎoshī jiào shénme míngzi?
5. Nǐmen Zhōngguórén yě ài liáo tiān ma?

Exercises for 8.2
1. gēn, lái
2. gēn, qù
3. gēn, qù
4. gēn, yìqǐ
5. gēn, yìqǐ qù
6. gēn, lái

Exercises for 8.3
1. sānbǎilíngjiǔ
2. èrlínglíngbānián
3. èrlíngyīlíngnián
4. wǔshíhào fángjiān
5. yīliùlínghào fángjiān

Exercises for 8.4
1. Qǐng jìnlái.
2. Wǒ māma chūqù le.
3. Wǒmen jìnqù ba.
4. Dìdi, gǎnkuài chūlái!
5. Bié jìnqù!

Exercises for 8.5
1. Yùshì hěn gānjìng.
2. Chuángdān tài zāng le.
3. Chuáng búgòu ruǎn.
4. Zhèijiān fángjiān yǒudiǎn xiǎo.
5. Nèizhāng zhuōzi duóme dà a!
6. Nèijiān yùshì nàme xiǎo.

Exercises for 8.6
1. Zhèr yǒu sìge rén.
2. Nǐ jiālǐ yǒu méiyǒu lǎoshǔ?
3. Zhèizhāng zhuōzi shàng méiyǒu diànhuà.
4. Nèijiān yùshì lǐ yǒu yìzhī zhāngláng.
5. Wǒ shúshu chuáng shàng yǒu sānběn shū.

CHAPTER 9

Exercises for 9.1
1. Wǒ jīnnián èrshíqī suì.
2. Wǒde shēngrì shì shíyīyuè sānshíhào.
3. A: Jīnnián shì něinián?
   B: èrlínglìngbānián
4. Wǒ bāshíjiǔ suì.
5. Jīntiān shì èryuè shísìhào.

Exercises for 9.2
1. sāntiān
2. sìshíwǔge xīngqī
3. shíèrnián
4. bāge yuè
5. Yíge xīngqī yǒu jǐtiān?

6. Yìnián yǒu jǐge yuè?

7. Qǐng (nǐ) zài shuō yícì.

8. Yìnián yǒu wǔshíèrge xīngqī.

Exercises for 9.3

1. kàndewán

2. kànbùwán

3. tīngdedǒng

4. tīngbùdǒng

5. kàndedǒng, kànbùdǒng

Exercises for 9.4

1. shì něinián shēngde?

2. shì yījiǔèrwǔnián jiéhūn de.

3. shì zěnme lái Měiguó de?

4. shì yījiǔjiǔsìnián sānyuè shíhào xiàwǔ liǎngdiǎn shēng de.

5. búshì zuò fēijī qù Zhōngguó de.

Exercises for 9.5

1. Nǐ shénme shíhòu yào jiào chūzū qìchē?

2. Nǐ dǎsuàn shénme shíhòu qù Zhōngguó?

3. Lín Xiǎojiě jīntiān zǎoshàng gěi wǒ yàoshi.

4. Tā dìdi jīnnián shíèryuè yào qù Yīngguó.

5. Nǐ zǔmǔ shì shénme shíhòu lái Měiguó de?

Exercises for 9.6

1. Bù, wǒ māma bú zài Měiguó zhù.

2. Bù, wǒ bàba bú zài yínháng gōngzuò.

3. Bù, nèige rén bù gěi wǒ kàn tāde hùzhào.

4. Bù, wǒ jiějie bú zài xuéxiào yóuyǒng.

5. Bù, wǒ péngyou bù gěi wǒ kàn tāde zhàopiàn.

Exercises for 9.7

1. Tā méiyǒu shēng háizi.

2. Wǒ hái méiyǒu jiào chūzū qìchē.

3. Nǐ méiyǒu qù fēijīchǎng ma?

4. Bǐdé méiyǒu gěi nèige zhíyuán kàn tāde hùzhào.

5. Wǒ péngyou méiyǒu gěi wǒ kàn tā chǒngwù de zhàopiàn.

Exercises for 9.8

1. zěnme shuō

2. zěnme qù fēijīchǎng

3. zěnme bù lái wǒmen jiā

4. zěnme nàme máng

5. zěnme nàme zāng

CHAPTER 10

Exercises for 10.1
1. cóng, wàng, běi, dōng
2. wàng, yòu, wàng, zuǒ
3. cóng, dào
4. xī, nán
5. Cóng, wàng, xī, yòu

Exercises for 10.2
1. fēijīchǎng, zěnme zǒu
2. wàng dōng zǒu
3. zěnme qù
4. Wǒ yào zuò chē qù. (OR Wǒ yào zuò gōnggòng qìchē qù.)
5. zěnme bàn

Exercises for 10.3
1. zài wàng běi zǒu
2. xiān wàng Běijīng Fàndiàn, (wàng) zuǒ zhuǎn
3. qù gōngyuán, zài qù tāde gōngsī
4. xiān qù fēijīchǎng, zài mǎi bàozhǐ
5. xiān (wàng) yòu zhuǎn, zài wàng dōng zǒu.

Exercises for 10.4
1. Nǐ jiā lí wǒ jiā hěn yuǎn ma?
2. Wǒ jiā lí gōngyuán hěn jìn.
3. Cóng zhèr dào wǒ jiā yǒu liǎnglǐ lù.
4. Nǐ jiā lí gōngsī hěn yuǎn ma?
5. Cóng wǒ jiā dào fēijīchǎng yǒu wǔshíbālǐ lù.

Exercises for 10.5
1. lǐbiān
2. zuǒbiān, yòubiān
3. dōngbiān
4. běibiān, nánbiān
5. xībiān

Exercises for 10.6
1. Wàng běi zǒu, bié wàng dōng zǒu.
2. (Nǐmen) búyòng xiè.
3. (Nǐ) bié mǎi shū.
4. Nǐ búyòng gěi qián.
5. Nǐ búyòng gěi wǒ kàn nǐde hùzhào.

Exercises for 10.7

1. Nèige bàba dài háizi qù gōngyuán.
2. Nǐmen kàndào hónglǜdēng zài zuǒ zhuǎn.
3. Tā jīnnián shíèryuè yào dài Mèimei lái Zhōngguó.
4. Wǒ kàndào tā dài tā dìdi qù shàng cèsuǒ.
5. Zhèige xiǎojiě yào dài wǒ zǔfù qù yínháng.

CHAPTER 11

Exercises for 11.1

1. Lìlián: Wéi?
   Bǐdé: Shì Lìlián ma?
   Lìlián: Duì, (shì wǒ).
   Bǐdé: Nǐ jīntiān yǒu méiyǒu kòng?
   Lìlián: Yǒu.
   Bǐdé: Wǒ xiǎng qǐng nǐ chī fàn.
   Lìlián: Tài hǎo le. Xièxie.
2. A: Wéi?
   Mínglěi: Qǐngwèn Lǐ Jīnglǐ zàibúzài?
   Lǐ Jīnglǐ: Wǒ jiù shì.
   Mínglěi: Lǐ Jīnglǐ, wǒ xiǎng qǐng nǐ lái wǒ jiā hē chá.
   Lǐ Jīnglǐ: Nǐ tài kèqi le. Kěshì jīntiān bútài fāngbiàn.
   Mínglěi: Nǐ xiànzài hěn máng ma?
   Lǐ Jīnglǐ: Duì, wǒ xiànzài hěn máng. Zhēn duìbùqǐ.

Exercises for 11.2

1. Tā jiù shì wǒ jiějie.
2. Wǒ jiù shì.
3. Zhèizhī jiù shì.
4. wǒ jiù shì (OR wǒ jiù shì Wèi Jiàoshòu)
5. Nèige xiǎojiě jiù shì (wǒmen de jiàoliàn).

Exercises for 11.3

1. Wǒ gāng mǎi le yìběn shū.
2. Lǐ Xiǎojiě gāng lái wǒ jiā.
3. Wáng Jīnglǐ gāng qù Zhōngguó.
4. Tā gāng mài le tāde chē.
5. Wǒde háizi gāng shàng le cèsuǒ.
6. Tā dìdi de diànhuà gāng huài le.
7. Wǒ xiānsheng gāng xiūlǐ le diànnǎo.

Exercises for 11.4

I. 1. Mèimei, Bàba zài jiào nǐ.

   2. Nǐmen zài chī fàn ma?

   3. Wǒ gēge zài xiūlǐ diànnǎo.

   4. Wǒ xiànzài zài kàn shū.

II. 1. Wǒ děngzhe nǐ.

   2. Wǒmen zhànzhe ba.

   3. Nèige xiǎojiě zěnme názhe bàozhǐ?

   4. Wǒ xiànzài zuòzhe fàn.

Exercises for 11.5

1. Nǐ zěnme bú guòlái gēn wǒmen chī (fàn)?

2. Tā yào guòqù gēn tā jiàoliàn shuō.

3. Qǐng nǐmen zǒuguòlái.

4. Tā zǒuguòqù kàn nèizhī māo.

5. Wǒmen yào guòqù gēn tāmen yóuyǒng ma?

Exercises for 11.6

1. Zhèiběn cídiǎn kěyǐ ma? (OR Zhèiběn cídiǎn kěyǐ bùkěyǐ?)

2. Nǐ kěyǐ zài nàr yóuyǒng.

3. Wǒ kěyǐ zài zhèr chōu yān ma?

4. Nǐ xiànzài bù kěyǐ kāi chē.

5. Nǐ kěyǐ gēn wǒde gǒu wán.

Exercises for 11.7

1. Nǐ yào búyào hē (yì)diǎnr shénme?

2. Lǐ Lǎoshī méi shénme xuéshēng.

3. Nǐ yào búyào chī (yì)diǎnr shénme?

4. Wǒ bàba méi shénme zhàopiàn.

5. Wǒ méi mǎi shénme (dōngxi).

CHAPTER 12

Exercises for 12.1

1. Wǒ zǔmǔ kuài zǒu le.

2. Fēijī kuài qǐfēi le.

3. Gēge kuài chī wǔfàn le.

4. Nèige xuéshēng kuài qù Zhōngguó le.

5. Wǒmen kuài dào gōngyuán le.

Exercises for 12.2

1. Nǐ māma zuòhǎo fàn le ma?

2. Nǐ shúshu kànwán bào le ma?

3. Wǒ bāo hǎole èrshísìge jiǎozi.

4. Nǐ gēge kànwán le jǐběn shū?

5. Nǐmen dōu zuòhǎo le shì (le) ma?

Exercises for 12.3
1. yìxiē zhuōzi
2. nèixiē jiǎozi
3. něixiē fēijī
4. yìxiē chūzū qìchē
5. zhèixiē shū
6. něixiē yǔsǎn

Exercises for 12.4
1. Nǐ mèimei huì yóuyǒng ma? (OR Nǐ mèimei huì búhuì yóuyǒng?)
2. Wǒ xiānsheng huì bāo jiǎozi.
3. Nèige jiàoliàn búhuì shuō Zhōngwén (OR Zhōngguóhuà).
4. Zhèixiē lǎoshī huì kàn Yīngwén bào.
5. Nǐde háizi huì shàng cèsuǒ ma?
6. Tāde nánpéngyou hěn huì chī cù.

Exercises for 12.6
1. Qǐng nǐ bǎ yǔsǎn jiègěi wǒ.
2. Qǐng nǐ bǎ yán nágěi wǒ māma.
3. Nèige fúwùyuán bǎ dìtú nágěi Lín Tàitai.
4. Wáng Lǎoshī bǎ nèixiē xuéshēng dàiqù Zhōngguó.
5. Wǒ bàba bù bǎ chē jiègěi nèixiē háizi.

Exercises for 12.7
I. 1. Nèixiē jīnglǐ míngtiān cái dào.
   2. Tā érzi yījiǔjiǔwǔ nián cái shēng.
   3. Hán Xiānsheng xiànzài cái xiū diànnǎo.
   4. Xiàwǔ liǎngdiǎn cái xià yǔ.
   5. Nèige Zhōngguó jiàoliàn míngnián cái lái Měiguó.
II. 1. Qǐng kāi mén. Wǒ yào jìnqù.
   2. Nǐ huì kāi chē ma?
   3. Nèixiē lǎoshī míngtiān cái kāi huì.
   4. Bàba xiān kāi dēng, zài kàn bào.
   5. Lǐ Jīnglǐ bú huì kāi wánxiào.

CHAPTER 13

Exercises for 13.1
1. Tā méi yòng dāochā.
2. Lín Xiǎojiě méi qù Xiānggǎng.
3. Nèixiē niánqīngrén méi wán diànnǎo.
4. Zhèige xuéshēng méi bāo sānshíge jiǎozi.
5. Wǒ méi xiǎngdào nǐ huì shuō Zhōngwén.
6. Tā māma méi xiǎngdào tā huì kāi chē.

Exercises for 13.2

1. yòng. (Peter knows very well how to eat with chopsticks.)
2. gēn. (Anna also went with us to buy dictionaries.)
3. yòng, yòng. (Mr. Lín writes with his right hand, yet he holds a fork with his left hand.)
4. gēn. (She likes to swim with her dog.)
5. yòng. (My grandfather doesn't write letters with a computer.)
6. Yòng. (Eating with a knife and fork is the habit of Americans.)

Exercises for 13.3

1. Tā gěi wǒ jiějie kāi mén.
2. Nèige māma hěn xǐhuān gěi tā háizi zuò fàn.
3. Wǒde Zhōngguó péngyou jīnnián méi gěi wǒ xiě xìn.
4. Jīntiān wǎnshàng bādiǎnbàn wǒ huì gěi jiàoliàn dǎ diànhuà.
5. Nǐ péngyou yǐjīng gěi nǐ bāohǎole sānshíliùge jiǎozi.

Exercises for 13.4

I. 1. zài yínháng gōngzuò.
   2. zài jiā xiūlǐ chē.
   3. zài gōngyuán wán.
   4. zài fēijīchǎng chī jiǎozi.
II. 1. tǎngzài yǐzishàng
   2. zhànzài chuángshàng
   3. zhùzài Běijīng Fàndiàn
   4. bù kěyǐ zuòzài zhuōzishàng

Exercises for 13.5

1. A: Nǐ wèishénme zuò tāde chē qù gōngyuán?
2. A: Nèige rén wèishénme yòng kuàizi chī shālā?
3. A: Nǐ māma wèishénme bāng Lǐ Xiǎojiě zuò fàn?
4. A: Nǐ zǔfù wèishénme bù dǎ zì?
5. A: Nǐ wèishénme zài xiào?

Exercises for 13.6

1. B: Yīnwèi nǐ jiā hěn yuǎn, suǒyǐ wǒ bú qù nǐ jiā yóuyǒng.
2. B: Yīnwèi tā yào qù fēijīchǎng, suǒyǐ tā yào jiào chūzū qìchē.
3. B: Yīnwèi tā nàme máng, suǒyǐ wǒ bāng tā xiūlǐ diànnǎo.
4. B: Yīnwèi tā gāng shēng háizi, suǒyǐ wǒ yào gǎnkuài gěi tā zuòfàn.
5. B: Yīnwèi wǒ xiǎng zhù nèijiā fàndiàn, suǒyǐ wǒ yào gěi nèige zhíyuán kàn wǒde hùzhào.

Exercises for 13.7

1. liǎngge yuè méi(yǒu) shuō huà
2. yìnián méi(yǒu) yóuyǒng
3. sìtiān méi(yǒu) dǎ diànnǎo

4. hěn jiǔ méi(yǒu) jiàn miàn, suǒyǐ wǒ gěi tā dǎ diànhuà
5. liǎngtiān méi(yǒu) hē niúnǎi

CHAPTER 14

Exercises for 14.1
1. Tā gēge jīnnián dàgài bú huì qù Zhōngguó.
2. Nèige fángjiān yóuqí gānjìng.
3. Zhūròu hé shēngcài dōu hěn guì.
4. Tā xǐhuān hē chá, yóuqíshi Zhōngguó chá.
5. Wǒmen dōu shì Měiguórén.
6. Zhèixiē háizi yóuqí xǐhuān yóuyǒng.
7. Nèixiē lǎoshī dàgài dào le.
8. Wǒ māma bǎ xìn dōu xiěwán (Or xiěhǎo) le.

Exercises for 14.2
1. Wǒ bù zhīdào nèixiē rén shì búshì Rìběnrén.
2. Wǒmen bù zhīdào nèige háizi huì búhuì yóuyǒng.
3. Lín Tàitai bù zhīdào nǐ xǐ(huān) bù xǐhuān hē chá.
4. Māma bù zhīdào nǐ yǒu méiyǒu piàoliàng de yīfu.
5. Wǒ jiějie bù zhīdào zhèixiē jiǎozi gòu búgòu.
6. Nèige zhíyuán bù zhīdào Wáng Jīnglǐ zài búzài jiā.

Exercises for 14.4
1. Nǐ xiǎng hē (yì)diǎnr chá ma? (OR Nǐ xiǎng bùxiǎng hē [yì]diǎnr chá?)
2. Māma, mèimèi hěn xǐhuān piàoliàng de yīfu.
3. Wǒ hěn xiǎng gěi wǒ péngyou dǎ diànhuà.
4. Nǐ hěn xǐhuān yòng diànnǎo xiě xìn ma?
5. Bàba, wǒ bùxiǎng chī nèixiē jiǎozi.

Exercises for 14.5
1. Tiānqì lěng de shíhòu, yóuqí xǐhuān hē tāng.
2. Zhōngguó de shíhòu, chī zhūròu jiǎozi.
3. gěi nǐ dǎ diànhuà de shíhòu, nǐ zài zuò shénme?
4. chūqù mǎi xīguā de shíhòu, fàn zuòhǎo le.
5. yìqǐ chūqù de shíhòu, tā xiānsheng hěn bù gāoxìng.

Exercises for 14.6
1. Zhèixiē yīfu yòu piàoliàng yòu piányi.
2. Tā yòu chī fàn yòu dǎ diànhuà.
3. Nèige fángjiān yòu xiǎo yòu zāng.
4. Lín Lǎoshī yòu xiǎng zuò fàn yòu xiǎng xiūlǐ diànnǎo.
5. Zhèizhī māo yòu gānjìng yòu kě'ài.
6. Nèixiē niánqīngrén yòu mǎi cídiǎn yòu mǎi dìtú.
7. Tā yòu yǎng háizi yòu yǎng yā.

CHAPTER 15

Exercises for 15.1
1. B: Wǒ jiějie xiǎng zuò chūzū qìchē qù (fēijīchǎng).
2. B: Nèige rén shì zuò fēijī dào Měiguó lái de.
3. B: tāmen shì zuò huǒchē qù Niǔyuē de.
4. B: Wǒmen shì xiān zuò chē, zài zǒu lù lái de.
5. B: Tā shì zuò chē qù Mòxīgē wán de.

Exercises for 15.2
1. Xièxie nǐ. Wǒmen děi zǒu le.
2. Duìbùqǐ, kěshì wǒ děi zuò chē huí jiā le.
3. Nǐ děi gǎnkuài xué Yīngwén.
4. Nǐmen děi xiān wàng nán zǒu, zài yòu zhuǎn.
5. Nǐ děi xiān xǐ shǒu, zài chī shuǐguǒ.

Exercises for 15.3
1. Wǒ māma de xìn zài zhuōzi shàngmiàn.
2. Bēizi lǐtou yǒu yìzhī zhāngláng.
3. Tāde gōngsī zài huǒchēzhàn hòumiàn.
4. Nèige háizi de yīfu bú zài bàozhǐ xiàmiàn.
5. Zhèige niánqīngrén zài qìchē (or chēzi) qiánmiàn zhànzhe.
6. Něijiā yínháng zài gōngyuán duìmiàn?
7. Nǐ zài yùshì wàitou děng nǐ dìdi ma?

Exercises for 15.4
1. Nǐ xìng Lǐ háishi Lín?
2. Nǐ xǐhuān gǒu háishi māo?
3. Tāmen yào zuò huǒchē háishi fēijī?
4. Nǐ shì Rìběnrén háishi Zhōngguórén?
5. Nèixiē pángxiè zài dàizi lǐtou háishi dàizi wàitou?

Exercises for 15.5
1. Tā xǐhuān de yínháng hěn yuǎn.
2. Wǒ zuò de huǒchē fēicháng gānjìng.
3. Nèixiē háizi zài kàn chī shēngcài de yā.
4. Huì shuō Zhōngwén de xuéshēng kěyǐ qù Zhōngguó.
5. Wǒ xiānsheng xiǎng chī nǐ dàizi lǐ de pángxiè.
6. Wǒ bàba zài xiūlǐ de diànnǎo shì wǒde.
7. Wáng Xiǎojiě jiè(gěi) nǐ de yīfu hǎokàn bù hǎokàn?

Exercises for 15.6
1. B: Nàme wǒmen zhǐhǎo mǎi zhūròu.
2. B: Wǒmen zhǐhǎo zài zhèr děngzhe.
3. B: Yīnwèi wǒ xiānsheng zhǐ huì shuō Zhōngwén, suǒyǐ wǒ zhǐhǎo xué Zhōngwén.

4. B: Yīnwèi wǒ xiàge yuè yào kǎoshì, suǒyǐ wǒ zhǐhǎo gǎnkuài kàn.
5. B: Yīnwèi wǒ tài pàng, děi jiǎnféi, suǒyǐ wǒ zhǐhǎo chī shēngcài.

CHAPTER 16

Exercises for 16.1
Māma: Nǐ xiǎng chī shénme?
A: Wǒ hěn xiǎng chī lóngxiā, kěshì lóngxiā tài guì le.
Māma: Méi guānxi. Wǒmen diǎn yìzhī lóngxiā ba. (To Bàba.) Nǐ nàme ài chī yāròu. Wǒmen diǎn zhī yā ba. Bù zhīdào tāmen yǒu méiyǒu Běijīng kǎoyā. (Called the waiter.) Fúwùyuán, qǐng nǐ guòlái. Wǒmen xiǎng diǎn jǐge cài, hái yào yíge tāng.
Fúwùyuán: Nǐmen yào diǎn něixiē cài?
Māma: Wǒmen yào chǎo lóngxiā, Běijīng kǎoyā, bōcài, hé hǎixiāntāng.
Fúwùyuán: Háiyào biéde ma?
Bàba: Zhèixiē cài gòu le. Yě qǐng nǐ gěi wǒmen jǐbēi shuǐ.
A (after eating the meal): Tāmen zuò de lóngxiā fēicháng hǎochī.
Māma: Tāng yě hěn hǎohē.
Bàba: Tāmen de Běijīng kǎoyā yǒudiǎn xián, kěshì hái búcuò.
A (to parents): Wǒ hěn xǐhuān zhèijiā fànguǎn. Xièxie nǐmen dài wǒ lái zhèr.

Exercises for 16.2
1. Nǐ xǐ bùxǐhuān chī kǎo huǒjī?
2. Nǐ māma zhī bùzhīdào nǐ hē píjiǔ?
3. Nèige xiǎojiě kě bùkěyǐ zài fángjiān chōu yān?
4. Nèixiē nánháizi yīng bùyīnggāi wán diànnǎo?
5. Nǐ zhī bùzhīdào tā zài nǎr?

Exercises for 16.3
1. Nǐ shì nánxuéshēng háishi nǚxuéshēng?
2. Jīròu huòzhě huǒjīròu dōu kěyǐ.
3. Ānnà shì Měiguórén háishi Zhōngguórén?
4. Wǒde háizi xǐhuān hē shuǐ huòzhě qìshuǐ.
5. Nǐ yào hē chá háishì kāfēi?

Exercises for 16.4
1. Nǐ xiǎng bùxiǎng hēhē kàn?
2. Nǐ qù nàr wènwèn kàn.
3. Nǐ yào búyào chīchī kàn?
4. Nǐ xiǎng bùxiǎng kāikāi kàn?
5. Nǐ shuōshuō kàn.

Exercises for 16.5

1. Māma zhīdào nèijiā fànguǎn hǎo bùhǎo.
2. Nǐ wèn tāmen yǒu méiyǒu suānlà tāng.
3. Bàba bù zhīdào nǐ yǒu méiyǒu diànnǎo.
4. Wǒmen xiǎng zhīdào nǐ huì búhuì shuō Zhōngwén.
5. Lǐ Lǎoshī wèn wǒ kǎo huǒjī hǎo(chī) bùhǎochī.

Exercises for 16.6

1. Tā yǐwéi nèige jīnglǐ shì Měiguórén.
2. Māma yǐwéi nèixiē háizi hěn huài.
3. Nǐ yǐwéi wǒ huì kāi chē ma?
4. Bàba yǐwéi nèijiā yínháng zài huǒchēzhàn hòumiàn.
5. Nǐ shúshu yǐwéi wǒde fángjiān hěn gānjìng ma?

CHAPTER 17

Exercises for 17.1

1. xīngqī'èr, xīngqīsì
2. Míngtiān
3. xīngqīyī, xīngqīwǔ
4. Qùnián, jīnnián, míngnián
5. Shànggeyuè, xià(ge) xīngqī
6. shàng(ge) xīngqītiān, zuótiān

Exercises for 17.2

1. Wǒde xīgài shàng xīngqīliù kāishǐ tòng, ránhòu wǒde jiǎo yě kāishǐ tòng.
2. Lìlián gēn tā nánpéngyou xiān qù gōngyuán, ránhòu qù yìjiā Fǎguó fànguǎn.
3. Xiǎo Wěi shuō tā dùzi tòng, ránhòu shuō tā yào hē qìshuǐ.
4. Wǒ shàng xīngqīsān kāishǐ fāshāo, ránhòu (wǒ) kāishǐ liú bíshuǐ.
5. Zhāng Xiānsheng shàngge xīngqī kāishǐ hóulóng tòng, ránhòu tā dé le qìguǎn yán.
6. Nèige lǎorén shàngge yuè dé le fèi yán, ránhòu tā sǐ le.

Exercises for 17.3

1. Nèige lǎorén zuò le yíge zhōngtóu.
2. Nǐde jīnglǐ gōngzuò le sìge xīngqī le.
3. Nǐ chī wǔfàn chī le duōjiǔ le?
4. Zhèige niánqīngrén xué Zhōngwén xué le wǔge yuè le.
5. Tāmen yóuyǒng yóu le duōjiǔ le?

Exercises for 17.4

1. Nèixiē lǎoshī ràng xuéshēng kàn zhèiběn shū.
2. Wǒ bàba bú ràng wǒ gēge kāi tāde chē.

3. Tā māma zhǐ ràng tā hē shuǐ hé guǒzhī.

4. Nǐ péngyou ràng nǐ jiè tāde cídiǎn ma?

5. Wǒ nánpéngyou bù xǐhuān ràng wǒ kàn tāde zhàopiàn.

Exercises for 17.5

1. Nǐ xǐhuān něizhǒng diànnǎo?

2. Wǒ xǐhuān zhèizhǒng diànnǎo.

3. Zhè shì něizhǒng píjiǔ?

4. Zhè shì Déguó píjiǔ?

5. Nèizhǒng cài hǎochī ma?

6. Bù, nèizhǒng cài bútài hǎochī.

Exercises for 17.6

1. Nèige māma duì tāde háizi fēicháng hǎo.

2. Wǒ xiǎng yóuyǒng duì nǐde shēntǐ hěn hǎo.

3. Chī qīngcài duì lǎorén hǎo bùhǎo?

4. Nǐ hóulóng tòng de shíhòu, suānlà tāng duì nǐ bútài hǎo.

5. Nǐ dé qìguǎnyán de shíhòu, fú kàngshēngsù duì nǐ hěn hǎo.

Exercises for 17.7

1. Qǐng duō chī yìdiǎnr cài.

2. Nǐ fāshāo de shíhòu, duō hē shuǐ duì nǐ hěn hǎo.

3. Wǒ duō kàn Zhōngwén shū, shǎo kàn Yīngwén shū.

4. Duō kàn diànyǐng hé diànshì duì nǐmen bù hǎo.

5. Wǒ míngnián yào kāishǐ duō xiě xìn, shǎo dǎ diànhuà.

CHAPTER 18

Exercises for 18.1

1. A: Nǐmen yígòng chī le sì jīn zhūròu.

2. A: Nǐ zhuāguò zhāngláng
   B: Wǒ zài jiālǐ zhuāguò yìzhī.

3. A: Nǐ māma hēguò Fǎguó jiǔ méiyǒu?
   B: Tā méiyǒu hēguò Fǎguó jiǔ.

4. B: Wǒ qùguò Rìběn yícì. (OR Wǒ qùguò yícì Rìběn.)

5. A: Nǐ kànguò zhèiběn shū méiyǒu?

Exercises for 18.2

1. Zhèr měiběn shū dōu hěn piányi.

2. Gōngyuán lǐ měige rén dōu hěn gāoxìng.

3. Měige háizi dōu yǎngguò lǎoshǔ ma?

4. Tā xíguàn měitiān wǎnshàng jiǔdiǎn shàng chuáng.

5. Chén Tàitai hé tā xiānsheng měige yuè dōu qù nèijiā fànguǎn chī fàn.

Exercises for 18.3

1. Nèige lǎorén zǒu de hěn kuài.
2. Wǒ bù zhīdào nǐmen chī de nàme duō.
3. Měizhī gǒu dōu wán de hěn gāoxìng.
4. Bàba méi xiǎngdào gēge kāi de nàme hǎo.
5. Tāde zǔfù cóng zhèr kěyǐ kàn de fēicháng qīngchǔ.

Exercises for 18.4

1. Zhèizhī gǒu kě sǐ le.
2. Nǐ kàn, nèige háizi è sǐ le.
3. Nèixiē yǎnyuán de biǎoyǎn hǎo jí le.
4. Tāde zǔfù qì sǐ le.
5. Zhèixiē pángxiè hǎochī jí le.

Exercises for 18.5

1. Nǐ chángcháng qù kàn Jīngjù.
2. bù cháng(cháng) qù.
3. Wǒ bù měige xīngqītiān qù.
   wǒ yǒu shíhòu gēn tā qù.
4. Wǒmen yǒu shíhòu diǎn tángcù yú, yǒu shíhòu diǎn chǎo qīngcài hé tāng.
5. Nǐ chángcháng tīng gǔdiǎn yīnyuè ma?
   Duì. Yīnwèi wǒ hěn xǐhuān gǔdiǎn yīnyuè, suǒyǐ wǒ chángcháng tīng.

Exercises for 18.6

1. Nèijiā yínháng hěn yuǎn, zhèijiā yínháng jìn yìdiǎnr.
2. Tā jīnglǐ de fēijī piào yǒu yìdiǎnr guì.
3. Nèige suānlà tāng bù suān, zhèige tāng suān yìdiǎnr.
4. Tāmen de yīfu dōu yǒu yìdiǎnr zāng.
5. Zhèige fángjiān xiǎo yìdiǎnr, yě piányi yìdiǎnr.

Exercises for 18.7

1. Wǒ zhēn duìbùqǐ nǐ.
2. Nǐ bù yīnggāi kànbùqǐ nèige rén.
3. Tā yǐwéi nǐ mǎibùqǐ diànnǎo.
4. Yīnwèi tā hé tā xiānsheng dōu méiyǒu gōngzuò, suǒyǐ tāmen yǎngbùqǐ háizi.
5. Yīnwèi tāmen zuòbùqǐ fēijī, suǒyǐ tāmen děi kāi chē qù Niǔyuē.

CHAPTER 19

Exercises for 19.1

1. Nèijiā fàndiàn zuì guì, tāmen de fúwù yě zuì hǎo.
2. Wǒ jiālǐ wǒ māma zuì máng, dànshì tā yìdiǎnr yě bú lèi.

3. Tā zuì ài chī chǎo qīngcài.

4. Wǒmen yìdiǎnr yě bù xǐhuān lǎoshǔ.

5. Zài fànguǎn lǐ, wǒ dìdi zhǐ chī jiǎozi. Biéde cài tā yìdiǎnr yě bù chī.

Exercises for 19.2

1. Tā māma pǎo de fēicháng kuài.

2. Nèige Měiguórén shuō Zhōngwén shuō de hěn màn.

3. Zhèixiē háizi ná dāochā ná de yóuqí hǎo.

4. Tā mèimei xiě zì xiě de piàoliàng jí le.

5. Nǐde nánpéngyou zuò fàn zuò de hǎo bùhǎo?

Exercises for 19.3

1. Zhèiběn shū bǐ nèiběn shū guì.

2. Suānlà tāng bǐ tángcù yú suān de duō.

3. Fēijī piào bǐ huǒchē piào guì duō le.

4. Wǒ xiǎng Zhōngguó bǐ Měiguó dà yìdiǎnr.

5. Tā yǐwéi nánrén de chènshān bǐ nǚrén de piàoliàng de duō.

Exercises for 19.4

1. Wǒ zǔmǔ mǎi dōngxi mǎide bǐ wǒ duō.

2. Tā shuō Zhōngguóhuà shuōde bǐ wǒde Rìběn péngyou kuài.

3. Bù, tā zhùde bǐ wǒ jìn.

4. Tā jiějie bāo jiǎozi bāode bǐ tā màn, kěshì bǐ tā hǎo.

5. Bù, wǒ māma kàn Zhōngwén bào kànde bǐ wǒ kuài.

Exercises for 19.5

1. Zhèige fēijīchǎng gēn nèige bù yíyàng.

2. Nèijiā yínháng gēn zhèijiā yíyàng fāngbiàn ma?

3. Wǒ xiǎng zhèizhī lù gēn nèizhī yíyàng kě'ài.

4. Lǐ Xiānsheng gēn Hán Xiānsheng yíyàng lèi.

5. Yòng shǒu xiě gēn yòng diànnǎo xiě yíyàng hǎokàn ma?

Exercises for 19.6

1. Yóuyǒng, mànpǎo, wǒde jīnglǐ dōu bù xǐhuān.

2. Zhōngguó cài, Měiguó cài, Wáng Xiǎojiě dōu xiǎng chī.

3. Píjiǔ, qìshuǐ, jiǔ, wǒ shúshu dōu bù kěyǐ hē.

4. Guì de dōngxi, méiyòng de dōngxi, nèige niánqīngrén dōu bù yīnggāi mǎi.

5. Zhōngwén xìn, Yīngwén xìn, zhèige zhíyuán dōu huì xiě.

Exercises for 19.7

A: Nǐ zuìjìn zěnme nàme piàoliàng?

B: Yīnwèi wǒ chángcháng liàn qìgōng, suǒyǐ wǒde shēntǐ jīnnián bǐ qùnián jiànkāng.

(After you climb up the mountain.)

A: Wǒ lèi jí le.

B: Wǒ yìdiǎnr yě bù juéde lèi.

A: Nǐ chī xiē shénmeyàng de dōngxi?

B: Wǒ zuì xǐhuān chī qīngcài.

A: Nǐ lǎoshì chī qīngcài ma?

B: Bù, qīngcài, ròu wǒ dōu chī. Zhèi liǎngzhǒng dōngxi duì nǐde shēntǐ dōu hěn hǎo.

A: Nǐ xiǎng wǒ yīnggāi zuò shénmeyàng de yùndòng?

B: Yěxǔ nǐ kěyǐ chángcháng mànpǎo, yǒu shíhòu nǐ yě kěyǐ qù yóuyǒng. Háiyǒu, wǒ huì jiāo nǐ qìgōng.

APPENDIX 2: CHINESE PĪNYĪN-ENGLISH GLOSSARY

This list includes all the vocabulary from the dialogues as well as some important words in the grammar notes and exercises. The number in parentheses after the English text indicates the chapter in which the vocabulary item is featured and in which more detailed information on its meaning and usage is available.

a [particle] (8)

ADJ + le have gotten ADJ (12)

ADJ-sǐ le be terribly adjective (18)

āi ya! yikes! egads! (8)

ài to love; love, affection (5)

Ānnà [name, Anna] (13)

ba [particle] (6)

bā eight (5)

bǎ [coverb for prestating the object] (12)

bǎ [measure] (14)

bàba dad, papa (3)

bái be white (16)

báifàn cooked white rice (16)

bǎihuò gōngsī department store (19)

bàn half (6)

bàn to handle, to do (10)

bāng to help (12)

bāo to wrap (12)

bàozhǐ newspaper (7)

bāyuè August (9)

bēi cup [measure] (6)

běi north (10)

bèi [OR **bèibù**] back (17)

Běijīng Fàndiàn the Běijīng Hotel (10)

bēizi cup (6)

běn [measure] (7)

bǐ compared to (19)

biān [localizer, "side"] (10)

biǎoyǎn to perform, to act (18)

bié + VERB don't VERB (6)

biéde another, something else (8)

bíkǒng nostril (17)

bǐjiào comparatively (10)

bìng sickness; be sick (17)

bíshuǐ nasal discharge (17)

bízi nose (17)

bózi [OR **jǐng**] neck (17)

bù no, not (3)

bù hǎo yìsi to be embarrassed (11)

bú yàojǐn It doesn't matter. (12)

bù yíyàng be different (19)

bù zhīdào NOUN-VERB-bù-VERB don't know whether noun verbs or not (14)

búcuò be pretty good, be not bad (19)

búgòu + ADJ be not adjective enough (8)

búhuì + VERB won't (likely) verb (8)

bútài + ADJ be not very ADJ (11)

búyòng + VERB no need to VERB (10)

búyòng xiè you needn't thank me (10)

cái only then, only (12)

cài vegetable, cooked dish, national cuisine (16)

càidān menu (16)

cèsuǒ toilet (10)

chá tea (6)

cháng be long (15)

chángcháng often (19)

Chángchéng Great Wall of China (15)

chǎo to sauté (16)

chǎo qīngcài sautéed green vegetables (16)

chéng wall, city wall, city (15)
chéng lǐtou inside the city (15)
chènshān shirt (19)
chēshàng on the bus (15)
chī to eat something (11)
chī cù to taste vinegar, be jealous (12)
chī fàn to eat (VERB-OBJ) (11)
chǒngwù pet (5)
chū to exit (8)
chuān to wear (clothing) (19)
chuáng bed (8)
chuángdān bed sheets (8)
chūntiān spring (14)
chūqù to go out (8)
chūzū qìchē taxicab (6)
cídiǎn dictionary (7)
cóng from (10)
cù vinegar (12)
cuò be wrong (7)

dǎ to hit, to manipulate by hand (13)
dà be big (8)
dǎ diànhuà to make a phone call (13)
dǎ gé to burp (19)
dà jiào to shout loudly (18)
dàgài probably (10)
dài to escort, to lead (10)
dàizi bag (15)
dāngrán of course, naturally (11)
dànshì but, however (18)
dào to, to arrive (10)
dāochā knife and fork (13)
dǎsuàn to plan (9)
de [particle] (4)
. . . de shíhòu, when . . . (14)
dé to contract, to get (17)
Déguó Germany (7)
děi + VERB must VERB, have to VERB (15)
dēng light, lamp (10)
děng to wait (11)
děng huǐr jiàn see you after awhile (11)
Déwén German language (7)
diǎn dot, point, o'clock (6); to order (16)
diàn electric, electricity (8)

diànhuà telephone (8)
diànnǎo computer (11)
diànyuán shop clerk (7)
dìdi younger brother (5)
dìtú map (7)
dōng east (10)
dǒng to understand (9)
dōngtiān winter (14)
dōngxi thing (19)
dōu all, both (14)
duì be correct, "That's right . . ." (13)
duì NOUN hěn hǎo be good for the noun (17)
duìbùqǐ sorry, excuse me (3)
duìmiàn the opposite side, across the way (15)
duō be many, numerous, much (bound form) (9)
duō VERB + OBJ verb more of the object (17)
duōjiǔ how long (in duration)? (9)
duóme + ADJ how adjective it is! (8)
duōshǎo how much?/how many? (7)
dùzi stomach (12)

è be hungry (12)
Éguó (OR Èguó) Russia (7)
èr two (5)
ěrduo ear (17)
èryuè February (9)
étóu forehead (17)
Éwén (OR Èwén) Russian language (7)

Fǎguó (OR Fàguó) France (7)
fàn cooked rice, food, a meal (11)
fàndiàn hotel (10)
fāngbiàn be convenient (11)
fángjiān room (8)
fànguǎn restaurant (16)
fāshāo to run a fever (17)
Fǎwén (OR Fàwén) French language (7)
fēicháng + ADJ extremely ADJ (10)
fēijī airplane (6)
fēijīchǎng airport (6)
fēn minute(s); cent(s) (6)
fú to take (as medicine) (17)
fùjìn in the vicinity (10)

fúwùyuán shop clerk, waiter (7, 16)

gāncǎo licorice root (17)
Gǎn'ēnjié Thanksgiving (16)
gāng + VERB has just verbed (11)
gānjìng be clean (8)
gǎnkuài hurriedly (6)
gāo be tall (19)
gāoxìng be happy, be glad (4)
ge [measure] (5)
gēge elder brother (5)
gěi to give (7)
gěi P xiě xìn to write P a letter (13)
gēn with, and (8)
gōngsī company (4)
gōngyuán park (10)
gōngzuò to work; job (9)
gǒu dog (5)
guài be strange (19)
guàibùdé no wonder . . . (19)
Guǎngdōnghuà Cantonese, spoken (7)
Gùgōng Old Imperial Palace (15)
guì be honorable (4), be expensive (7)
guìxìng? What is your family name? (4)
guò to cross, to exceed (11)
guòlái to come over (11)

hái still, in addition (5)
hái méiyǒu + VERB haven't yet verbed (9)
háishi either A or B? (15)
háiyǒu what's more, moreover (18)
háizi child(ren) (9)
Hán [surname] (6)
Hànyǔ Hàn Chinese language (7)
hǎo be good, be well (3)
hào [measure] (8)
hǎochī be tasty (14)
hǎokàn be nice-looking (15)
hǎole, hǎole okay, okay (9)
hǎoxiàng seems as though . . . (6)
hǎoxiào be funny, be laughable (18)
hē to drink (6)
hé and, with (5)
hěn very (3)
hěn jiǔ a (very) long time (13)
hóng be red (10)

hónglǜdēng traffic light (10)
hóulóng throat (17)
hòumiàn behind (15)
huà speech, spoken words (8)
huài be bad, be broken (11)
huānyíng welcome (12)
huānyíng nǐ lái (We) welcome your visit. (12)
huì to know how to, can (12)
huì + VERB will (likely) verb (8)
huǐr (or yìhuǐr) awhile (11)
huǒchē train (15)
huǒchēzhàn train station (15)
huǒjī turkey (16)
huǒjì waiter (16)
huòzhě or (16)
hùzhào passport (9)

jí be anxious (6)
jǐ how many? (5)
jǐ be crowded (15)
jiā family, home (5), [measure] (9)
jiālǐ in home, at home (8)
jiàn [measure] (19)
jiàn miàn to meet somebody in person (13)
Jiānádà Canada (7)
jiānbǎng shoulder (17)
jiǎng to recount, to talk, to explain (18)
jiànkāng be healthy (19)
jiāo to teach (19)
jiǎo foot (17)
jiào to call, to order, to shout (4, 6)
jiàoliàn coach (4)
jiǎozi dumplings (12)
jǐdiǎn, jǐdiǎn zhōng What time is it? (6)
jiē street (10)
jié festival, holiday (16)
jiè to borrow, to lend (12)
jiègěi to lend to somebody (12)
jiéhūn to marry (9)
jiějie elder sister (4)
jiěmèi sister(s) (5)
jīn [weight measure] (14)
jìn to enter (8)
jìn be close, be near (10)
Jīngjù Běijīng Opera (18)

jīnglǐ manager (4)
jìnlái to come in (8)
jīnnián this year (9)
jīntiān today (9)
jīròu chicken (16)
jǐsuì how many years old? (9)
jǐtiān how many days? (9)
jiǔ nine (5)
jiǔ a long time (13)
jiǔ liquor, alcoholic beverage (16)
jiù then (8)
jiù gòu le would (then) be enough (14)
jiù shì to be none other than (11)
jiǔyuè September (9)
juéde to feel (18)

kāi to open, to turn on, to wisecrack, to drive, to convene (12)
kāi wánxiào to crack a joke (12)
kāishǐ to start, to begin (17)
kàn to look at, to read (5)
kàndào to see (10)
kàngshēngsù antibiotic(s) (17)
kànkan to take a look (6)
kǎo to roast (16)
kǎo huǒjī roast turkey (16)
ké to cough (17)
kě be thirsty (16)
kě'ài be cute, be lovable (5)
kèqi be polite, be considerate (11)
kěshì but, yet (7)
késòu to cough (17)
kěyǐ to be permitted, to be able, to be okay (11)
kòng free time, leisure time (11)
kǔ be bitter (16)
kuài [measure] (7)
kuài be fast (12)
kuài + VERB + le about to verb, on the verge of verbing (12)
kuàizi chopsticks (13)
kuàngquán shuǐ spring water (19)
kùzi pants (19)

là be hot, be spicy (16)
lái to come (8, 12), to bring (16)
lǎo be old (8)

Lǎo + surname Ol' [surname] (8)
lǎorén old person (15)
lǎoshī teacher (3)
lǎoshì VERB always (19)
lǎoshǔ mouse (3)
le [particle] (6)
lèi be tired (19)
lěng be cold (19)
lí distance from (15)
lǐ in (8)
lǐ [measure] (10)
liǎn face (17)
liàn to practice (19)
liǎng two (6)
liǎnjiá cheek (17)
liáo tiān to chat (6)
lǐbiān inside (10)
Lìlián [name] (4)
Lín [surname] (6)
líng zero (5)
lǐtou inside (15)
liú to flow (17)
liú bíshuǐ to have a runny nose (17)
liù six (5)
liùyuè June (9)
lù deer (5)
lù road, [as measure, "route"] (10, 15)
lǜ be green (10)
lǜ de green, a green one (17)

ma [particle] (3)
mǎi to buy (7)
mài to sell (7)
māma mom, mama (3)
màn be slow (19)
máng be busy (3)
mànpǎo to jog (19)
māo cat (5)
máo dime [measure] (7)
máoyī sweater (19)
méi not (5)
méi guānxi It doesn't matter. (8)
měi-MEAS-NOUN every noun, each noun (18)
méi shénme It's nothing to speak of. (11)
méi VERB guò have never verbed (18)

méi xiǎngdào didn't realize . . . (13)

Měiguó America (7)

Měiguórén American person(s), an American (13)

méimáo eyebrows (17)

mèimei younger sister (5)

měitiān zǎoshàng every morning (19)

méiyǒu + NOUN have no noun, don't have (5)

méiyǒu + VERB haven't verbed, didn't verb (9)

Mínglěi [name] (3)

míngzi name (4)

Mòxīgē Mexico (7)

ná to hand, to hold, to take or bring (10, 13)

nà that (5)

nà fùjìn in that vicinity (10)

nágěi to hand to somebody, to pass (12)

nǎlǐ where?/"How could that be?" (12)

nàlǐ there (8)

nàme in that case, so (7)

nán male (4)

nánfāng the South (of a country), southern (12)

nánfāngrén southerner (12)

nǎr where? (9)

nàr there (8)

ne [particle] (3, 12)

nèi that (5)

něinián which year? (9)

néng to be able (11)

nǐ you (3)

nǐ hǎo hi, hello (3)

nǐ māma your mom (3)

nián year (bound form) (9)

niánxīn annual salary (9)

nǐde your (4)

nǐmen you (plural) (7)

nín you (honorific) (3)

Niǔyuē New York (13)

nǚ female (4)

NUM + cì NUM times (9)

NUM + hào the NUMth day of the month (9)

NUM + suì NUM years old (9)

nǚpéngyou girlfriend (4)

Ō Oh (12)

pángxiè crab (15)

pǎo to run (19)

péngyou friend (4)

piányi be cheap (14)

piào ticket (6)

piàoliàng be pretty (14)

píjiǔ beer (16)

píng [measure] (16)

qī seven (5)

qì vapor (16)

qì breath, air (19)

qián money (7)

qìchē automobile (6)

qǐfēi to take off (6)

qìgōng deep-breathing exercises (19)

qìguǎn bronchial tubes (17)

qìguǎnyán bronchitis (17)

qīng be green, be blue (16)

qǐng please (8, 9), to invite, to request (11)

qǐng zuò please have a seat (12)

qīngchǔ be clear (18)

qǐngwèn May I ask. . . ? (4)

qìshuǐ soda pop (16)

qiūtiān autumn (fall) (14)

qīyuè July (9)

qù to go, to go to (6)

qùnián last year (19)

qúnzi skirt (19)

ràng to permit, to let (17)

ránhòu afterward, later (17)

rè be hot (14)

rén person(s) (5)

rènshì to be acquainted with, to recognize (4)

Rìběn Japan (7)

Rìběnhuà spoken Japanese (7)

Rìwén Japanese language (7)

ròu meat (14)

ruǎn be soft (8)

sān three (5)

Sānjiě Third Elder Sister (4)

sānyuè March (9)

shàng on (8)

shàng to go to, to get on (10)

shàng + time words last, previous (17)

shàng cèsuǒ to go to the toilet (10)

shéi who? (4)

shēng to be born (9)

shēng bìng le have fallen ill, have gotten sick (17)

shēngcài lettuce (14)

shēngyì business, commerce (13)

shénme what? (4)

shénme shíhòu when? (9)

shénmeyàng de NOUN what kind of NOUN? (19)

shēntǐ body, physique (19)

shí ten (5)

shì to be, is, am, are (3)

shì things to do (6)

shíèryuè December (9)

shīfu sir, ma'am, master (used in PRC) (14)

shíhòu time (9)

shíjiān time (duration) (15)

shíyīyuè November (9)

shíyuè October (9)

shǒu hand (13)

shòu be thin (19)

shǒubì arm (17)

shǒuzhǐ finger (17)

shū book (7)

shuǐ water (16)

shuō to say, to speak (5)

shúshu paternal uncle (5)

sì four (5)

sìyuè April (9)

suān be sour, be tart (16)

suānlà tāng hot-and-sour soup (16)

suànle the heck with it, enough already (10)

suǒyǐ therefore (13)

tā he, she, it (3)

tài + ADJ too adjective (8)

tàitai Mrs. (after surname), a married lady (11)

Táiwān Taiwan (7)

Táiwānhuà Taiwanese, spoken (7)

tán phlegm, coughed-up mucus (17)

tāng soup (16)

táng sugar (16)

tángcù yú sweet-and-sour fish (16)

tiān day (bound form) (9)

tián be sweet (16)

tiānqì weather (14)

tiáo [measure] (5)

tīng to listen (9, 12)

tīngbùdǒng cannot understand (through listening) (9)

tòng to ache, to hurt (17)

tóu head (17)

tóu tòng to have a headache (17)

tóufà [or tóufǎ] hair (17)

tuǐ leg (15)

túnbù [OR pìgǔ] buttocks (17)

tūrán suddenly (18)

VERB-bùqǐ can't afford to verb (18)

VERB + guò have verbed before (18)

VERB + hǎo to finish verbing (12)

VERB + zhe is verbing (11)

wàitou outside (15)

wán to play (12)

wán pill (17)

wǎn bowl (16)

wàng toward, to (10)

wǎnshàng evening, night (6)

wánxiào joke (12)

wàzi socks (19)

wéi hello (used at start of phone calls) (11)

wèi [measure] (8)

wèishēng be sanitary (10)

wèishēng zhǐ toilet paper (10)

wèishénme why? (13)

wèn to ask (4)

wèntí question, problem (9)

wènwen kàn to try asking about something (16)

wǒ I, me (3)

wǒ jiù shì It's none other than I; "Speaking" (11)

wǒmen we, us (6)

wǔ five (5)

wǔyuè May (9)

xī west (10)

xià to get off (bus), to fall (rain), below (12)

xià yǔ It's raining. (12)

xiàbā chin (17)

xiān + VERB first verb (6)

xiān VERB1, zài VERB2 first VERB1, then VERB2 (10)

xián be salty (16)

xiǎng to think, to miss somebody (13)

xiǎng + VERB would like to verb, want to verb (11)

xiǎngdào to realize (13)

Xiānggǎng Hong Kong (7)

Xiānggǎngrén Hong Kong person(s) (13)

xiānsheng Mr. (6), sir (8), husband (11)

xiànzài now (6)

xiǎo be young, be little (6), be small (8)

xiào to laugh (12)

xiǎojiě Miss, young woman (4)

xiàsǐ le to be scared to death (18)

xiàtiān summer (14)

xiàwǔ afternoon (6)

Xībānyáwén Spanish (7)

xiē [plural measure] (12)

xiē (short for yìxiē) some (16)

xiě to write (something in particular) (13)

xiě zì to write (VERB-OBJ) (13)

xiézi shoes (19)

xīgài knee (17)

xīguā watermelon (14)

xíguàn to be accustomed; habit (13)

xǐhuān to like, to be fond of (12)

xìn letter; to believe (13)

xíng okay, all right (14)

xìng to be surnamed (4)

xīngqī week (17)

xīngqī'èr Tuesday (17)

xīngqīliù Saturday (17)

xīngqīsān Wednesday (17)

xīngqīsì Thursday (17)

xīngqītiān [OR xīngqīrì] Sunday (17)

xīngqīwǔ Friday (17)

xīngqīyī Monday (17)

Xīnjiāpō Singapore (7)

xiōng [or xiōngbù] chest (17)

xiōngdì brother(s) (5)

xiūlǐ to repair (11)

xiūxi to rest (17)

xué to learn, to study (4)

xuéshēng student (4)

yā, yāzi duck (14)

yáchǐ teeth (17)

yǎng to raise (children, pets, livestock, and so on) (14)

yǎnjīng eyes (17)

yánsè color (17)

yǎnyuán actor (18)

yǎo to bite (8)

yào want, going to, must (6), to order (16)

yào medicine (17)

yàojǐn be important (12)

yàoshi key (9)

yě also, too (3)

yěxǔ perhaps, maybe (19)

yī, yì, yí one, a (5)

yíbàn half, halfway (18)

yícì once, one time (9)

yìdiǎnr yě bù ADJ not even a little bit ADJ (19)

yīfu clothing (14)

yígòng altogether, in toto (5)

yìhuǐr (huǐr) awhile (11)

yíkuàir together (11)

yǐjīng already (6)

yìliǎng + MEAS one or two of them (8)

yīnggāi should (15)

Yīngguó England (9)

Yīngwén English-language (7)

yínháng bank (9)

yīnwèi because (13)

yīnwèi A, suǒyǐ B because A, . . . B (13)

yìqǐ together (8)

yīshēng medical doctor (17)

yìsi meaning (11)

yǐwéi to have mistakenly thought that (16)

yìxiē some (of them) (12)

yíyàng be the same (19)

yīyuè January (9)

yìzhǒng NOUN a kind of noun (17)

yòng to use (10), with (instrumental) (13)

yǒu to have, there is, there are (5)

yòu right (side) (10)

yǒu rén (as SUBJ) . . . there's somebody . . . (15)

yǒu (de) shíhou sometimes (18)

yòu VERB1 yòu VERB2 both VERB1 and VERB2 (14)

yǒu yìsī be interesting, be fun (18)

yǒudiǎn + ADJ be a bit ADJ (8)

yóuqíshi especially (14)

yóuyǒng to swim (4)

yóuyǒng jiàoliàn swimming coach (4)

yǔ rain (12)

yuǎn be far, be distant (10)

yuánlái originally (11)

yuè month (bound form) (9)

yùndòng exercise; to exercise (19)

yǔsǎn umbrella (12)

yùshì bathroom (8)

zài another, again (7)

zài to be at, to be there (11)

zài + PW + VERB verb at PW (9)

zài shuō yícì Say it once again; say it one more time. (9)

zài + VERB is verbing (11)

zàijiàn see you later, good-bye (3)

zāng be dirty (8)

zāogāo! darn! (6)

zěnme how? / how come? (5)

zěnme bàn? What'll I do? (10)

zěnme nàme ADJ how come so ADJ? (9)

zěnmeyàng How was it? / How are things? (18)

zhàn to stand (15)

zhāngkāi to open (mouth) (17)

zhànzhe to be standing, to remain standing (15)

zhǎo to return in change, to look for (7)

zhème + ADJ be so ADJ (8)

zhāng [measure] (5)

zhāngláng cockroach (8)

zhàopiàn photograph (5)

zhè this (7)

zhèi this (5)

zhèlǐ here (8)

zhēn truly, really (5, 11)

zhèr here (8)

zhī [measure] (5)

zhǐ only (7)

zhǐ paper (10)

zhīdào to know (something) (14)

zhǐhǎo the only thing to do is (15)

zhíyuán employee (8)

zhōng clock (6)

zhǒng [measure for "type of"] (17)

Zhōng yào Chinese medicine (17)

Zhōngguó China (7)

Zhōngguóhuà spoken Chinese (7)

Zhōngwén Chinese language (5, 7)

zhū pig (14)

zhù to stay, to live (8)

zhuā to pinch, to grab (15)

zhuǎn to turn (10)

zhuōzi table (8)

zhūròu pork (14)

zhùzài + PW to live at PW (13)

zì Chinese character, word (13)

zǒu to go, to leave, to walk (10)

zǔfù grandfather (5)

zuǐ mouth (17)

zuì + ADJ the most ADJ (19)

zuǐba mouth (17)

zuǐchún lips (17)

zuìjìn recently (19)

zǔmǔ grandmother (5)

zuǒ left (10)

zuò to do, to make (11)

zuò to sit, to ride a conveyance (12, 15)

zuò fàn to cook (VERB-OBJ) (11)

zuò shēngyì to do business (13)

zuò yùndòng to do exercises (19)

zuòwèi seat, place to sit (15)

APPENDIX 3: ENGLISH-CHINESE PĪNYĪN GLOSSARY

This list includes all the vocabulary from the dialogues as well as some important words in the grammar notes and exercises. The number in parentheses in each entry indicates the chapter in which the vocabulary item is featured and in which more detailed information on its meaning and usage is available.

a yī, yì, yí (5)
a bit + ADJ yǒudiǎn + ADJ (8)
able to kěyǐ (11)
about to VERB, on the verge of verbing
  kuài + VERB + le (12)
accustomed, be used to xíguàn (13)
ache, hurt tòng (17)
act biǎoyǎn (18)
actor yǎnyuán (18)
afternoon xiàwǔ (6)
afterward, later ránhòu (17)
again zài (7)
air qì (19)
airplane fēijī (6)
airport fēijīchǎng (6)
alcoholic beverage jiǔ (16)
all, both dōu (14)
already yǐjīng (6)
also yě (3)
altogether yígòng (5)
always lǎoshì VERB (19)
am shì (3)
America Měiguó (7)
American person(s), an American
  Měiguórén (13)
and (connects nouns) hé (5), gēn (8)
annual salary niánxīn (9)
another biéde (8)
antibiotic kàngshēngsù (17)
anxious jí (6)
approximately, about dàgài (14)
April sìyuè (9)

are shì (3)
arm shǒubì (17)
arrive dào (10)
ask (for information) wèn (4)
at home jiālǐ (8)
at PW zài + PW (9)
August bāyuè (9)
automobile qìchē (6)
autumn qiūtiān (14)
awhile huǐr (or yìhuǐr) (11)

back bèi [or bèibù] (17)
bad huài (11)
bag dàizi (15)
bank yínháng (9)
bathroom yùshì (8)
be acquainted with rènshi (4)
be at, be there zài (11)
be born shēng (9)
be called jiào (4)
be embarrassed bù hǎo yìsi (11)
be none other than jiù shì (11)
be permitted kěyǐ (11)
because yīnwèi (13)
because A, . . . B yīnwèi A, suǒyǐ B (13)
bed chuáng (8)
bedsheets chuángdān (8)
beer píjiǔ (16)
begin kāishǐ (17)
behind hòumiàn (15)
Běijīng Hotel Běijīng Fàndiàn (10)
Běijīng Opera Jīngjù (18)

309

below xià (12)

big dà (8)

bite yǎo (8)

bitter kǔ (16)

body, physique shēntǐ (19)

book shū (7)

borrow, lend jiè (12)

both dōu (14)

both VERB1 and VERB2 yòu VERB1
   yòu VERB2 (14)

bowl wǎn (16)

breath, air qì (19)

bring ná (12), lái (16)

broken huài (11)

bronchial tubes qìguǎn (17)

bronchitis qìguǎnyán (17)

brother(s) xiōngdì (5)

burp dǎ gé (19)

business, commerce shēngyì (13)

busy máng (3)

but, yet kěshì (7) dànshì (18)

buttocks túnbù [or pìgǔ] (17)

buy mǎi (7)

call jiào (6)

can huì (12)

Canada Jiānádà (7)

cannot afford to verb VERB-bùqǐ (18)

cannot hear clearly tīngbùqīngchǔ (18)

cannot see kànbújiàn (18)

cannot understand (through listening)
   tīngbùdǒng (9)

Cantonese, spoken Guǎngdōnghuà (7)

cat māo (5)

cent(s) [measure] fēn (7)

chat liáo tiān (6)

cheap piányi (14)

cheek liǎnjiá (17)

chest xiōng [or xiōngbù] (17)

chicken jīròu (16)

child(ren) háizi (9)

chin xiàbā (17)

China Zhōngguó (7)

Chinese Zhōngwén (5, 7)

Chinese character, word zì (13)

Chinese medicine Zhōng yào (17)

Chinese, spoken Zhōngguóhuà (7)

chopsticks kuàizi (13)

city, city wall chéng (15)

clean gānjìng (8)

clear qīngchǔ (18)

clock zhōng (6)

close, near jìn (10)

clothing yīfu (14)

coach jiàoliàn (4)

cockroach zhāngláng (8)

cold lěng (19)

color yánsè (17)

come lái (8, 12)

come in jìnlái (8)

come over guòlái (11)

company gōngsī (4)

comparatively bǐjiào (10)

compared to bǐ (19)

computer diànnǎo (11)

considerate kèqi (11)

contract, get dé (17)

convene (meeting) kāi (12)

convenient fāngbiàn (11)

cook (VERB) zuò fàn (11)

cooked rice fàn (11)

cooked white rice báifàn (16)

correct, "That's right . . ." duì (13)

cough késòu, ké (17)

crab pángxiè (15)

crack a joke kāi wánxiào (12)

cross, exceed guò (11)

crowded jǐ (15)

cuisine, national cài (16)

cup bēi, bēizi (6)

cute kě'ài (5)

dad bàba (3)

darn! zāogāo! (6)

day (bound form) tiān (9)

December shí'èryuè (9)

deep-breathing exercises qìgōng (19)

deer lù (5)

department store bǎihuò gōngsī (19)

dictionary cídiǎn (7)

didn't realize . . . méi xiǎngdào (13)

didn't verb méiyǒu + VERB (9)

different bù yíyàng (19)
dime [measure] máo (7)
dirty zāng (8)
dish, cooked cài (16)
distance from lí (15)
do exercises zuò yùndòng (19)
do, make zuò (11)
doesn't matter bú yàojǐn (12)
dog gǒu (5)
don't VERB bié + VERB (6)
dot diǎn (6)
drink hē (6)
drive (vehicle) kāi (12)
duck yā, yāzi (14)
dumplings jiǎozi (12)

ear ěrduo (17)
east dōng (10)
eat food chī fàn (11)
eat something chī (11)
eight bā (5)
elder brother gēge (5)
elder sister jiějie (4)
electric, electricity diàn (8)
employee zhíyuán (8)
England Yīngguó (9)
English language Yīngwén (7)
enter jìn (8)
escort dài (10)
especially yóuqíshi (14)
evening wǎnshàng (6)
ever verbed OBJ before VERB-guò-OBJ (18)
every morning měitiān zǎoshàng (19)
every noun, each noun měi-MEAS-NOUN (18)
exercise, to exercise yùndòng (19)
exit (VERB) chū (8)
expensive guì
extremely ADJ fēicháng + ADJ (10)
eyebrows méimáo(17)
eyes yǎnjīng (17)

face liǎn (17)
fall (rain, snow) xià (12)
fall ill shēng bìng (17)

family jiā (5)
far, distant yuǎn (10)
fast kuài (12)
February èryuè (9)
feel juéde (18)
female nǚ (4)
festival, holiday jié (16)
fever, to run a fāshāo (17)
finger shǒuzhǐ (17)
finish verbing VERB + hǎo (12)
first VERB xiān + VERB (6)
first VERB1, then VERB2 xiān VERB1, zài VERB2 (10)
five wǔ (5)
flow liú (17)
food fàn (11)
foot jiǎo (17)
forehead étóu (17)
four sì (5)
France Fǎguó (OR Fàguó) (7)
free time, leisure time kòng (11)
French language Fǎwén (OR Fàwén) (7)
Friday xīngqīwǔ (17)
friend péngyou (4)
from cóng (10)
funny hǎoxiào (18)

German language Déwén (7)
Germany Déguó (7)
get off (bus) xià (12)
girlfriend nǚpéngyou (4)
give gěi (7)
go, go to qù (6)
go out chūqù (8)
go to, get on shàng (10)
go to the toilet shàng cèsuǒ (10)
good hǎo (3)
good for the noun duì NOUN hěn hǎo (17)
good-bye zàijiàn (3)
grandfather zǔfù (5)
grandmother zǔmǔ (5)
Great Wall of China Chángchéng (15)
green lǜ (10), qīng (16)
green, a green one lǜ de (17)
green vegetables qīngcài (16)

habit, custom xíguàn (13)

hair tóufà [or tóufǎ] (17)

half bàn (6)

half, halfway yíbàn (18)

Hàn Chinese language Hànyǔ (7)

hand shǒu (13)

hand, hold, take ná (10, 12)

hand to somebody, pass nágěi (12)

handle, do bàn (10)

happy gāoxìng (4)

have yǒu (5)

have a headache tóu tòng (17)

have a runny nose liú bíshuǐ (17)

have just verbed gāng + VERB (11)

have no NOUN, don't have méiyǒu + NOUN (5)

haven't verbed, didn't verb méiyǒu + VERB (9)

haven't yet verbed hái méiyǒu + VERB (9)

he tā (3)

head tóu (17)

healthy jiànkāng (19)

heck with it, the suànle (10)

hello nǐ hǎo (3)

hello (used at start of phone calls) wéi (11)

help (VERB) bāng (12)

here zhèr, zhèlǐ (8)

hit, manipulate by hand dǎ (13)

hold, take or bring ná (10, 13)

holiday jié (16)

home jiā (5)

Hong Kong Xiānggǎng (7)

Hong Kong person(s) Xiānggǎngrén (13)

honorable guì (4)

hot rè (14)

hot-and-sour soup suānlà tāng (16)

hotel fàndiàn (10)

how ADJ it is! duóme + ADJ (8)

how come? zěnme (5)

how come so ADJ? zěnme nàme ADJ (9)

How is it? / How are things? zěnmeyàng (18)

how long (in duration)? duōjiǔ (9)

how many? jǐ (5), duōshǎo (7)

how many days? jǐtiān (9)

how many years old? jǐsuì (9)

how much? duōshǎo (7)

however kěshì (7), dànshì (18)

hungry è (12)

hurriedly gǎnkuài (6)

hurt, ache tòng (17)

husband xiānsheng (11)

I wǒ (3)

important yàojǐn (12)

in lǐ (8)

in addition hái (5)

in that case nàme (7)

in that vicinity nà fùjìn (10)

in the vicinity fùjìn (10)

inside lǐbiān (10), lǐtou (15)

interesting, fun yǒu yìsi (18)

invite qǐng (11)

is shì (3)

it tā (3)

It doesn't matter. méi guānxi (8)

January (9) yīyuè (9)

Japan Rìběn (7)

Japanese language Rìwén (7)

Japanese, spoken Rìběnhuà (7)

jealous chī cù (12)

jog mànpǎo (19)

joke wánxiào (12)

July qīyuè (9)

June liùyuè (9)

key yàoshi (9)

kind, type zhǒng [measure] (17)

knee xīgài (17)

knife and fork dāochā (13)

know (something) zhīdào (14)

know how to, can huì (12)

lamp dēng (10)

last, previous + time word shàng + time word (17)

last year qùnián (19)

laugh xiào (12)
laughable hǎoxiào (18)
learn xué (4)
leave, go, walk zǒu (10)
left (side) zuǒ (10)
leg tuǐ (15)
lend jiè (12)
lend to somebody jiègěi (12)
let, permit ràng (17)
letter, to believe xìn (13)
lettuce shēngcài (14)
licorice root gāncǎo (17)
like, be fond of xǐhuān (12)
lips zuǐchún (17)
liquor jiǔ (16)
listen tīng (9)
little xiǎo (6)
live at PW zhùzài + PW (13)
live, stay zhù (8)
long cháng (15)
long time, a jiǔ (13)
look at kàn (5)
look for zhǎo (7)
love ài (5)

make zuò (11)
make a phone call dǎ diànhuà (13)
male nán (4)
malfunction (VERB) huài (11)
manager jīnglǐ (4)
many duō (9)
map dìtú (7)
March sānyuè (9)
marry jiéhūn (9)
master shīfu (14)
May wǔyuè (9)
May I ask . . . ? qǐngwèn (4)
me wǒ (3)
meal fàn (11)
meaning yìsi (11)
meat ròu (14)
medical doctor yīshēng (17)
medicine yào (17)
meet somebody in person jiàn miàn (13)
menu càidān (16)

Mexico Mòxīgē (7)
minute(s) fēn (6)
Miss xiǎojiě (4)
miss somebody xiǎng (13)
mistakenly thought that, have yǐwéi (16)
mom māma (3)
Monday xīngqīyī (17)
money qián (7)
month (bound form) yuè (9)
more of the object, VERB duō VERB OBJ (17)
moreover háiyǒu (18)
most adjective, the zuì + ADJ (19)
mouse lǎoshǔ (3)
mouth zuǐ [or zuǐba] (17)
Mr. xiānsheng (6)
Mrs. (after surname), a married lady tàitai (11)
much duō (15)
must yào (6), děi (15)

name míngzi (4)
nasal discharge bíshuǐ (17)
naturally dāngrán (11)
neck bózi [or jǐng] (17)
New York Niǔyuē (13)
newspaper bàozhǐ (7)
nice-looking hǎokàn (15)
night wǎnshàng (6)
nine jiǔ (5)
no bù (3), méi (5)
no need to VERB búyòng + VERB (10)
no wonder . . . guàibùdé (19)
north běi (10)
nose bízi (17)
nostril bíkǒng (17)
not bù (3), méi (5)
not ADJ enough búgòu + ADJ (8)
not even a little bit ADJ yìdiǎnr yě bù ADJ (19)
not very ADJ bútài + ADJ (11)
nothing to speak of méi shénme (11)
November shíyīyuè (9)
now xiànzài (6)

NUM times NUM + cì (9)
NUM years old NUM + suì (9)
NUMth day of the month NUM + hào (9)
numerous duō (a bound form) (15)

o'clock diǎn (6)
October shíyuè (9)
of course dāngrán (11)
often chángcháng (19)
okay kěyǐ (11), xíng (14)
okay, okay hǎole, hǎole (9)
old lǎo (8)
Old Imperial Palace Gùgōng (15)
old person lǎorén (15)
on shàng (8)
once, one time yícì (9)
one yī, yì, yí (5)
one or two of them yìliǎng + MEAS (8)
only zhǐ (7)
only then, only cái (12)
only thing to do is zhǐhǎo (15)
open (mouth) zhāngkāi (17)
open, turn on kāi (12)
opposite side, across the way duìmiàn (15)
or huòzhě (16)
or (in exclusive question) háishi (15)
order (dishes) jiào, diǎn, yào (16)
originally yuánlái (11)
outside wàitou (15)

pants kùzi (19)
paper zhǐ (10)
park gōngyuán (10)
passport hùzhào (9)
perform biǎoyǎn (18)
perhaps, maybe yěxǔ (19)
permit, let ràng (17)
person(s) rén (5)
pet chǒngwù (5)
phlegm, coughed-up mucus tán (17)
photograph zhàopiàn (5)
pig zhū (14)
pill wán (17)
pinch, grab zhuā (15)

plan dǎsuàn (9)
play wán (12)
please qǐng (8, 9)
polite kèqi (11)
pork zhūròu (14)
practice liàn (19)
pretty piàoliàng (14)
pretty good, not bad búcuò (19)
probably dàgài (10)

question, problem wèntí (9)

rain yǔ (12)
raise (children, pets, livestock, and so on) yǎng (14)
read kàn (5)
realize xiǎngdào (13)
really zhēn (5, 11)
recently zuìjìn (19)
recount jiǎng (18)
red hóng (10)
repair xiūlǐ (11)
request qǐng (11)
rest xiūxi (17)
restaurant fànguǎn (16)
return in change, look for zhǎo (7)
ride a conveyance, sit zuò (12, 15)
right, correct duì (13)
right (side) yòu (10)
road lù (10)
roast kǎo (16)
room fángjiān (8)
route, bus lù (15)
run pǎo (19)
Russia Éguó (OR Èguó) (7)
Russian language Éwén (OR Èwén) (7)

salty xián (16)
same yíyàng (19)
sanitary wèishēng (10)
Saturday xīngqīliù (17)
sauté chǎo (16)
say shuō (5)
say it once again zài shuō yícì (9)
scared to death xiàsǐ le (18)
seat, place to sit zuòwèi (15)

see kàndào (10)

see you after awhile děng huǐr jiàn (11)

seems as though . . . hǎoxiàng (6)

sell mài (7)

September jiǔyuè (9)

seven qī (5)

she tā (3)

shirt chènshān (19)

shoes xiézi (19)

shop clerk fúwùyuán, diànyuán (7)

should yīnggāi (15)

shoulder jiānbǎng (17)

shout jiào

shout loudly dà jiào (18)

sickness, sick bìng (17)

Singapore Xīnjiāpō (7)

sir xiānsheng (8)

sister(s) jiěmèi (5)

sit zuò (12, 15)

six liù (5)

skirt qúnzi (19)

slow màn (19)

small xiǎo (8)

so + ADJ zhème + ADJ (8), nàme + ADJ (9)

socks wàzi (19)

soda pop qìshuǐ (16)

soft ruǎn (8)

some (of them) yìxiē (12)

sometimes yǒu (de) shíhòu (18)

sorry duìbùqǐ (3)

soup tāng (16)

sour, tart suān (16)

South, southern nánfāng (12)

southerner nánfāngrén (12)

Spanish language Xībānyáwén (7)

speak shuō (5)

speech, spoken words huà (8)

spicy hot là (16)

spring chūntiān (14)

spring water kuàngquán shuǐ (19)

stand zhàn (15)

start, begin kāishǐ (17)

stay, live zhù (8)

still hái (5)

stomach dùzi (12, 17)

strange guài (19)

street jiē (10)

student xuéshēng (4)

study xué (4)

suddenly tūrán (18)

sugar táng (16)

summer xiàtiān (14)

Sunday xīngqītiān, xīngqīrì (17)

surname xìng (4)

sweater máoyī (19)

sweet tián (16)

sweet-and-sour fish tángcù yú (16)

swim yóuyǒng (4)

table zhuōzi (8)

Taiwan Táiwān (7)

Taiwanese, spoken Táiwānhuà (7)

take a look kànkan (6)

take (medicine) fú (17)

take off (in flight) qǐfēi (6)

take or bring ná (13)

talk, explain jiǎng (18)

tall gāo (19)

tasty hǎochī (14)

taxicab chūzū qìchē (6)

tea chá (6)

teach jiāo (19)

teacher lǎoshī (3)

teeth yáchǐ (17)

telephone diànhuà (8)

ten shí (5)

terribly ADJ ADJ-sǐ le (18)

Thanksgiving Gǎn'ēnjié (16)

that nà, nèi (5)

then jiù (8)

there nàr, nàlǐ (8)

therefore suǒyǐ (13)

thin shòu (19)

thing dōngxi (19)

things to do shì (6)

think xiǎng (13)

Third Elder Sister Sānjiě (4)

thirsty kě (16)

this zhèi (5) zhè (7)

this year jīnnián (9)

three sān (5)

throat hóulóng (17)

Thursday xīngqīsì (17)

ticket piào (6)

time shíhòu (9)

time (duration) shíjiān (15)

tired lèi (19)

to + PW dào + PW (10)

today jīntiān (9)

together yìqǐ (8), yíkuàir (11)

toilet cèsuǒ (10)

toilet paper wèishēng zhǐ (10)

toward, to wàng (10)

traffic light hónglǜdēng (10)

train huǒchē (15)

train station huǒchēzhàn (15)

truly zhēn (5,11)

try asking about something wènwen kàn (16)

Tuesday xīngqī'èr (17)

turkey huǒjī (16)

turn zhuǎn (10)

turn on (appliance) kāi (12)

two èr (5), liǎng (6)

type zhǒng [measure] (17)

umbrella yǔsǎn (12)

uncle (paternal) shúshu (5)

understand dǒng (9)

us wǒmen (6)

use yòng (10)

used to, be xíguàn (13)

vapor qì (16)

vegetable cài (16)

verbing zài + VERB (11); VERB + zhe (11)

very hěn (3)

vinegar cù (12)

wait (VERB) děng (11)

waiter huǒjì, fúwùyuán (16)

walk, leave, go zǒu (10)

want yào (6)

water shuǐ (16)

watermelon xīguā (14)

we wǒmen (6)

wear (clothing) chuān (19)

weather tiānqì (14)

Wednesday xīngqīsān (17)

week xīngqī (17)

welcome huānyíng (12)

west xī (10)

what? shénme (4)

what kind of NOUN? shénmeyàng de NOUN (19)

What time is it? jǐdiǎn, jǐdiǎn zhōng (6)

What'll I do? zěnme bàn? (10)

when . . . . . . de shíhòu (14)

when? shénme shíhòu (9)

where? nǎr (9)

where?/"How could that be?" nǎlǐ (12)

which year? něinián (9)

white bái (16)

who? shéi? (4)

why? wèishénme (13)

will (likely) verb huì + VERB (8)

winter dōngtiān (14)

wisecrack kāi wánxiào (12)

with gēn (8)

with (instrumental) yòng (13)

won't (likely) verb búhuì + VERB (8)

work gōngzuò (9)

would like to VERB, want to VERB xiǎng + VERB (11)

wrap bāo (12)

write xiě, xiě zì (13)

wrong cuò (7)

year (bound form) nián (9)

yikes! āi ya! (8)

you nǐ, nín (3)

you (plural) nǐmen (7)

younger brother dìdi (5)

younger sister mèimei (5)

your nǐde (4)

zero líng (5)

APPENDIX 4: CHINESE PĪNYĪN-CHINESE CHARACTER GLOSSARY

This list includes all the vocabulary from the dialogues as well as some important words in the grammar notes and exercises. The entries in this glossary exactly match those in Appendix Two, where the English words are given. Traditional or long-form characters appear first; when a simplified-character counterpart exists, it is given in parentheses to the right of its long-form equivalent.

a	啊
ADJ + le	ADJ + 了
ADJ-sǐ le	ADJ + 死了
āi ya!	哎呀！
ài	愛（爱）
Ānnà	安娜
ba	吧
bā	八
bǎ	把
bàba	爸爸
bái	白
báifàn	白飯（饭）
bǎihuò gōngsī	百貨（货）公司
bàn	半
bàn	辦（办）
bāng	幫（帮）

bāo	包
bàozhǐ	報紙 (报纸)
bāyuè	八月
bēi	杯
běi	北
bèi (or bèibù)	背，背部
Běijīng Fàndiàn	北京飯 (饭) 店
bēizi	杯子
běn	本
bǐ	比
biān	邊 (边)
biǎoyǎn	表演
bié + VERB	別 + VERB
biéde	別的
bǐjiào	比較 (较)
bíkǒng	鼻孔
bìng	病
bíshuǐ	鼻水
bízi	鼻子
bózi (or jǐng)	脖子，頸 (颈)
bù	不
bù hǎo yìsī	不好意思
bú yàojǐn	不要緊 (紧)
bù yíyàng	不一樣 (样)
bù zhīdào NOUN-VERB-bù-VERB	不知道 NOUN - VERB - 不 - VERB

búcuò	不錯（错）
búgòu + ADJ	不夠 + ADJ
búhuì + VERB	不會（会）+ VERB
bútài + ADJ	不太 + ADJ
búyòng + VERB	不用 + VERB
búyòng xiè	不用謝（谢）
cái	才
cài	菜
càidān	菜單（单）
cèsuǒ	廁（厕）所
chá	茶
cháng	長（长）
chángcháng	常常
Chángchéng	長（长）城
chǎo	炒
chǎo qīngcài	炒青菜
chéng	城
chéng lǐtou	城裏頭（里头）
chènshān	襯（衬）衫
chēshàng	車（车）上
chī	吃
chī cù	吃醋
chī fàn	吃飯（饭）
chǒngwù	寵（宠）物

chū	出
chuān	穿
chúang	床
chuángdān	床單（单）
chūntiān	春天
chūqù	出去
chūzū qìchē	出租汽車（车）
cídiǎn	詞（词）典
cóng	從（从）
cù	醋
cuò	錯（错）
dǎ	打
dà	大
dǎ diànhuà	打電話（电话）
dǎ gé	打嗝
dà jiào	大叫
dàgài	大概
dài	帶（带）
dàizi	袋子
dāngrán	當（当）然
dànshì	但是
dào	到
dāochā	刀叉
dǎsuàn	打算

de	的
dé	得
. . . de shíhòu,	的 時 (时) 候
Déguó	德國 (国)
děi + VERB	得 + VERB
dēng	燈 (灯)
děng	等
děng huǐr jiàn	等會 (会) 兒 (儿) 見 (见)
Déwén	德文
diǎn	點 (点)
diàn	電 (电)
diànhuà	電話 (电话)
diànnǎo	電腦 (电脑)
diànyuán	店員 (员)
dìdi	弟弟
dìtú	地圖 (图)
dōng	東 (东)
dǒng	懂
dōngtiān	冬天
dōngxi	東 (东) 西
dōu	都
duì	對 (对)
duì NOUN hěn hǎo	對 (对) NOUN 很好
duìbùqǐ	對 (对) 不起
duìmiàn	對 (对) 面
duō	多

duō VERB + OBJ	多 VERB + OBJ
duōjiǔ	多久
duóme + ADJ	多麼 (么) + ADJ
duōshǎo	多少
dùzi	肚子
è	餓 (饿)
Éguó (or Èguó)	俄國 (国)
èr	二
ěrduo	耳朵 (朵)
èryuè	二月
étóu	額頭 (额头)
Éwén (or Èwén)	俄文
Fǎguó (or Fàguó)	法國 (国)
fàn	飯 (饭)
fàndiàn	飯 (饭) 店
fāngbiàn	方便
fángjiān	房間 (间)
fànguǎn	飯館 (饭馆)
fāshāo	發燒 (发烧)
Fǎwén (or Fàwén)	法文
fēicháng + ADJ	非常 + ADJ
fēijī	飛機 (飞机)
fēijīchǎng	飛機場 (飞机场)

fēn	分
fú	服
fùjìn	附近
fúwùyuán	服務 (务) 員 (员)
gāncǎo	甘草
Gǎn'ēnjié	感恩節 (节)
gāng + VERB	剛 (刚) + VERB
gānjìng	乾淨 (干净)
gǎnkuài	趕 (赶) 快
gāo	高
gāoxìng	高興 (兴)
ge	個 (个)
gēge	哥哥
gěi	給 (给)
gěi PERSON xiě xìn	給 (给) PERSON 寫 (写) 信
gēn	跟
gōngsī	公司
gōngyuán	公園 (园)
gōngzuò	工作
gǒu	狗
guài	怪
guàibùdé	怪不得
Guǎngdōnghuà	廣東話 (广东话)
Gùgōng	故宮

guì	貴（贵）
guìxìng?	貴（贵）姓？
guò	過（过）
guòlái	過來（过来）
hái	還（还）
hái méiyǒu + VERB	還（还）沒有 + VERB
háishi	還（还）是
háiyǒu	還（还）有
háizi	孩子
Hán	韓（韩）
Hànyǔ	漢語（汉语）
hǎo	好
hào	號（号）
hǎochī	好吃
hǎokàn	好看
hǎole, hǎole	好了，好了
hǎoxiàng	好像（象）
hǎoxiào	好笑
hē	喝
hé	和
hěn	很
hěn jiǔ	很久
hóng	紅（红）
hónglǜdēng	紅綠燈（红绿灯）
hóulóng	喉嚨（咙）

hòumiàn	後（后）面
huà	話（话）
huài	壞（坏）
huānyíng	歡（欢）迎
huānyíng nǐ lái	歡（欢）迎 你 來（来）
huì	會（会）
huì + VERB	會（会）+ VERB
huǐr (or yìhuǐr)	會兒（会儿），一會兒（会儿）
huǒchē	火車（车）
huǒchēzhàn	火車（车）站
huǒjī	火雞（鸡）
huǒjì	伙計（计）
huòzhě	或者
hùzhào	護（护）照

jí	急
jǐ	幾（几）
jǐ	擠（挤）
jiā	家
jiālǐ	家裏（里）
jiàn	件
jiàn miàn	見（见）面
Jiānádà	加拿大
jiānbǎng	肩膀
jiǎng	講（讲）

jiànkāng	健康
jiāo	教
jiǎo	腳（脚）
jiào	叫
jiàoliàn	教練（练）
jiǎozi	餃（饺）子
jǐdiǎn	幾點（几点）
jǐdiǎn zhōng	幾點鐘（几点钟）
jiē	街
jié	節（节）
jiè	借
jiègěi	借給（给）
jiéhūn	結（结）婚
jiějie	姊姊（姐姐）
jiěmèi	姊（姐）妹
jīn	斤
jìn	進（进）
jìn	近
Jīngjù	京劇（剧）
jīnglǐ	經（经）理
jìnlái	進來（进来）
jīnnián	今年
jīntiān	今天
jīròu	雞（鸡）肉
jǐsuì	幾歲（几岁）

jǐtiān	幾（几）天
jiǔ	九
jiǔ	久
jiǔ	酒
jiù	就
jiù gòu le	就夠了
jiù shì	就是
jiǔyuè	九月
juéde	覺（觉）得
kāi	開（开）
kāi wánxiào	開（开）玩笑
kāishǐ	開（开）始
kàn	看
kàndào	看到
kàngshēngsù	抗生素
kànkan	看看
kǎo	烤
kǎo huǒjī	烤火雞（鸡）
ké	咳
kě	渴
kě'ài	可愛（爱）
kèqi	客氣（气）
kěshì	可是
késòu	咳嗽

kěyǐ	可以
kòng	空
kǔ	苦
kuài	塊（块）
kuài	快
kuài + VERB + le	快 + VERB + 了
kuàizi	筷子
kuàngquán shuǐ	礦（矿）泉水
kùzi	褲（裤)子
là	辣
lái	來（来）
lǎo	老
Lǎo + surname	老 + surname
lǎorén	老人
lǎoshī	老師（师）
lǎoshì + VERB	老是 + VERB
lǎoshǔ	老鼠
le	了
lèi	累
lěng	冷
lí	離（离）
lǐ	裏（里）
lǐ	里
liǎn	臉（脸）

liàn	練（练）
liǎng	兩（两）
liǎnjiá	臉頰（脸颊）
liáo tiān	聊天
lǐbiān	裏邊（里边）
Lìlián	麗蓮（丽莲）
Lín	林
líng	零
lǐtou	裏頭（里头）
liú	流
liú bíshuǐ	流鼻水
liù	六
liùyuè	六月
lù	鹿
lù	路
lǜ	綠（绿）
lǜ de	綠（绿）的
ma	嗎（吗）
mǎi	買（买）
mài	賣（卖）
māma	媽媽（妈妈）
màn	慢
máng	忙
mànpǎo	慢跑

māo	貓（猫）
máo	毛
máoyī	毛衣
méi	沒
méi guānxi	沒關（关）係（系）
měi + MEAS + NOUN	每 + MEAS + NOUN
méi shénme	沒什麼（么）
méi VERB guò	沒 VERB 過（过）
méi xiǎngdào	沒想到
Měiguó	美國（国）
Měiguórén	美國（国）人
méimáo	眉毛
mèimei	妹妹
měitiān zǎoshàng	每天早上
méiyǒu + NOUN	沒有 + NOUN
méiyǒu + VERB	沒有 + VERB
Mínglěi	銘（铭）磊
míngzi	名字
Mòxīgē	墨西哥
ná	拿
nà	那
nà fùjìn	那附近
nágěi	拿給（给）
nǎlǐ	哪裏（里）
nàlǐ	那裏（里）

nàme	那麼（么）
nánfāng	南方
nánfāngrén	南方人
nǎr	哪兒（儿）
nàr	那兒（儿）
ne	呢
nèi	那
něinián	哪年
nǐ	你
nǐ hǎo	你好
nǐ māma	你媽媽（妈妈）
nián	年
niánxīn	年薪
nǐde	你的
nǐmen	你們（们）
nín	您
Niǔyūe	紐約（纽约）
nǚ	女
NUM + cì	NUM + 次
NUM + hào	NUM + 號（号）
NUM + suì	NUM + 歲（岁）
nǚpéngyou	女朋友
Ō	哦

pángxiè	螃蟹
pǎo	跑
péngyou	朋友
piányi	便宜
piào	票
piàoliàng	漂亮
píjiǔ	啤酒
píng	瓶
qī	七
qì	汽
qì	氣（气）
qián	錢（钱）
qìchē	汽車（车）
qǐfēi	起飛（飞）
qìgōng	氣（气）功
qìguǎn	氣（气）管
qìguǎnyán	氣（气）管炎
qīng	青
qǐng	請（请）
qǐng zuò	請（请）坐
qīngchǔ	清楚
qǐngwèn	請問（请问）
qìshuǐ	汽水
qiūtiān	秋天

qīyuè	七月
qù	去
qùnián	去年
qúnzi	裙子
ràng	讓（让）
ránhòu	然後（后）
rè	熱（热）
rén	人
rènshì	認識（认识）
Rìběn	日本
Rìběnhuà	日本話（话）
Rìwén	日文
ròu	肉
ruǎn	軟（软）
sān	三
Sānjiě	三姊（姐）
sānyuè	三月
shàng	上
shàng + TIME WORD	上 + TIME WORD
shàng cèsuǒ	上廁（厕）所
shéi	誰（谁）
shēng	生
shēng bìng le	生病了

shēngcài	生菜
shēngyì	生意
shénme	什麼（么）
shénme shíhòu	什麼（么）時（时）候
shénmeyàng de + NOUN	什麼（么）樣（样）的 + NOUN
shēntǐ	身體(体)
shí	十
shì	是
shì	事
shíèryuè	十二月
shīfu	師（师）傅
shíhòu	時（时）候
shíjiān	時間（时间）
shíyīyuè	十一月
shíyuè	十月
shǒu	手
shòu	瘦
shǒubì	手臂
shǒuzhǐ	手指
shū	書（书）
shuǐ	水
shuō	說（说）
shúshu	叔叔
sì	四
sìyuè	四月

suān	酸
suānlà tāng	酸辣湯 (汤)
suànle	算了
suǒyǐ	所以
tā	他，她，它
tài + ADJ	太 + ADJ
tàitai	太太
Táiwān	台灣 (湾)
Táiwānhuà	台灣 (湾) 話 (话)
tán	痰
tāng	湯 (汤)
táng	糖
tángcù yú	糖醋魚
tiān	天
tián	甜
tiānqì	天氣 (气)
tiáo	條 (条)
tīng	聽 (听)
tīngbùdǒng	聽 (听) 不懂
tòng	痛
tóu	頭 (头)
tóu tòng	頭 (头) 痛
tóufà [or tóufǎ]	頭髮 (头发)
tuǐ	腿

túnbù [or pìgǔ]	臀部 ，屁股
tūrán	突然
VERB + bùqǐ	VERB + 不起
VERB + guò	VERB + 過 (过)
VERB + hǎo	VERB + 好
VERB + zhe	VERB + 著
wàitou	外頭 (头)
wán	玩
wán	丸
wǎn	碗
wàng	往
wǎnshàng	晚上
wánxiào	玩笑
wàzi	襪 (袜) 子
wéi	喂
wèi	位
wèishēng	衛 (卫) 生
wèishēng zhǐ	衛 (卫) 生紙 (纸)
wèishénme	爲 (为) 什麼 (么)
wèn	問 (问)
wèntí	問題 (问题)
wènwen kàn	問問 (问问) 看
wǒ	我

wǒ jiù shì	我就是
wǒmen	我們（们）
wǔ	五
wǔyuè	五月
xī	西
xià	下
xià yǔ	下雨
xiàbā	下巴
xiān + VERB	先 + VERB
xiān VERB1, zài VERB2	先 VERB1, 再 VERB2
xián	鹹（咸）
xiǎng	想
xiǎng + VERB	想 + VERB
xiǎngdào	想到
Xiānggǎng	香港
Xiānggǎngrén	香港人
xiānsheng	先生
xiànzài	現（现）在
xiǎo	小
xiào	笑
xiǎojiě	小姐
xiàsǐ le	嚇（吓）死了
xiàtiān	夏天
xiàwǔ	下午

Xībānyáwén	西班牙文
xiē	些
xiē (short for yìxiē)	些，一些
xiě	寫（写）
xiě zì	寫（写）字
xíezi	鞋子
xīgài	膝蓋（盖）
xīguā	西瓜
xíguàn	習慣（习惯）
xǐhuān	喜歡（欢）
xìn	信
xíng	行
xìng	姓
xīngqī	星期
xīngqī'èr	星期二
xīngqīliù	星期六
xīngqīsān	星期三
xīngqīsì	星期四
xīngqītiān, xīngqīrì	星期天，星期日
xīngqīwǔ	星期五
xīngqīyī	星期一
Xīnjiāpō	新加坡
xiōng [or xiōngbù]	胸，胸部
xiōngdì	兄弟
xiūlǐ	修理

xiūxi	休息
xué	學（学）
xuéshēng	學（学）生
yā, yāzi	鴨（鸭），鴨（鸭）子
yáchǐ	牙齒（齿）
yǎng	養（养）
yǎnjīng	眼睛
yánsè	顏色
yǎnyuán	演員（员）
yǎo	咬
yào	要
yào	藥（药）
yàojǐn	要緊（紧）
yàoshi	鑰（钥）匙
yě	也
yěxǔ	也許（许）
yī, yì, yí	一
yíbàn	一半
yícì	一次
yìdiǎnr yě bù + ADJ	一點（点）兒（儿）也不 + ADJ
yīfu	衣服
yígòng	一共
yìhuǐr (huǐr)	一會（会）兒（儿）
yíkuàir	一塊（块）兒（儿）

yǐjīng	已經 (经)
yìliǎng + MEAS	一兩 (两) + MEAS
yīnggāi	應該 (应该)
Yīngguó	英國 (国)
Yīngwén	英文
yínháng	銀 (银) 行
yīnwèi	因 為 (为)
yīnwèi A, suǒyǐ B	因 為 (为) A, 所以 B
yìqǐ	一起
yīshēng	醫 (医) 生
yìsi	意思
yǐwéi	以為 (为)
yìxiē	一些
yíyàng	一樣 (样)
yīyuè	一月
yìzhǒng + NOUN	一種 (种) + NOUN
yòng	用
yǒu	有
yòu	右
yǒu rén (as SUBJ) ...	有人 (as SUBJ) ...
yǒu (de) shíhòu	有 (的) 時 (时) 候
yòu + V1 + yòu + V2	又 + VERB1 + 又 + VERB2
yǒu yìsi	有 意思
yǒudiǎn + ADJ	有 點 (点) + ADJ
yóuqíshi	尤其是

yóuyǒng	游泳
yóuyǒng jiàoliàn	游泳教練（练）
yǔ	雨
yuǎn	遠（远）
yuánlái	原來
yuè	月
yùndòng	運動（运动）
yǔsǎn	雨傘（伞）
yùshì	浴室
zài	再
zài	在
zài + PLACE WORD + VERB	在 + PLACE WORD + VERB
zài shuō yícì	再說（说）一次
zài + VERB	在 + VERB
zàijiàn	再見（见）
zāng	髒（脏）
zāogāo!	糟糕
zěnme	怎麼（么）
zěnme bàn?	怎麼（么）辦（办）
zěnme nàme + ADJ	怎麼（么）那麼（么）+ ADJ
zěnmeyàng	怎麼（么）樣（样）
zhàn	站
zhāngkāi	張開（张开）
zhànzhe	站著

zhǎo	找
zhāng	張（张）
zhāngláng	蟑螂
zhàopiàn	照片
zhè	這（这）
zhèi	這（这）
zhèlǐ	這裏（这里）
zhème + ADJ	這麽（这么）+ ADJ
zhēn	眞
zhèr	這兒（这儿）
zhī	隻（只）
zhǐ	只
zhǐ	紙（纸）
zhīdào	知道
zhǐhǎo	只好
zhíyuán	職員（职员）
zhōng	鐘（钟）
zhǒng	種（种）
Zhōng yào	中藥（药）
Zhōngguó	中國（国）
Zhōngguóhuà	中國（国）話（话）
Zhōngwén	中文
zhū	豬（猪）
zhù	住
zhuā	抓

zhuǎn	轉（转）
zhuōzi	桌子
zhūròu	豬（猪）肉
zhùzài + PLACE WORD	住在 + PLACE WORD
zì	字
zǒu	走
zǔfù	祖父
zuǐ	嘴（咀）
zuì + ADJ	最 + ADJ
zuǐba	嘴（咀）巴
zuǐchún	嘴（咀）唇
zuìjìn	最近
zǔmǔ	祖母
zuǒ	左
zuò	做（作）
zuò	坐
zuò fàn	做飯（作饭）
zuò shēngyì	做（作）生意
zuò yùndòng	做運動（作运动）
zuòwèi	座位

APPENDIX 5: CHINESE CHARACTER VERSION OF DIALOGUES AND VOCABULARY

第三课, **CHAPTER 3:** 老鼠好

生词 *Vocabulary, Chapter 3*

1. 老鼠
2. 好
3. 我
4. 不
5. 是
6. 老师
7. 对不起
8. 你好
9. 你
10. 你妈妈

11. 妈妈
12. 他 (he), 她 (she), 它 (it)
13. 很
14. 爸爸
15. 呢
16. 也
17. 忙
18. 吗
19. 您
20. 再见

对话 *Dialogue, Chapter 3*

铭磊： 老鼠好！
李老师： 我不是老鼠。我是老师。
铭磊： 对不起。老师好！
李老师： 你好！你妈妈好吗？
铭磊： 她很好。
李老师： 你爸爸呢？
铭磊： 他也很好。
李老师： 你忙吗？
铭磊： 我不忙。您呢？
李老师： 我很忙。再见！
铭磊： 老师再见！

第四课, CHAPTER 4: 很高兴认识您

生词 *Vocabulary, Chapter 4*

1. 经理
2. 谁
3. 的
4. 你的
5. 女朋友
6. 女
7. 朋友
8. 姐姐
9. 三姐
10. 公司
11. 请问
12. 问
13. （您）贵姓？
14. 贵

15. 姓
16. 高兴
17. 认识
18. 小姐
19. 叫
20. 什么
21. 名字
22. 学生
23. 学
24. 游泳教练
25. 游泳
26. 教练
27. 男

对话 *Dialogue, Chapter 4*

王经理：　她是谁？她是不是你的女朋友？
铭磊：　　不是。她是我姐姐。三姐，他是我公司的经理。
丽莲：　　您好！请问，您贵姓？
王经理：　我姓王。
丽莲：　　王经理，很高兴认识您。
王经理：　小姐，你叫什么名字？
丽莲：　　我叫韩丽莲。
王经理：　你是不是学生？
丽莲：　　不，我是游泳教练。

第五课, CHAPTER 5: 你有没有兄弟姐妹？

生词 *Vocabulary, Chapter 5*

1. 有		21. 和	
2. 没		22. 叔叔	
3. 兄弟姐妹		23. 看	
4. 兄弟		24. 这	
5. 姐妹		25. 张	
6. 三		26. 照片	
7. 个		27. 那	
8. 哥哥		28. 一	
9. 弟弟		29. 条	
10. 妹妹		30. 鹿 (deer), 路 (road)	
11. 家		31. 只	
12. 一共		32. 中文	
13. 几		33. 怎么	
14. 人		34. 说	
15. 九		35. 宠物	
16. 还		36. 那	
17. 爸爸		37. 真	
18. 妈妈		38. 可爱	
19. 祖父		39. 爱	
20. 祖母			

对话 *Dialogue, Chapter 5*

李老师： 你有没有兄弟姐妹？

铭磊： 我有三个姐姐。我没有哥哥，也没有弟弟、妹妹。

李老师： 你家一共有几个人？

铭磊： 我家有九个人。我还有爸爸、妈妈、祖父、祖母、和一个叔叔。老师，您
看这张照片。

李老师： 那是什么？

铭磊： 那是一条鹿 (deer) [路 (road)]

李老师： 不是一条鹿 (deer) [路 (road)]，是一只鹿。

铭磊： 老师, pet, 中文怎么说？

李老师： 宠物。

铭磊： 那只鹿是我的宠物。它真可爱。

第六课, CHAPTER 6: 你现在有没有事？

生词 *Vocabulary, Chapter 6*

1. 林先生	25. 两点
2. 先生	26. 两 + Measure Word + Noun
3. 小韩	27. 了
4. 小	28. 赶快 + Verb
5. 现在	29. 叫
6. 事	30. 出租汽车
7. 要 + Verb	31. 汽车
8. 要 (as Verb)	32. 看看
9. 去	33. 飞机票
10. 去 + Verb	34. 票
11. 飞机场	35. 下午
12. 飞机	36. 晚上
13. 几点	37. 八点二十分
14. 起飞	38. 别 + Verb
15. 好像	39. 急
16. 三点半	40. 我们 ..... 吧
17. 三点	41. 我们
18. 几点钟	42. 先 + Verb
19. 钟	43. 喝
20. 一点五十五分	44. 杯
21. 一点	45. 杯子
22. 五十五分	46. 茶
23. 糟糕	47. 聊聊天
24. 已经	48. 聊天

对话 *Dialogue, Chapter 6*

林先生： 小韩，你现在有没有事？
铭磊：　　我要去飞机场。
林先生： 你的飞机几点起飞？
铭磊：　　好像是三点半。现在几点钟？
林先生： 一点五十五分。
铭磊：　　糟糕！已经两点了。我要赶快叫出租汽车。
林先生： 我看看你的飞机票。不是下午三点半，是晚上八点二十分。你别急，我们
　　　　　先去喝一杯茶，聊聊天吧！

第七课, CHAPTER 7: 那么，你们卖什么？

生词 *Vocabulary, Chapter 7*

1. 你们
2. 美国
3. 报纸
4. 服务员
5. 中国
6. 地图
7. 那么
8. 卖
9. 只
10. 中文
11. 书
12. 英文的
13. 英文
14. 这
15. 汉语
16. 词典

17. 本
18. 多少钱
19. 多少
20. 钱
20. 十二块五毛
22. 块
23. 毛
24. 贵
25. 买
26. 给
27. 可是
28. 不是……吗？
29. 错
30. 再
31. 找

对话 *Dialogue, Chapter 7*

铭磊：　　你们有没有美国报纸？
服务员：　对不起，我们没有。
铭磊：　　有没有中国地图？
服务员：　对不起，我们也没有。
铭磊：　　那么你们卖什么？
服务员：　我们只卖中文书和中文报纸，不卖英文的，也不卖地图。
铭磊：　　那是什么？
服务员：　这是汉语词典。
铭磊：　　一本多少钱？
服务员：　一本十二块五毛。不贵。
铭磊：　　我买两本，给你五十块。
服务员：　可是，这不对。这是二十块，不是五十块。
铭磊：　　哦，那不是五十块吗？对不起，我错了。再给你十块。
服务员：　好，找你五块。

第八课, CHAPTER 8: 你们有房间吗？

生词 *Vocabulary, Chapter 8*

1. 先生	19. 不会	37. 脏
2. 房间	20. 咬人	38. 干净
3. 职员	21. 咬	39. 还是　不
4. 位	22. 就	40. 出去
5. 我们两个人	23. 请	41. 出
6. 住	24. 进去	42. 别的
7. 老	25. 进	43. 进来
8. 老	26. 不够	44. 多么
9. 跟	27. 大	45. 啊
10. 一起	28. 浴室	46. 桌子上
11. 二零九号	29. 这么	47. 桌子
12. 零	30. 小	48. 上
13. 号	31. 床	49. 电话
14. 蟑螂	32. 太	50. 电
15. 家里	33. 软	51. 话
16. 里	34. 哎呀	52. 这儿；这里
17. 一两	35. 床单	53. 那儿；那里
18. 没关系	36. 有点	

对话 *Dialogue, Chapter 8*

彼得：　先生，你们有房间吗？
职员：　有。几位？
彼得：　我们两个人，要住一个房间。
职员：　老张，你跟他们一起去看看二零九号。
丽莲：　你们的房间有没有蟑螂？
老张：　没有。我们的房间没有蟑螂。我家里有一两只蟑螂。可是，没关系，
　　　　它们不会咬人。
丽莲：　房间里没有蟑螂就好。　我们不要蟑螂。
老张：　请进去看看。
彼得：　这间好像不够大。浴室这么小。
丽莲：　床太软了。哎呀！床单有点脏。
老张：　可是这个房间很干净，　也没有蟑螂。
丽莲：　我还是不要。我们出去吧！
老张：　那么，去看看别的吧！
老张：　你们进来看看，这间多么干净啊！桌子上还有电话。
彼得：　我们就住这儿吧！

第九课, CHAPTER 9: 你们打算住多久？

生词 *Vocabulary, Chapter 9*

1. 今天
2. 天
3. 七月四号
4. 七月
5. 月
6. 四号
7. 号
8. 打算
9. 多久
10. 听不懂
11. 听
12. 懂
13. 请
14. 再说一次
15. 一次
16. 次
17. 几天
18. 今年
19. 年
20. 几岁
21. 岁
22. 什么时候

23. 时候
24. 生
25. 给我看
26. 护照
27. 哪年
28. 结婚
29. 孩子
30. 还没有
31. 没有
32. 在
33. 哪儿；哪里
34. 工作
35. 家
36. 英国
37. 银行
38. 年薪
39. 问题
40. 怎么那么
41. 多
42. 好了，好了
43. 不问了
44. 钥匙

对话 *Dialogue, Chapter 9*

职员：今天是七月四号。你们打算住多久？
彼得：对不起，我听不懂。请你再说一次。
职员：你们要住几天？
彼得：五天。
职员：你今年几岁？是什么时候生的？
彼得：我二十三岁。是一九八六年生的。
职员：请给我看看你们的护照。你们是哪年结婚的？有没有孩子？
彼得：我们还没有结婚。
职员：你在哪儿工作？
彼得：我在一家英国银行工作。
职员：你年薪多少？
彼得：你的问题怎么那么多？
职员：好了，好了，不问了。这是你们房间的钥匙。

第十课, CHAPTER 10: 厕所在哪儿?

生词 *Vocabulary, Chapter 10*

1.	上厕所	25.	近
2.	厕所	26.	西边
3.	上	27.	西
4.	从	28.	边
5.	往	29.	公园
6.	北	30.	里边
7.	走	31.	先…再…
8.	大概	32.	右
9.	里	33.	转
10.	路	34.	看到
11.	到	35.	红绿灯
12.	东长安街	36.	红
13.	东	37.	绿
14.	街	38.	灯
15.	那附近	39.	左
16.	附近	40.	算了
17.	北京饭店	41.	带
18.	饭店	42.	卫生纸
19.	非常	43.	纸
20.	卫生	44.	拿
21.	远	45.	用
22.	怎么办	46.	不用谢
23.	办	47.	不用
24.	比较	48.	年轻人

对话 *Dialogue, Chapter 10*

铭磊:　　请问，厕所在哪儿？我要上厕所。
年轻人：你从这儿往北走，大概半里路，就到东长安街。那附近有北京饭店。
　　　　　他们的厕所非常卫生。
铭磊:　　太远了！怎么办？有没有比较近的？
年轻人：有。西边有个公园。里边也有厕所。
铭磊:　　怎么走？
年轻人：先右转，看到红绿灯再左转…算了，我带你去吧！
铭磊:　　厕所里会有卫生纸吗？。
年轻人：厕所里会有卫生纸。我这儿也有。你拿去用吧！
铭磊:　　谢谢你！
年轻人：不用谢。

第十一课, CHAPTER 11: 我想请你们吃饭。

生词 *Vocabulary, Chapter 11*

1. 太太		19. 在	
2. 喂		20. 修理	
3. 在		21. 做饭	
4. 我就是		22. 做	
5. 就是		23. 着	
6. 空		24. 过来	
7. 想		25. 过	
8. 请		26. 一块儿	
9. 吃饭		27. 可以	
10. 吃		28. 当然	
11. 饭		29. 真	
12. 客气		30. 不好意思	
13. 不太		31. 意思	
14. 方便		32. 原来	
15. 电脑		33. 没什么	
16. 刚		34. 等会儿见	
17. 坏		35. 等	
18. 先生		36. 会儿	

对话 *Dialogue, Chapter 11*

林太太： 喂？

铭磊： 请问，林太太在不在？

林太太： 我就是。

铭磊： 你们今天有空吗？我想请你们吃饭。

林太太： 谢谢。你太客气了。可是今天不太方便。

铭磊： 哦，你们现在很忙吗？

林太太： 我们的电脑刚坏了，我先生在修理电脑。我现在做着饭。
你要不要过来跟我们一块儿吃？

铭磊： 可以吗？

林太太： 当然可以啊！

铭磊： 那真不好意思。我原来想请你，现在你请我了。

林太太： 没什么。等会儿见。

第十二课, CHAPTER 12: 请你把醋拿给我

生词 *Vocabulary, Chapter 12*

1. 欢迎你来
2. 欢迎
3. 请坐
4. 坐
5. 饺子
6. 快包好了
7. 快
8. 快…了
9. 包
10. 好
11. 我肚子饿了
12. 肚子
13. 饿
14. 了
15. 帮
16. 一些
17. 些
18. 南方人
19. 南方
20. 会
21. 听
22. 下雨了
23. 下
24. 雨
25. 下雨
26. 不要紧
27. 要紧
28. 把
29. 雨伞
30. 借给
31. 借
32. 醋
33. 拿给
34. 那么喜欢
35. 喜欢
36. 吃醋
37. 哦
38. 啊
39. 哪里
40. 才
41. 呢
42. 开玩笑
43. 开
44. 玩
45. 笑
46. 玩笑

对话 *Dialogue, Chapter 12*

林太太： 请进。欢迎你来。请坐。
铭磊： 谢谢。
林太太： 饺子快包好了。
铭磊： 我肚子饿了。我帮你包一些。
林太太： 哦，南方人也会包饺子吗？
铭磊： 当然会。…你听，下雨了。
林太太： 不要紧。我会把雨伞借给你。
林太太： 请你把醋拿给我。
铭磊： 哦，你那么喜欢吃醋啊？
林太太： 哪里，我先生才喜欢呢！
林先生： 你们真会开玩笑。

第十三课, CHAPTER 13: 你为什么给他写信？

生词 *Vocabulary, Chapter 13*

1. 没想到		18. 美国人	
2. 想		19. 纽约	
3. 想到		20. 做生意	
4. 用		21. 生意	
5. 手		22. 为什么	
6. 写字		23. 给...写信	
7. 写		24. 因为	
8. 字		25. 很久	
9. 对		26. 久	
10. 拿		27. 没见面	
11. 筷子		28. 见面	
12. 习惯		29. 很想他	
13. 刀叉		30. 因为...所以...	
14. 信		31. 所以	
15. 住在		32. 打电话	
16. 香港		33. 打	
17. 香港人			

对话 *Dialogue, Chapter 13*

安娜：　哦，我没想到，你用左手写字。
丽莲：　对，可是我用右手拿筷子
安娜：　你习惯用筷子吃饭吗？
丽莲：　对，可是我也会用刀叉。
安娜：　你在给谁写信？
丽莲：　我给我的男朋友写信。
安娜：　他住在哪儿？
丽莲：　他住在香港。
安娜：　他是香港人吗？
丽莲：　不，他是美国人。他是从纽约来的。
安娜：　他在香港做什么？
丽莲：　他在做生意。
安娜：　你为什么给他写信？
丽莲：　因为我们很久没见面，我很想他，所以给他写信。
安娜：　你为什么不给他打电话？
丽莲：　因为我比较喜欢给我男朋友写信。我们也打电话。可是，他也很喜欢给我写
　　　　信。

第十四课, **CHAPTER 14:** 大概两三斤就够了。

生词 *Vocabulary, Chapter 14*

1. 师傅
2. 衣服
3. 漂亮
4. 猪肉
5. 猪
6. 肉
7. 斤
8. 大概
9. 两三斤
10. 就够了
11. 不知道
12. 知道
13. 生菜
14. 把

15. 养
16. 鸭
17. 都
18. 尤其是
19. 天气热的时候
20. 天气
21. 热
22. ...的时候
23. 夏天
24. 西瓜
25. 又...又...
26. 便宜
27. 好吃
28. 行

对话 *Dialogue, Chapter 14*

师傅： 小姐，你的衣服真漂亮！
丽莲： 哪里，哪里。师傅，我想买一点儿猪肉。多少钱一斤？
师傅： 十六块一斤。你要几斤？
丽莲： 大概两三斤就够了。
师傅： 还要什么？
丽莲： 我不知道你们卖不卖生菜。我还要五把生菜。
师傅： 要这么多啊？你们养鸭吗？
丽莲： 不是。可是我们都喜欢吃生菜，尤其是天气热的时候。
师傅： 现在夏天西瓜很多，又便宜，又好吃。你要不要买？
丽莲： 行，我买一个。

第十五课, CHAPTER 15: 我要坐几路车？

生词 *Vocabulary, Chapter 15*

1. 长城
2. 长
3. 城
4. 坐
5. 得 (děi)
6. 老人
7. 火车站
8. 火车
9. 时间
10. 故宫
11. 城里头
12. 里头
13. 还是
14. 外头
15. 离
16. 好看
17. 应该
18. 对面

19. 十三路车
20. 车上的人
21. 车上
22. 很多
23. 多
24. 挤
25. 座位
26. 只好
27. 站着
28. 站
29. 有人
30. 抓
31. 腿
32. 后面
33. 袋子里
34. 袋子
35. 螃蟹

对话 *Dialogue, Chapter 15*

丽莲： 请问，到长城去要坐几路车？
老人： 你得去火车站坐火车。
丽莲： 那太远了。我们今天没有时间去。
      请问，故宫在城里头还是在城外头？
老人： 在城里头。离这儿不远。故宫非常好看，你们应该去看看。
丽莲： 从这儿怎么走？
老人： 你到对面去等十三路车。
丽莲： 谢谢。
老人： 不用客气。
丽莲： 车上的人很多。
彼得： 真挤。没有座位。我们只好站着。
丽莲： 好像有人在抓我的腿。
彼得： 不是。是后面那个人袋子里的螃蟹。

第十六课, CHAPTER 16: 汽水或者啤酒都可以

生词 *Vocabulary, Chapter 16*

1. 饭馆
2. 菜单
3. 点
4. 些
5. 要
6. 酸辣汤
7. 酸
8. 辣
9. 汤
10. 糖醋鱼
11. 糖
12. 碗
13. 白饭
14. 白
15. 炒青菜
16. 炒
17. 青
18. 菜
19. 渴

20. 汽水
21. 汽
22. 水
23. 啤酒
24. 酒
25. 或者
26. 来
27. 瓶
28. 感恩节
29. 节
30. 问问看
31. 烤火鸡
32. 烤
33. 火鸡
34. 知道
35. 以为
36. 伙计
37. 鸡肉

对话 *Dialogue, Chapter 16*

铭磊：　我们可（以）不可以看看菜单？

服务员：当然可以。菜单在这儿。

服务员：先生，小姐，你们要点些什么菜？

铭磊：　我们要一个酸辣汤，一个糖醋鱼，两碗白饭。

服务员：还要别的吗？

丽莲：　还要一个炒青菜。

铭磊：　你渴不渴？　你要喝汽水还是啤酒？

丽莲：　汽水或者啤酒都可以。

铭磊：　来两瓶汽水。

丽莲：　今天是感恩节。我们问问看他们有没有烤火鸡。

服务员：你们在叫我吗？

丽莲：　不，我们没有叫你。我们想知道你们有没有烤火鸡。

服务员：噢，我以为你们说"伙计"。对不起，我们没有火鸡。你们要不要来一个
　　　　鸡肉？

铭磊：　不用了。我们的菜够了。

第十七课, CHAPTER 17: 你咳嗽咳了多久了？

生词 *Vocabulary, Chapter 17*

1. 医生
2. 生病了
3. 病
4. 上星期一
5. 星期一
6. 星期
7. 开始
8. 发烧
9. 头痛
10. 头
11. 痛
12. 流鼻水
13. 流
14. 鼻水
15. 然后
16. 喉咙
17. 咳嗽
18. 咳
19. 张开
20. 嘴巴
21. 让

22. 痰
23. 颜色
24. 绿的
25. 绿
26. 得
27. 气管炎
28. 气管
29. 服
30. 抗生素
31. 干草丸
32. 干草
33. 丸
34. 不是…吗？
35. 一种
36. 种
37. 中药
38. 药
39. 对…很好
40. 多
41. 休息

对话 *Dialogue, Chapter 17*

丽莲： 医生，我生病了。我上星期一开始发烧，头痛，流鼻水，然后喉咙痛。
医生： 你咳嗽咳了多久了？
丽莲： 已经咳了一个星期了。
医生： 张开嘴巴让我看看。痰是什么颜色的？
丽莲： 是绿的。
医生： 你得了气管炎。你要服抗生素跟干草丸。
丽莲： 干草不是一种糖吗？
医生： 不，这是中药。对你的喉咙很好。你也要多喝水，多休息。

第十八课, CHAPTER 18: 你看过京剧没有？

生词 *Vocabulary, Chapter 18*

1. 看过
2. 过... 没有？
3. 京剧
4. 没看过
5. 觉得
6. 怎么样
7. 有意思
8. 没...
9. 演员
10. 表演
11. 得
12. 但是
13. 看到一半
14. 一半
15. 突然

16. 大叫
17. 吓死了
18. 死了
19. 讲
20. 好笑
21. 还有
22. 坐得太远
23. 有(的)时候
24. 看不见
25. 听不清楚
26. 清楚
27. 坐得近一点儿
28. 座位
29. 买不起
30. 不起

对话 *Dialogue, Chapter 18*

李老师： 你们看过京剧没有？
安娜： 我没看过。
铭磊： 我看过一次。
李老师： 你觉得怎么样？
铭磊： 我觉得很有意思。每个演员都表演得很好。但是，我看到一半，突然有个
演员大叫。我吓死了！
李老师： 你讲得那么好笑！
铭磊： 还有，我坐得太远，有时候看不见，也听不清楚。
李老师： 你怎么没坐得近一点儿？
铭磊： 近的座位太贵了。我买不起。

第十九课, CHAPTER 19: 你怎么比我瘦?

生词 *Vocabulary, Chapter 19*

1. 穿		22. 每天早上	
2. 件		23. 运动	
3. 衬衫		24. 作运动	
4. 不错		25. 什么样的	
5. 错		26. 常常	
6. 百货公司		27. 慢跑	
7. 东西		28. 慢	
8. 最		29. 跑	
9. 冷		30. 练气功	
10. 毛衣		31. 气功	
11. 最近		32. 气	
12. 累		33. 高	
13. 跟你不一样		34. 比	
14. 不一样		35. 也许	
15. 一样		36. 快	
16. 一点儿也不		37. 瘦	
17. 身体		38. 矿泉水	
18. 比		39. 怪不得	
19. 去年		40. 怪	
20. 健康		41. 老是	
21. 都没		42. 打嗝	

对话 *Dialogue, Chapter 19*

彼得: 铭磊，你穿的那件衬衫很不错。在哪儿买的？

铭磊: 在北京一家百货公司买的。他们的东西最便宜。彼得，今天不冷，
你为什么穿毛衣？

彼得: 我觉得有点冷。我最近也很累。

铭磊: 那我就跟你不一样了。我一点儿也不累。我的身体今年比去年健康。
我都没生病，因为我每天早上都运动。

彼得: 你作什么样的运动？

铭磊: 我常常慢跑。有时候跟我三姐去游泳，有时候练气功。

彼得: 你比丽莲高，也许跑得比她快。

铭磊: 对。可是我游泳游得比她慢。彼得，你不作运动，怎么比我瘦？

彼得: 因为我汽水、酒、都不喝。我只喝矿泉水。

铭磊: 怪不得你老是打嗝！

NOTES

NOTES

NOTES

NOTES